A Policy for Scientific
and Professional Manpower

NATIONAL MANPOWER COUNCIL

A Policy for Scientific and Professional Manpower

A STATEMENT BY THE COUNCIL
with
FACTS AND ISSUES PREPARED
BY THE RESEARCH STAFF

New York 1953

COLUMBIA UNIVERSITY PRESS

65

The National Manpower Council

Preface

THE NATIONAL MANPOWER Council has been engaged in studying scientific and professional manpower problems for over a year. In this study, as well as in its earlier consideration of student deferment policy and its current investigation of technical and skilled manpower, the Council is dealing with closely related aspects of the problem of the quality of the nation's manpower resources.

The objectives of the National Manpower Council are to evaluate manpower problems of crucial concern to the United States in this period of enduring emergency and to recommend constructive policies for their solution.

In developing the facts required for the determination of policy, the Council has sought the active cooperation of those whose knowledge and experience can illuminate the issues which the Council has under consideration. Such success as the Council has had stems in the first instance from the remarkable response of many individuals and groups to the Council's requests for assistance.

The chapters which make up Part Two of this book, "Facts and Issues about Scientific and Professional Manpower," grew out of studies which the staff developed for the Council, and the Council gratefully acknowledges the generous assistance of many individuals and organizations in their preparation. The basic data underlying Chapter II, "The Growth of the Professions," was prepared by the Bureau of Labor Statistics of the Department of

Labor under the guidance of Dr. Harold Goldstein and Dr. Seymour Wolfbein. Dr. Dael Wolfle, Director of the Commission on Human Resources and Advanced Training, made available unpublished data for Chapter IV, "The Potential for Higher Education." Essential materials for Chapter V, "Research and Development," were provided by the Atomic Energy Commission through Mr. McKay Donkin, Special Assistant to the Chairman, and by the Research and Development Board, Department of Defense, through Mr. Kenneth S. Colmen of the staff.

Chapter VIII, "The Engineering Profession," owes much to the cooperation of the Engineering Manpower Commission of Engineers Joint Council and to the work of Mr. Thomas Marshall, Jr., its Executive Secretary. The American Institute of Physics, through its Director, Dr. Henry Barton, was helpful in the preparation of Chapter XI, "Physicists." Dr. George B. Pegram of Columbia University acted as advisor on this chapter, and Dr. Lee A. DuBridge, a member of the Council, assisted greatly in the preparation of the final version. The basic draft of Chapter X, "Physicians," was prepared by Dr. Herbert Klarman, formerly of the staff of the National Security Resources Board and currently Assistant Director of the Hospital Council of Greater New York. Dr. Stanhope Bayne-Jones, a member of the Council, acted as a consultant in the preparation of this chapter.

As in its previous study, the Council made effective use of the conference technique in developing important information and ideas about various facets of scientific and professional manpower. In April 1952, Mr. Robert Clark, Director of the Manpower Office of the National Security Resources Board, called a meeting of governmental and non-governmental experts to explore problems in this field. In the same month, Mr. Wilbur C. Munnecke, a member of the Council, arranged a small conference in Chicago. In June, the Council, under the sponsorship of one of its members, Dr. Charles S. Johnson, held a conference at Fisk University, Nashville, Tennessee, which dealt with selected problems of scientific and professional manpower from a regional point of view. In June, through the assistance of Mr. Frank Pierce, another Council member, Dr. Mervin Kelly, President of the Bell Telephone Laboratories, called a conference of experts from industry and engineering education to assist the Council in clarifying the bearing of industrial research and development on current and future manpower problems.

At its December, 1952, meeting, the Council benefited substantially from the critical discussion of the first draft of its Policy Statement by the following experts: Dean J. Douglas Brown of Princeton University; Mr. T. Keith Glennan, former Commissioner of the Atomic Energy Commission and President of the Case Institute of Technology; Dr. Francis Wheeler Loomis, Professor of Physics, University of Illinois; Mr. E. Duer Reeves, Executive Vice President of the Standard Oil Development Company. A Presidential assignment prevented Dr. Arthur S. Flemming, Director of the Office of Defense Mobilization, from attending this meeting, but his views were made known to the Council. These five individuals also reviewed a later draft of the Council's Statement.

Special note must also be made of the contribution by Dr. Moses Abramovitz, Professor of Economics, Stanford University, who acted as consultant to the Council's staff during the formative period when the basic approach was being developed. Mr. Alden H. Emery, Executive Secretary of the American Chemical Society, made available a large amount of material and read all of the staff chapters. Mr. J. R. Killian, Jr., President of the Massachusetts Institute of Technology, not only submitted his own critical suggestions on an early draft of the Council Statement and on Chapters V, VIII and IX, but also elicited comments from his associates, Dr. K. T. Compton, Chairman of the Board of the Corporation, and Dean George R. Harrison, which he made available to the Council's staff. Mrs. Margaret Hickey, Public Affairs Editor of the *Ladies Home Journal*, assisted significantly in the editing of the Council's Statement. Dr. John Richards, Director of the Office of Research Service, New York University, was helpful at almost every stage of the Council's work.

The Council is also grateful for the assistance provided by many other individuals and organizations. Their names are listed in the Acknowledgments which follow this Preface.

Although the Council has been able to draw liberally on the present store of knowledge and expert opinion in the field of scientific and professional manpower, and although it has studied the problem for more than a year, it considers its current work to be exploratory rather than definitive. The Council's objectives have been to frame the problem, to identify its most important facets, to evaluate the existing evidence, to indicate the lines of policy where the evidence appears adequate, and to suggest where additional research and evaluation must be undertaken before balanced judgment can be reached. The Council is sponsoring a conference in October to explore further the important problem of the utilization of scientific and professional manpower. Moreover, it will deal with additional facets of scientific and professional manpower problems in the course of its investigation into technical and skilled manpower and other related issues.

There have been important changes in the membership of the Council in recent months. With his appointment as Secretary of the Navy, Mr. Robert B. Anderson, who participated in the preparation of the basic draft of the Council's Statement, will not be an active member of the Council for the duration of his government service. Dr. Stanhope Bayne-Jones is leaving the Council because of his assumption of full-time duties as Director of Research of the Army Medical Department. In March, the following members joined the Council: Dr. Leo Bartemeier, Mr. Erwin D. Canham, Dr. Douglas Southall Freeman, and Mr. W. H. Harrison. The new members did not participate in the Council's work on scientific and professional manpower.

JAMES D. ZELLERBACH
Chairman, National Manpower Council

San Francisco

Acknowledgments

ORGANIZATIONS

Business
American Management Association
Bell Telephone Laboratories
National Association of Manufacturers

Educational
American Council on Education
Educational Testing Service
National Education Association
Southern Regional Education Board
University of California, Radiation Laboratory

Governmental
Atomic Energy Commission
Civil Service Commission
Department of Commerce, Bureau of the Census
Department of Defense, Research and Development Board
Department of Labor, Bureau of Apprenticeship and Bureau of Labor Statistics
Department of the Air Force
Department of the Army
Department of the Navy
Federal Security Agency, Office of Education
Industrial College of the Armed Forces
Interdepartmental Committee on Scientific Research and Development
Los Alamos Scientific Laboratory
National Science Foundation
National Security Resources Board
Office of Defense Mobilization
Selective Service System
Tennessee Valley Authority

Other

American Chemical Society
American Institute of Physics
Commission on Financing Higher Education
Commission on Human Resources and Advanced Training
Engineers Joint Council, Engineering Manpower Commission
National Research Council
Thomas Alva Edison Foundation

INDIVIDUALS

Albert Abrahamson, Bowdoin College, Brunswick, Me.
W. Earl Armstrong, Office of Education, Washington, D.C.
Thomas C. Blaisdell, University of California, Berkeley, Calif.
Major General R. W. Bliss (ret.), Chocorua, N.H.
D. B. Bridgman, American Telephone and Telegraph Company, New York, N.Y.
Lyman Bryson, Teachers College, Columbia University, New York, N.Y.
Ambrose Caliver, Office of Education, Federal Security Agency, Washington, D.C.
Harry J. Carman, Columbia University, New York, N.Y.
Henry Chauncey, Educational Testing Service, Princeton, N.J.
Harold Clark, Teachers College, Columbia University, New York, N.Y.
J. M. Clark, Columbia University, New York, N.Y.
Isaac Cogan, Office of the Surgeon General, Department of the Army, Washington, D.C.
George B. Corless, Standard Oil Company of New Jersey, New York, N.Y.
Bowen C. Dees, National Science Foundation, Washington, D.C.
Frank Dickinson, American Medical Association, Chicago, Ill.
John R. Dunning, Columbia University, New York, N.Y.
Willard S. Elsbree, Teachers College, Columbia University, New York, N.Y.
Colonel J. C. Evers, Office of the Deputy Chief of Staff, Personnel, Department of the Air Force, Washington, D.C.
Frederick Fassett, Massachusetts Institute of Technology, Cambridge, Mass.
Paul D. Gard, Office of the Assistant Chief of Staff (G-1), Department of the Army, Washington, D.C.
Harold V. Gaskill, Office of the Chief of Staff, Department of the Army, Washington, D.C.
Major Billy B. Geery, Office of the Assistant Chief of Staff (G-4), Department of the Army, Washington, D.C.
Dr. Sol W. Ginsburg, New York, N.Y.

Major Estel E. Gohn, Office of the Assistant Chief of Staff (G-3), Department of the Army, Washington, D.C.

Lt. Colonel F. B. Gregory, Office of the Assistant Chief of Staff (G-1), Department of the Army, Washington, D.C.

Colonel Joel D. Griffing, Selective Service Headquarters, Washington, D.C.

George V. Haythorne, Department of Labour, Ottawa, Canada

Alexander R. Heron, Crown Zellerbach Corporation, San Francisco, Calif.

David B. Hertz, Columbia University, New York, N.Y.

Robert K. Herz, Office of the Assistant Chief of Staff (G-3), Department of the Army, Washington, D.C.

Dr. Herman Hilleboe, State Department of Health, Albany, N.Y.

John Hilliard, Defense Manpower Administration, Department of Labor, Washington, D.C.

Joseph Hinsey, Medical College, Cornell University, New York, N.Y.

Captain H. T. Hoffman, Office of the Assistant Secretary (Manpower and Reserve Forces), Department of the Army, Washington, D.C.

Ralph M. Hogan, Office of Naval Research, Department of the Navy, Washington, D.C.

Hon. Earl D. Johnson, Under Secretary of the Army, Washington, D.C.

David B. Kaplan, Bureau of the Census, Department of Commerce, Washington, D.C.

Donald B. Keyes, National Association of Manufacturers, New York, N.Y.

Charles V. Kidd, United States Public Health Service, Bethesda, Md.

Dr. Stockton Kimball, School of Medicine, University of Buffalo, Buffalo, N.Y.

George B. Kistiakowsky, Harvard University, Cambridge, Mass.

Harold D. Lasswell, Yale University, New Haven, Conn.

Dr. Paul A. Lembcke, John Hopkins University, Baltimore, Md.

Major Robert D. Lent, Office of the Deputy Chief of Staff, Development, Department of the Air Force, Washington, D.C.

Colonel W. D. McCahan, Office of the Assistant Chief of Staff (G-1), Department of the Army, Washington, D.C.

John Macy, Office of the Under Secretary, Department of the Army, Washington, D.C.

Lt. Colonel Walter E. Mather, Office of the Assistant Secretary (Manpower and Reserve Forces), Department of the Army, Washington, D.C.

Ray C. Maul, National Education Association, Washington, D.C.

John D. Millett, Commission on Financing Higher Education, New York, N.Y.

Thomas B. Nolan, Geological Survey, Department of the Interior, Washington, D.C.

James C. O'Brien, Office of Education, Federal Security Agency, Washington, D.C.

G. St. J. Perrott, Public Health Service, Federal Security Agency, Washington, D.C.

Lt. Colonel W. D. Perry, Office of the Deputy Chief of Staff, Personnel, Department of the Air Force, Washington, D.C.

Emanuel Piore, Office of Naval Research, Department of the Navy, Washington, D.C.

Russell S. Poor, Medical Center Study, University of Florida, Gainesville, Fla.

Matthew Radom, Standard Oil Company of New Jersey, New York, N.Y.

Jerome Rothenberg, Amherst College, Amherst, Mass.

Arthur L. H. Rubin, New York, N.Y.

Dr. Howard Rusk, Health Resources Advisory Committee, Office of Defense Mobilization, Washington, D.C.

Stanley H. Ruttenberg, Department of Education and Research, Congress of Industrial Organizations, Washington, D.C.

Eugene W. Scott, Interdepartmental Committee on Scientific Research and Development, Washington, D.C.

Norman A. Shepard, American Cyanamid Company, New York, N.Y.

Lt. Colonel J. L. Spooner, Office of the Deputy Chief of Staff, Personnel, Department of the Air Force, Washington, D.C.

Dr. John M. Stallnaker, Association of American Medical Colleges, Chicago, Ill.

B. R. Stanerson, American Chemical Society, Washington, D.C.

Commander W. A. Stevenson, Bureau of Naval Personnel, Department of the Navy, Washington, D.C.

Cora E. Taylor, Bureau of Labor Statistics, Department of Labor, Washington, D.C.

James D. Teller, Office of the Deputy Chief of Staff, Personnel, Department of the Air Force, Washington, D.C.

M. H. Trytten, National Research Council, Washington, D.C.

Stephen L. Tyler, American Institute of Chemical Engineers, New York, N.Y.

Fletcher G. Watson, Harvard University, Cambridge, Mass.

Marsh W. White, Pennsylvania State College, State College, Penna.

J. F. Wellemeyer, American Council of Learned Societies, Washington, D.C.

Kenneth Williamson, Health Information Foundation, New York, N.Y.

Captain L. Williamson, Bureau of Naval Personnel, Department of the Navy, Washington, D.C.

Helen Wood, Bureau of Labor Statistics, Department of Labor, Washington, D.C.

Solly Zuckerman, University of Birmingham, Birmingham, England

CONFERENCE PARTICIPANTS [a]

APRIL MEETINGS

Washington, D.C.

Mark Colburn, National Security Resources Board, Washington, D.C.

Kenneth L. Heaton, Richardson, Bellows, Henry & Co., Inc., New York, N.Y.

Buton Klein, RAND Corporation, Washington, D.C.

Lowell G. Kraegel, National Science Foundation, Washington, D.C.

Philip N. Powers, Monsanto Chemical Company, St. Louis, Mo.

Everett Reimer, Syracuse University, Washington Research Office, Washington, D.C.

Robert E. Robinson, Jr., National Research Council, Washington, D.C.

H. M. Somers, Haverford College, Haverford, Penna.

Chicago, Illinois

Garrett L. Bergen, Marshall Field & Company, Chicago, Ill.

John T. Bobbitt, Argonne National Laboratory, Lemont, Ill.

Warren C. Johnson, University of Chicago, Chicago, Ill.

Robert Kennedy, Chicago Sun-Times, Chicago, Ill.

JUNE MEETINGS

Nashville, Tennessee

Paul R. Christopher, CIO Organizing Committee, Knoxville, Tenn.

Frank T. deVyver, Duke University, Durham, N.C.

Ernest J. Eberling, Vanderbilt University, Nashville, Tenn.

James L. Gabbard, Union Carbide and Carbon Corporation, Oak Ridge, Tenn.

George F. Gant, Southern Regional Education Board, Atlanta, Ga.

Henry Haller, International Harvester Company, Memphis, Tenn.

David L. Hill, Vanderbilt University, Nashville, Tenn.

John Hope II, Fisk University, Nashville, Tenn.

John E. Ivey, Jr., Southern Regional Education Board, Atlanta, Ga.

Howard K. Menhinick, Georgia Institute of Technology, Atlanta, Ga.

Alonzo G. Moron, Hampton Institute, Hampton, W. Va.

Richard O. Niehoff, Tennessee Valley Authority, Knoxville, Tenn.

F. D. Patterson, Tuskegee Institute, Tuskegee, Ala.

[a] Not previously listed.

J. J. Ray, General Shoe Corporation, Nashville, Tenn.

Rupert B. Vance, University of North Carolina, Chapel Hill, N. C.

Charles B. Wade, Jr., Reynolds Tobacco Company, Winston-Salem, N.C.

Kendall Weisiger, Rotary Educational Foundation of Atlanta, Atlanta, Ga.

Edward H. Weyler, Kentucky State Federation of Labor, AFL, Louisville, Ky.

Columbia University, New York

William A. Bittendender, Merck and Company, Rahway, N.J.

Cole Coolidge, E. I. DuPont de Nemours and Company, Wilmington, Del.

George O. Curme, Union Carbide and Carbon Corporation, New York, N.Y.

S. W. Davidson, Eastman Kodak Company, Rochester, N.Y.

Glen Giddings, General Electric Company, Schenectady, N. Y.

Solomon C. Hollister, School of Engineering, Cornell University, Ithaca, N.Y.

Elmore Northy, American Cyanamid Company, New York, N.Y.

Earl T. Stevenson, Arthur D. Little Company, Inc., Cambridge, Mass.

Julius A. Stratton, Massachusetts Institute of Technology, Cambridge, Mass.

W. J. Sweeney, Standard Oil Development Company, New York, N.Y.

The figures and map in Part Two were prepared by Mr. Vincent Kotschar, American Geographical Society, New York, N. Y.

Contents

Tables

Figures

PART ONE

A Policy for Scientific
and Professional Manpower

Summary of Recommendations by the National Manpower Council

ONLY a purposeful and sustained effort can insure that the United States will have adequate resources of scientific and professional manpower to meet its needs. Neither reliance upon a single course of action nor the pursuit of separate and unrelated policies will enable the nation to attain this goal.

Supported by an informed public opinion, a cooperative effort —involving government, industry, the educational institutions, and professional and other groups—can provide the nation with the scientific and professional manpower it requires through the achievement of five broad and related objectives. These are:

To develop more reliable knowledge about our human resources

To strengthen the institutions which educate and train our scientists and professionals

To maintain a continuous, large flow of students through our colleges and universities

To expand the opportunities for capable young persons to secure a higher education

To improve the utilization of the available supply of scientific and professional personnel

With respect to developing more reliable knowledge about our human resources, the National Manpower Council recommends that:

1. The foundations and the universities encourage and support research designed to increase our understanding of the processes of educational and career choices; of the factors facilitating the development of talent and intellectual ability; and of the conditions contributing to superior performance

2. Private and governmental agencies concerned with the development and utilization of scientific and professional manpower intensify their efforts to collect and analyze significant information about these critical resources

3. The Federal government, because of its specific responsibilities and unique facilities, provide leadership for these cooperative tasks under the guidance of the Office of Defense Mobilization

With respect to strengthening the institutions which educate and train our scientists and professionals, the National Manpower Council recommends that:

4. State and local governments, alumni, business, labor, and other interested groups and individuals intensify their efforts to provide the financial support required by the colleges and universities to improve their faculties and facilities

5. The President appoint a commission composed of representatives of government, universities, and industry to review the impact of governmental research and development contracts upon the primary responsibilities of the colleges and universities to advance fundamental knowledge and train tomorrow's scholars and scientists

6. Colleges and universities recognize that a dynamic society requires the kind of education and training that equips students to meet not only the demands of their first jobs but also the challenges of new tasks and problems which they will face many years later

With respect to maintaining a continuous, large flow of students through our colleges and universities, the National Manpower Council recommends that:

7. The public continue to support the present program of deferring qualified students in order to enable them to complete their education before they discharge their obligation of military service, and the President remove dependency, except in cases of hardship, as a ground for deferment in order to insure that postponement of service does not turn into exemption

8. The Secretary of Defense direct the Secretaries of the Army, the Navy, and the Air Force to provide sufficient flexibility in their policies governing the calling to active duty of students enrolled in Reserve Officers Training Corps programs, so that well-qualified students are permitted to pursue graduate work prior to their military service

With respect to expanding the opportunities for capable young persons to secure a higher education, the National Manpower Council recommends that:

9. The public and its elected officials fulfill their responsibility to maintain good elementary and secondary schools by providing the financial and personnel resources necessary to remedy the present weaknesses in our educational system

10. The schools, professional societies, governmental agencies, and other interested groups act together to strengthen the information and counseling services for high school and college students to assist them in the sound selection of schools, courses of instruction, and careers

11. Scholarship and fellowship programs, supported by private and public funds, be maintained and expanded to help more young people of ability to acquire a higher education

With respect to improving the utilization of the available supply of scientific and professional personnel, the National Manpower Council recommends that:

12. The President initiate a review of the existing legislation and administrative procedures governing the recall of reservists to active duty in order to develop a system that will provide for civilian participation in determining the

distribution of scientific and professional personnel required to meet military and civilian needs

13. Management intensify its efforts to determine the most effective balance among the different types of manpower it employs—scientific and professional, technical, skilled, and semi-skilled—in order to insure efficient and economical operations and to provide for the further training of the manpower for which it is responsible

14. Business and government intensify their efforts to develop executives who understand the importance of insuring that each highly trained person has the opportunity to utilize his capacities as fully as possible

A Statement by the
National Manpower Council

THIS NATION's economic and social well-being and its continued progress depend to a striking degree upon a small group of men and women who work in scientific and professional fields. The tense world situation gives our resources of scientific and professional manpower a special importance. In achieving national security and in strengthening the free world, many different kinds of scientists and professional persons—agricultural experts, international specialists, nuclear physicists, aeronautical engineers, psychologists, and a host of others—play key roles.

The National Manpower Council was established at Columbia University in the spring of 1951, under a grant from the Ford Foundation, to study significant manpower problems in this period of crisis and to contribute to the improved development and utilization of the country's human resources. The Council's primary concern is the training, skills, capacities, competence, and creativeness of the American people—that is, the *quality* of our human resources.

The Council first investigated the problem of *Student Deferment and National Manpower Policy,* on which it reported in April, 1952, and took as its second study *A Policy for Scientific and Professional Manpower.* The Council's third subject, *A Policy for Technical and Skilled Manpower,* is now under study. Each of these reflects the Council's concern with the quality of the nation's human resources.

SCIENTIFIC AND PROFESSIONAL PERSONNEL

Since 1900, the number of men and women who work in the sciences and the professions has been growing almost twice as fast as our total population. Today, over a million teachers are engaged in the education of our 32 million school children. We have over half a million engineers, one for every 120 in the nation's working force. Eighty years ago, there was only one engineer for every 2,000 in the working force. There are some 200,000 physicians and another 700,000 dentists, nurses, and other health workers in the country. Half a century ago, there were a little over a million men and women employed in scientific, professional, and related fields. Today, there are about 5 million.

We encounter the work of our physicians, teachers, clergymen, social workers, lawyers, and many other professionally trained persons in our daily lives. The functions performed by physical and natural scientists are not as directly familiar. We know that scientists and engineers have helped to bring about great changes in the food we eat, in the clothes we wear, and in the ways in which we produce goods, travel, and spend our leisure time. But we have less understanding of the work done by the small number of scientists which has revolutionized man's whole relationship to his physical universe.

American industry's increasing use of scientific advances has stimulated the growth of scientific and technological manpower in recent decades. Nevertheless, our 155,000 scientists still constitute a minute part—about two-tenths of one percent—of a working population of 63 million. Moreover, only about 15,000 of our scientists—one out of every 4,200 persons in the nation's working force—are primarily engaged in the fundamental research which opens up new frontiers of knowledge.

IMPACT OF THE WORLD CRISIS

During the latter part of World War II, some experts feared that the country's resources of scientific and professional manpower would be inadequate to meet the military challenge. After the war, there were scattered warnings that unless we took special action the nation would not have the highly trained personnel to meet the expanding needs of industry and government. Only after Korea became a battleground, however, was the critical importance of these limited manpower resources widely recognized.

As a result of the outbreak of hostilities in Korea, a program of partial mobilization was undertaken to deter aggression and build a solid foundation for a peaceful world. This program has created a heavy new demand for various kinds of scientists and professional persons. They are sought to man the nation's defense production program and its greatly expanded research and development activities. They are needed by the armed forces, and they are called upon to staff the technical assistance programs through which the United States is aiding its allies. Over 2,000 American scientists, professionals, and other highly trained persons are now working overseas to strengthen the free world.

Since the beginning of the fighting in Korea, the high demand for certain kinds of scientifically and professionally trained personnel has resulted in shortages. Current shortages and warnings of future shortages have spotlighted the importance of scientific and professional manpower for the security and well-being of the nation.

SHORTAGES

Newspaper advertisements of employment opportunities reflect the current high demand for engineers, physicists, and chemists. Delays in defense production have been blamed upon shortages of highly trained manpower. The scarcity of expert design engineers is said to result in the manufacture of some military items which are costly to operate and maintain. It is also reported that shortages of scientists and engineers have been responsible for the slow progress of research and development projects vital to the nation's security. It has been difficult to secure qualified Far Eastern and Russian experts for government service and university research projects.

Other current shortages have a longer history. For some years, the demand for nurses has exceeded the supply. For a decade, there have been shortages of qualified teachers. Rural communities have long been handicapped by shortages of doctors, and listings of unfilled positions for psychiatrists and other physicians in state hospitals have become fixed items in the medical journals. The scarcity of competent administrators has long been a cause of special concern to government and business.

Various attempts have been made to express the extent of current shortages in numerical terms. On the basis of studies by the Engineering Manpower Commission of Engineers Joint Council, a shortage of 25,000 newly graduated engineers was estimated at the end of 1952. If the number of emergency teaching licenses is used as a measure, there was a shortage of some 65,000 qualified elementary school teachers at the close of 1952.

In addition to shortages of physicians in certain rural areas and in most state hospitals, there are many positions for physicians in public health agencies which cannot be filled. There is, however, no commonly accepted estimate of the current shortage of doctors because there is no agreement on a standard of medical care or on the number of doctors required to provide any given level of medical care. The report of the President's Commission on the Health Needs of the Nation, submitted in December, 1952, emphasized the seriousness of current shortages and estimated that by 1960 the country will lack from 22,500 to 45,000 doctors. The President's Commission has also estimated that there will be a shortage of at least 50,000 registered nurses by that date.

Some authorities assert that there is little to be gained by trying to assess the extent of existing shortages in quantitative terms. They maintain that quality is the key factor in the demand for and the supply of scientific and professional personnel. For this reason the American Chemical Society, for example, has called attention to the unmet demand for various kinds of competent chemists, but it has not attempted to estimate the size of the current shortage.

In the case of physicists, too, there is little point in estimating the size of the shortage. Because of their great importance for national security, even a relatively small shortage of physicists is particularly critical. For some time, mature leaders for research projects as well as creative research physicists have been in particularly high demand.

ANALYSIS OF SHORTAGES

To contribute to the making of sound policies for relieving present and preventing future shortages, the National Manpower Council sought to learn how current shortages arose and to develop criteria for evaluating their significance. To accomplish this purpose, the Council, with the assistance of the staffs of professional societies and of other experts, undertook detailed studies of three groups of professionals—engineers, teachers, and physicians—and one group of scientists—physicists.

It is easy to demonstrate the existence of shortages, if the term is defined as the inability of employers to secure all the additional qualified personnel they are willing to hire at prevailing salary levels. It is far more difficult to determine the causes and full significance of shortages and their remedies. The basic information concerning the demand for and the supply and utilization of scientific and professional personnel is grossly inadequate, and a theoretical framework for the analysis of manpower problems still remains to be developed.

The emergency created by Communist aggression in Korea provides the key to many current shortages. The ensuing very sudden increases in expenditures for defense production and research and development came at a time of high civilian employment. These increases were quickly reflected in additional demands for scientists and engineers. However, the supply of scientists and engineers available to meet the new and expanding demands of industry and government was reduced after mid-1950. The peak college graduating classes of the post-war years were over; the draft had been reinstituted; and the armed services were forced to recall a large number of reservists.

Many employers, apprehensive about the future availability of highly trained personnel, hired engineers and scientists with an eye to anticipated rather than actual requirements. The tax structure and the cost-plus provision in government contracts encouraged employers to be uneconomical in the employment and utilization of manpower.

Since 1950, moreover, the United States has sought to have both more defense and more goods. In contrast to World War II, when the output of goods for civilian use was curtailed, civilian output since Korea has actually increased. Under these conditions, there has been a high demand for all kinds of physical and human resources. As the supply of highly trained manpower cannot be expanded quickly, these sudden and large increases in demand inevitably resulted in shortages.

A particularly important factor in the heavy demand for scientific and technological manpower has been the sharp rise in expenditures for research and development purposes. These expenditures doubled between 1949 and 1952. Current research and development projects, employing about 160,000 scientists and engineers, represent an annual cost of about $3.5 billion. The Federal government provides three-fifths of this money, most of which is being spent on applied research and development for defense purposes, and not on the basic research which aims at extending scientific knowledge.

The current high demand for physicists, chemists, and other scientists, however, cannot be attributed solely to the sudden expansion in research and development activities for defense. One consequence of the enormous strides taken in nuclear physics, electronics, and other fields in recent years has been the establishment of a higher demand for scientific personnel by industry. Private industrial research, moreover, has been steadily growing

in importance for several decades. Just as technological progress
has led to the greater use of engineers, so the practical application of scientific discoveries has increased the use of scientists by
industry.

In this period of partial mobilization, the United States has
resorted to a minimum of governmental control over manpower
and has made limited use of priorities for the allocation of other
scarce resources. As a result, the difficulties of transferring required resources to defense purposes have been multiplied. In
the absence of a system of governmental controls and priorities,
it has been both possible and profitable for industry to continue
to stress production for the civilian market, with the result that
there has been some delay in achieving defense goals.

Nevertheless, the gain in the nation's economic and military
strength since the fighting in Korea has been remarkable. Made
possible by the richness of our human and physical resources,
that gain has been attained with no reduction in civilian goods
and services and without resorting to compulsion except for building up the strength of the armed forces. In avoiding controls
over manpower and civilian industry, the nation has been willing
to risk delays in meeting its defense goals as well as shortages
of scientific and technological manpower.

Unlike the current shortages of engineers and scientists, those
of teachers and physicians are not primarily the result of demands produced by superimposing a program of partial mobilization upon a civilian economy operating at a high level of employment.

Shortages of qualified elementary school teachers have been
a continuing problem since World War II, when many teachers
left their posts for military service or for better paying jobs in
industry. For more than a decade, attractive opportunities in
private industry and the relatively low salaries and prestige of
teachers have discouraged many from entering or continuing in
the profession. Few communities have been sufficiently farsighted
or resourceful to protect their supply of competent teachers. The

total number of qualified teachers available is influenced by the steady rise in standards of licensing and by the fact that 90 percent of the elementary school teachers are women. Many women view teaching as a temporary occupation before marriage rather than as a lifetime career. The demand for teachers has been affected by the sharp rise in births during the 1940's, which is now reflected in increased elementary school enrollments and is beginning to be felt at the high school level. The spectacular population growth of new industrial and suburban areas has also created unusual demands for teachers in many communities.

Higher standards of health and a growing national income have increased the demand for medical service. At the same time, the limited capacities and the admission requirements of the medical schools have restricted the total number of doctors trained each year. Moreover, the supply of qualified physicians has been unevenly distributed throughout the country. For economic and other reasons, medical practice in rural areas has long been relatively unattractive. Although the ratio of doctors to population does not provide an accurate measure of medical care, it is significant that in 1949 there was one physician to about 500 people in the State of New York and one to almost 1,600 in Mississippi. The fact that 13,000 physicians—7 percent of the total supply—are in the armed forces also contributes to the current shortage of doctors.

ALLEVIATING SHORTAGES

There is no magic formula for the relief of manpower shortages. Each shortage requires separate analysis in order to determine how it can best be alleviated. Imbalances between supply and demand result from various causes and call for different kinds of corrective action.

Some shortages of scientific and professional personnel have been alleviated by improvements in the utilization of manpower which have had the effect of stretching the existing supply. Thus, auxiliary workers have been employed to relieve qualified engineers from routine tasks so that they can perform at a higher level of skill. For practical purposes, this change in utilization practice is equivalent to expanding the supply of engineers. The use of emergency licenses increases the available supply of teachers, although it may be criticized for sacrificing quality for quantity.

Certain manpower shortages are the inevitable reflections of scientific discovery and technological change. For example, recent advances have resulted in a shortage of solid-state physicists. Young men and women cannot be specifically trained for fields of work which may open up in the future. The scope and quality of their education and work experience, however, can prepare them to convert their skills to work on problems in new fields. Such convertibility provides in effect a potential reserve that can be drawn upon to meet demands for new kinds of personnel.

Manpower is never the only factor required for the production of goods, services, and ideas. It is necessary to determine for each shortage how limitations in personnel are related to other factors required to increase output. In addition to a shortage of scientists, for example, there may also be in a specific situation a shortage of capital, facilities, strategic materials, or technical workers. If such other shortages exist, it might be impossible to increase output even if additional scientific manpower were available. Thus, the scale of research and development activities is limited not only by the supply of scientists and engineers, but also by the willingness and ability of civilian industry and the armed forces to finance the production of new items in light of large investments in existing processes and stocks of finished goods.

Shortages of scientific and professional manpower always have qualitative as well as quantitative aspects. While some shortages involve an unfilled demand for hundreds or thousands of qualified personnel, others consist in the lack of a few individuals who possess rare and unusual qualities. Consequently, an increase in the gross supply alone may provide no solution for a specific shortage. Two second-rate engineers are not a substitute for the one first-rate man required. The addition of ten mediocre teachers to the staff will not relieve a school's need for several inspiring instructors. More general practitioners in a community do not make up for the lack of a competent neuro-surgeon or psychiatrist. The fact that all fields can always benefit from the work of men of outstanding ability underlines the limitations of considering scientific and professional manpower shortages solely as a problem in numbers.

THE PROBLEM OF FUTURE SHORTAGES

The consequences of current shortages warn of the dangers which would result from inadequate resources of scientific and professional manpower in the future. These potential dangers have stimulated efforts to increase the number of students in engineering, physics, chemistry, teaching, and other fields. The future supply of scientists and professional persons is directly dependent upon college enrollments. The current decline in the college age population, resulting from the low number of births in the 1930's, and the demand of the armed forces for manpower intensify the concern over future shortages. Not until the closing years of this decade will there be a substantial increase in the population of college age and in the number of college graduates.

The difficulties in measuring the extent of present shortages are minor compared to those involved in appraising future shortages. Estimates of college enrollment and graduation during the remainder of this decade permit forecasts of the future supply of scientific and professional manpower which are far more reliable than any predictions of future demand that can be ventured. There is no way to calculate the influence of all the key factors that will affect the demand for each group of scientific and professional workers.

At present all the signs point to a continuing strong demand for scientifically and professionally trained manpower. The cold war between the free world and the Soviet Union and its satellites will not terminate with the ending of hostilities in Korea. As long as the cold war continues, a significant share of our productive effort will be directed to the strengthening of the United States and its allies. Governmental expenditures for research and development will remain large, and the armed forces will probably be maintained at approximately their present size. Continuing advances in science and technology promise gains in productivity at least as great as those of past decades and a growing national income. The consumption of educational, health, and other services provided by professional personnel, therefore, is likely to increase whether conditions of partial mobilization continue or genuine peace is established. These considerations support the judgment that the total demand for the services of scientifically and professionally trained manpower in the future will be high.

PREVENTING FUTURE SHORTAGES

Demands for scientific and professional manpower can fluctuate sharply and unpredictably. The size of the supply, however, can be modified only slowly. Young men and women make decisions about their future careers in terms of life plans. Preparation for scientific and professional work requires many years of education and training. Within any limited time period, therefore, the demand for scientific and professional personnel is subject to far greater variations than the supply. There is real danger, consequently, in estimating future manpower requirements on the basis of current shortages or surpluses. Immediately before the outbreak of hostilities in Korea, the graduating classes of engineering schools were much larger than normal. In the light of the industrial demand then existing for engineers, many experts feared that some of the 50,000 engineering graduates in the record class of 1950 would find it difficult to secure satisfactory employment. After the Communist aggression in Korea, however, the possibility of a surplus of engineers was replaced by the actuality of a shortage.

Scientists and professional persons cannot be stockpiled like commodities against future shortages or hastily trained in response to sudden surges in demand. The problem of preventing future shortages, therefore, raises the question of what methods are available to a democratic society to insure a reasonable balance between supply and demand. Several factors that exercise major influence on supply and demand are not amenable to direct control by a free society. These include the dynamic character of modern science and technology, the expansion and contraction of the economy, irregularities in the birth rate, changes in educational institutions, and the values which affect the career decisions of individuals.

The nation can follow two broad courses of action in attempting to prevent future shortages:

We can try to alter the distribution of young men and women among fields of scientific and professional study so as to increase the numbers preparing for work in fields where shortages are anticipated, and

We can try to expand the size of the total college population so that more young men and women of ability will be educated and trained in each field.

Efforts are now being made to induce more students to select careers in fields where continuing shortages are expected, such as engineering, physics, chemistry, industrial management, and teaching. When energetically pursued, this course of action has the advantage of producing results in a relatively short time by influencing the career decisions of students about to enter or already in college. But, if the total college population remains stable, altering the distribution of students among fields of specialization means the growth of some fields at the expense of others. Thus, engineering may gain at the expense of chemistry, or physics at the expense of mathematics. If able students are channeled into scientific and technological fields, the social sciences and the humanities will inevitably suffer.

In a democratic society, the individual decides for himself the kind of education and career he will pursue. Since they determine the individual's future life, career choices should grow out of long-range considerations. Many students decide upon their careers quite early, sometimes before graduation from high school. Others make their choice during the first two years of college. Wise counseling and reliable information can contribute to sound educational and career choices. Hasty and uninformed decisions result in serious wastes of the individual's abilities and of the community's resources. These considerations point to the serious responsibilities assumed by schools, professional societies, employers, and others when they make special efforts to induce young men and women to select particular fields of study.

OUR UNDEVELOPED HUMAN RESOURCES

Today, less than half of those capable of acquiring a college degree enter college. About two-fifths of those who start college —many with superior ability—do not graduate. For every high school graduate who eventually earns a doctoral degree, there are twenty-five others who have the intellectual ability to achieve that degree but do not.

Because there are so many more young men and women in the nation capable of profiting from higher education than are currently obtaining it, future shortages can be guarded against by increasing the proportion of young men and women who graduate from college. An increase in the number of college graduates would expand the source of supply from which the nation's scientists and professional persons come and would help to reduce the loss represented by the failure to train many able individuals.

Three groups can readily be identified in the reserve of individuals capable of pursuing advanced education: high school graduates who do not enter college, those who start college but do not graduate, and those who graduate but do not pursue postgraduate training. There is an additional hidden reserve made up of capable individuals who achieve low scores on standard tests of intellectual ability primarily because of serious deficiencies in their early schooling. These individuals live, for the most part, in poor communities which spend little on education, and are

found particularly among such racial and ethnic minorities as
Negroes and Spanish-speaking Americans. The barriers which
limit the educational and occupational opportunities of these
groups have been substantially reduced in recent years. Many
Negroes, however, are still handicapped by poor education in
early life, and others are frequently prevented from using the
skills they do acquire by discriminatory employment practices.

GUIDES FOR ACTION

There is no easy way to insure that the United States will
have adequate resources of scientific and professional manpower
to meet its needs. Neither reliance upon a single course of action,
nor the pursuit of uncoordinated policies is sufficient. Nothing
short of a determined, cooperative effort involving government,
industry, the educational institutions, and professional and other
groups will attain this goal.

Supported by an informed public opinion, such a cooperative
effort can provide the nation with the scientific and professional
manpower it requires through the achievement of five broad and
related objectives. These are:

To develop more reliable knowledge about our human resources

To strengthen the institutions which educate and train our
scientists and professionals

To maintain a continuous, large flow of students through our
colleges and universities

To expand the opportunities for capable young persons to
secure a higher education

To improve the utilization of the available supply of scientific
and professional personnel

IMPROVING KNOWLEDGE ABOUT OUR HUMAN RESOURCES

The lack of a theoretical framework for manpower analysis
and the inadequacy of the information concerning our human
resources have made it difficult for the nation to appraise current

scientific and professional manpower problems and to work out sound policies for their solution.

The recent concern with shortages, however, has stimulated constructive action. Professional organizations such as the Engineering Manpower Commission of Engineers Joint Council and the American Chemical Society have developed more comprehensive information on their members and have improved their estimates of current and future demand. The Office of Defense Mobilization, in conjunction with other Federal agencies, has played a key role in preparing more reliable information on the demand for and supply of almost all groups of scientific and professional personnel. The Bureau of the Census has new data available in a form that will facilitate future research on professional, technical, and kindred workers.

In 1950, the Conference Board of Associated Research Councils established the Commission on Human Resources and Advanced Training. This Commission has been seeking to determine how many persons in the United States have been trained for scientific and professional work, the probable future demand for such personnel, and the number of individuals potentially capable of pursuing advanced education at college and post-graduate levels.

These and related developments are of great value, but much remains to be done before we possess the knowledge and tools we require. The National Manpower Council, therefore, recommends that:

1. The foundations and the universities encourage and support research designed to increase our understanding of the processes of educational and career choices; of the factors facilitating the development of talent and intellectual ability; and of the conditions contributing to superior performance

2. Private and governmental agencies concerned with the development and utilization of scientific and professional manpower intensify their efforts to collect and analyze significant information about these critical resources

3. The Federal government, because of its specific responsibilities and unique facilities, provide leadership for these cooperative tasks under the guidance of the Office of Defense Mobilization

STRENGTHENING THE EDUCATIONAL INSTITUTIONS

Our colleges and universities are the training centers for the nation's scientific and professional manpower. A decline in the quality of their teaching and research staffs or in other resources necessary for the effective performance of this function would injure the nation irreparably. At the end of 1952, the Commission on Financing Higher Education reported "a growing and serious discrepancy between the resources available to institutions of higher education and the costs of the services they are expected to perform."

In recent years the colleges and universities have seen effective teachers and gifted research personnel drawn away by the higher salary scales of industry and government. More important, low salaries are discouraging promising young men from entering upon academic careers.

Some relief from the financial problems faced by colleges and universities, particularly in the case of the larger institutions, is provided by their research and development contracts with the Federal government and industry. These contracts, in addition to contributing to the improved security of the country, have enabled many institutions to expand their staffs and research facilities.

But there is a serious danger that large-scale contracts for applied research may ultimately deflect the colleges and universities from their primary responsibilities for basic research and teaching. If basic research and teaching are neglected, the education of undergraduate and particularly of graduate students, must suffer. The heavy emphasis of contract research on the natural sciences also reduces the relative importance of the social sciences and the humanities within the university structure.

Reporting in March, 1953, the Committee on Institutional Research Policy of the American Council on Education pointed out that "both Government and higher education have a special obligation to continue a sound program of basic research . . . . This is a function of funds, of emphasis, of environment, and of men. This is another way of saying that it is a problem of maintaining the academic integrity of our educational institutions, of adhering to the primary objectives of higher education, and of not being beguiled by the temporary attractiveness of sponsored research that does not meet these long-term objectives." The staff of the National Science Foundation is now studying the impact of Federal funds for scientific research on the institutions of higher education.

With the country faced by the possibility of long-term shortages of scientific and professional personnel, the intellectual resourcefulness and convertibility of our scientists and professional persons to meet new problems assume great importance. Hence, there is special need for the institutions of higher education to reexamine their curricula and teaching methods to determine how effectively they contribute to the breadth as well as the depth of specialized training. Such a reexamination is, of course, a continuing responsibility of all educational institutions.

The National Manpower Council recommends that:

1. State and local governments, alumni, business, labor, and other interested groups and individuals intensify their efforts to provide the financial support required by the colleges and universities to improve their faculties and facilities

2. The President appoint a commission composed of representatives of government, universities, and industry to review the impact of governmental research and development contracts upon the primary responsibilities of the colleges and universities to advance fundamental knowledge and train tomorrow's scholars and scientists

3. Colleges and universities recognize that a dynamic society requires the kind of education and training that equips stu-

dents to meet not only the demands of their first jobs but also the challenges of new tasks and problems which they will face many years later

MAINTAINING THE FLOW OF STUDENTS

A sharp reduction in the number of students who enter and graduate from college will reduce the future supply of scientific and professional manpower. This occurred during World War II, when many young men were drawn out of the colleges for military service and many more did not enter. In 1948, the President's Commission on Higher Education found that the country had not adequately protected its resources of scientific personnel during the war, and that there was in consequence an insufficient number of qualified persons to meet the expanding manpower needs of government, industry, and the universities.

When the Congress amended the Universal Military Training and Service Act in 1951, it specifically recognized the importance of maintaining a continuous supply of highly skilled, scientific, and professional persons by providing for the deferment of qualified students. The deferment of students insures a continuing and large flow of young men into college and post-graduate study. By permitting students to postpone the time of their military service, but not to escape their obligation to serve, the student deferment program makes it easier for young men to plan for a career in science or the professions.

The growth of the Reserve Officers Training Corps programs has created a special problem in connection with graduate study. Reserve Officers Training Corps units are heavily concentrated in engineering and technological schools. In 1952, about one out of every six engineering school seniors was in the ROTC, and the ratio is expected to be one in four in 1953. A significant number of talented engineers and young scientists who are commissioned in the armed forces immediately on graduation from college may never return to the university to take an advanced degree.

In order to maintain a large and continuous flow of students

into the institutions of higher education, the National Manpower
Council recommends that:

1. The public continue to support the present program of defer-
    ring qualified students in order to enable them to complete
    their education before they discharge their obligation of
    military service, and the President remove dependency,
    except in cases of hardship, as a ground for deferment
    in order to insure that postponement of service does not turn
    into exemption

2. The Secretary of Defense direct the Secretaries of the Army,
    the Navy, and the Air Force to provide sufficient flexibility
    in their policies governing the calling to active duty of stu-
    dents enrolled in Reserve Officers Training Corps programs
    so that well-qualified students are permitted to pursue
    graduate work prior to their military service

EXPANDING THE OPPORTUNITIES FOR EDUCATION

In recent years, the United States has been spending less
than one percent of its national income on higher education. We
spend about 2 percent of our national income on elementary and
high school education. In contrast, we spend more than 4 percent
on recreation. The nation has the economic resources and the
reserves of intellectually capable young men and women to increase its college-educated population and thereby to provide
for an expansion of its scientific and professional manpower. We
have the need and the means, but we must develop the understanding and the will to attack the problem.

To encourage more able young men and women who do not
now undertake advanced education and training to do so will
require the accomplishment of at least the following four objectives:

Increased opportunities for and marked improvement in the
    quality of elementary and secondary schooling so as to elimi-
    nate gross educational deficiencies where they now exist

The reduction of financial barriers which currently prevent able persons from attending college and pursuing post-graduate work

The determination of the constructive measures that must be taken to insure that a larger percentage of able college students graduate from college

The creation of a more favorable climate of opinion for intellectual work and the reward of intellectual achievement

These goals will not be quickly attained, but they can be realized if the nation has the will to do so. The work of many local and state groups and such national organizations as the National Citizens Commission for the Public Schools has helped to impress upon the country that it has not matched its professed belief in education with deeds.

Considerable progress toward these objectives has already been made in recent years. Discriminatory barriers have been reduced. Scholarship and fellowship programs and veterans' benefits have made it possible for many able young persons, who otherwise would have lacked the means, to attend college and graduate school. A constantly larger number of business corporations and some trade unions have made funds available for scholarships. The foundations, which have long played a key role in the development of scientific and professional manpower, support a large number of specialized training programs. In creating the National Science Foundation in 1950, Congress recognized the importance of providing governmental assistance for advanced education and training in the physical, biological, and medical sciences.

To expand the opportunities for capable young persons to secure a higher education, the National Manpower Council recommends that:

1. The public and its elected officials fulfill their responsibility to maintain good elementary and secondary schools by providing the financial and personnel resources necessary to remedy the present weaknesses in our educational system

2. The schools, professional societies, governmental agencies, and other interested groups act together to strengthen the information and counseling services for high school and college students to assist them in the sound selection of schools, courses of instruction, and careers

3. Scholarship and fellowship programs, supported by private and public funds, be maintained and expanded to help more young people of ability to acquire a higher education

UTILIZING MANPOWER EFFECTIVELY

During World War II, and again after the outbreak of hostilities in Korea, manpower shortages encouraged the search for new and more effective ways of utilizing available trained personnel. Under normal conditions, the weight of tradition and habit discourages changes in manpower practices and contributes to the ineffective use of personnel. Many steps have recently been taken to insure more effective utilization of our limited resources of scientific and professional personnel, but much remains to be done before this objective is fully realized.

The armed forces are the largest single employer of manpower in the nation. By improving their selection and assignment procedures, they have tried to prevent waste of the capacities of scientists and professionals as well as of technical and skilled personnel. There is need, however, for the armed forces to take additional steps to improve the effective utilization of their trained manpower.

Policies governing the recall of reservists with scientific and professional training have not yet received adequate attention. Under present legislation, sole responsibility for the recall of reservists rests with the armed forces. Even though an extensive recall of reservists who are qualified scientists and professional persons would have the most far-reaching consequences for civilian work and life, there is no provision for civilian participation in the recall process.

The National Manpower Council recommends that:

1. The President initiate a review of the existing legislation and administrative procedures governing the recall of reservists to active duty in order to develop a system that will provide for civilian participation in determining the distribution of scientific and professional personnel required to meet military and civilian needs

2. Management intensify its efforts to determine the most effective balance among the different types of manpower it employs—scientific and professional, technical, skilled, and semi-skilled—in order to insure efficient and economical operations and to provide for the further training of the manpower for which it is responsible

3. Business and government intensify their efforts to develop executives who understand the importance of insuring that each highly trained person has the opportunity to utilize his capacities as fully as possible

PART TWO

Facts and Issues about Scientific and Professional Manpower

PREPARED BY THE RESEARCH STAFF

ELI GINZBERG, Director of Research
HENRY DAVID, Executive Secretary

SIDNEY E. ROLFE
I. PEGGY MOSES

JAMES K. ANDERSON
DOUGLAS W. BRAY
ROBERT W. SMUTS

CHAPTER I

Introduction

In the first optimistic years after World War II, it seemed reasonable for a group of social scientists to observe that the United States had "reached a stage of economic development and technical competence where inadequate industrial and commercial capacities can be quickly overcome through the construction of new facilities. We have more than enough manpower and resources and possess potential productive facilities to fulfill our requirements under every conceivable circumstance." This judgment appeared in the Twentieth Century Fund's comprehensive study, *America's Needs and Resources*, published in 1947. Since that date, and particularly since the midsummer of 1950, the country has had to learn that only specially directed, concerted efforts can provide the productive facilities, the material resources, and the manpower required by circumstances which had earlier seemed inconceivable.

The necessity of checking Communist aggression in Korea and of assuring a posture of readiness against the eventuality of a full-scale war without sacrificing the country's future well-being has led to widespread fear that the nation would be hard pressed to find the required manpower. Nevertheless, most of the manpower demands arising from the program of economic and military mobilization have been met with relative ease. The exceptions are the requirements for certain major groups of scientists and professional persons. In the *Eighth Quarterly Report to the President* on January 1, 1953, the Director of Defense Mobilization declared that "Acute shortages are continuing among highly skilled professional, scientific, and technical workers needed in defense and essential civilian activities. Under full mobilization," he warned, "the lack of such workers would be critical."

The cold war and the responsibilities which fall to the United States as the most powerful nation in the free world have inspired a unique concern with the adequacy of its resources of scientific and professional manpower. There is a growing appreciation of the significance of these highly trained persons in the country's normal life and its future progress, as well as in the present program of partial mobilization. This is the first step toward a public recognition that the development and effective utilization of the nation's resources of scientific and professional manpower constitute a new and challenging issue of public policy.

A little over a half century ago, a new approach to the country's physical resources began to develop because a few farsighted individuals realized that they were not inexhaustible. The work of the National Conservation Commission resulted, early in 1909, in the first of many attempts to inventory the natural resources of the United States. The exhaustive Report of the President's Materials Policy Commission, *Resources for Freedom,* submitted in 1952, reveals how much more is known at present about the country's physical resources than about its human resources. The unusually large demand for scientific and professional manpower during World War II and since Korea has highlighted the fact that much of the information essential for sound policy-making is lacking. It has also stimulated a fresh approach to problems concerning human resources.

In the past, the concern with human resources centered largely on the span of human life, health, and immigration. Efforts to conserve human resources aimed mainly at the elimination of preventable deaths. Disease and accidents were the specific targets, and improved hygiene, preventive medicine, and industrial and other safety measures were the major means relied upon. Until quite recently, questions of the effective use of the country's human resources, the development of skills and capacities, and the waste of ability received relatively little attention.

Since there seemed to be no ground for doubting the qualitative and quantitative adequacy of the country's resources of scientific and professional manpower as a whole, there was no reason to consider special measures to augment the supply and competence of such personnel. At the same time, of course, there were efforts to raise the standards of competence of professional groups, and to improve the quality of their formal education and training, as in the case of lawyers, doctors, and teachers. Evidence of these developments appears in the growth of professional and graduate schools, the striking rise in their admission requirements, and the improvement of their courses of instruction during the past half century. In general, however, it was taken for granted that the publicly supported educational system, the normal play of economic incentives, the social mobility of the American people, and immigration would provide the professional and scientific personnel required by a growing and increasingly complex society. Special provision for the relatively free admission of professional personnel in the restrictive immigration laws of the 1920's was an unusual expression of national concern with the supply of highly trained manpower.

America's wealth and the standard of living of its people, which were both a cause and a consequence of the growth of its scientifically and professionally trained personnel, had apparently been achieved without concerted attempts to insure an adequate supply of these kinds of manpower. Other societies, such as Germany and Japan, had consciously planned for their development, as has Soviet Russia since the 1920's. The experience of the United States, however, provided no compelling reasons to regard the supply of scientists and professionals as a question requiring long-range national policy.

THE NEW ATTITUDE TOWARD HUMAN RESOURCES

Since 1940, American attitudes toward the development and use of the nation's manpower resources have been challenged repeatedly. Even before Pearl Harbor, the importance of having an inventory of the highly trained manpower in the country was realized. In 1940, work on a national roster of scientists was begun. This kind of undertaking was renewed in the spring of 1950 with plans for an expanded and current National Scientific Register. Since then other rosters listing social scientists, recent graduates in engineering and scientific fields, and other groups have been prepared.

Reflection on the manpower policies of World War II raised the question of how a continuous, large supply of college-trained young men could be maintained under conditions of compulsory military service. Thus, the President's Commission on Higher Education reported at the close of 1948 that the country had failed to "safeguard its scientific manpower during . . . [World War II] as other nations did, and consequently we now do not have enough trained personnel to staff the research and development laboratories of industry, government, and the universities." At the same time, a number of individuals with intimate knowledge of the importance of scientific manpower for national security were warning that it was no longer safe to rely upon "normal" processes to produce the highly trained people which the country required. In *Modern Arms and Free Men*, published in 1949, Dr. Vannevar Bush declared: "In a world where the prosecution of war or the avoidance of war demands that we be in the forefront in the applications of science to public health, industry, and preparations for fighting effectively in the modern sense, we can no longer afford to drift with a slow current."

A new awareness of the role of basic scientific research and of scientific manpower in the country's strategic position as a world power, as well as in its economic welfare, was revealed in several developments during the latter half of 1950. In October of that year, the Six Scientific Advisory Committees to the Director of Selective Service, which had been appointed in 1948, recommended the establishment of a system of deferring students, so that a large and continuous supply of college-trained manpower would be available to the nation. In December, the National Security Resources Board established a Scientific Manpower Advisory Committee. Its report, *Plans for the Development and Use of Scientific Manpower,* popularly known as the Thomas Report, also urged the adoption of a student deferment plan. In addition, it recommended a special policy for the recall of members of the armed forces reserves who were scientifically and technically trained. It also suggested the creation of a National Scientific Personnel Board.

After several years of debate, the Congress finally acted at the close of 1950 to establish the National Science Foundation. In seeking to develop a broad national policy to insure that work in basic scientific research is adequate for the country's continued technological progress and security, the National Science Foundation has devoted considerable attention to problems of scientific manpower. The new place of science in American life and, consequently, the crucial position which scientific manpower occupies have been effectively indicated by Chester I. Barnard, the present chairman of the National Science Board of the National Science Foundation. In the Foreword to the Foundation's report for 1952, he wrote that "until comparatively recently, it has been generally impossible to look for practical results from application of science except to various specific problems and quite sporadically. This is still true, of course, in many branches of science, where the density of knowledge is low and the comprehensiveness and utility of theory is restricted. But we have now reached the stage of social organization and scientific development where these earlier limitations are being much reduced. This justifies the expenditure to a degree not possible earlier of manpower, resources, and money, solely to extend our knowledge and develop fundamental scientific ideas for their potential, if not immediately apparent, practical significance. Thus, we have reached the stage where the maintenance of an expanding pool of tested scientific knowledge is good economics as well as indispensable in the effective utilization of the world's natural resources for the needs of an increasing and largely half-starved population and necessary for maintaining the competitive position of this Nation for military or economic purposes.

"Whether such competition is desirable or merely unavoidable depends on the point of view. In any event, the bottleneck in the future will be men. The proportion of our population potentially capable of assimilating the training required of scientists, or having the curiosity, interest, and ambition to pursue effective scientific careers, is narrowly limited compared with the need for such trained individuals in the development of basic science."

The manpower implications of the continuing revolution in technology, which is so characteristic a facet of the history of the United States, were never fully grasped until the country was faced with the frightening possibility of another world war in the next decade or two. The full importance of highly trained personnel was not appreciated earlier largely because their major role in American life is so recent. It seems almost incredible, for example, that the first professionally trained chemist in the American petroleum industry was employed less than sixty-five years ago, and that up to 1900 there was not a single industrial research laboratory in the country.

New commodities, new skills, new processes, and new techniques are part of the American cultural experience. Increasing control over the physical world, the outcome of advances in technology, is taken for granted by Americans. No other society has gone quite so far in organizing its scientific and financial resources to solve specific problems in applied research. What the nation is capable of accomplishing when it marshals these resources is written in the history of the atomic bomb. The country's pride in its "know-how" is understandable. But this pride can also create undue optimism about the superiority of American technology, the progress of which rests upon the growth of basic scientific knowledge and upon a large supply of competent scientific and technological personnel. A failure in either would jeopardize, not only the country's technological position, but also its security and future economic development.

Other highly trained professional groups have also been the subjects of growing concern in recent years. Serious questions have been raised about the adequacy of the supply of teachers, doctors, and nurses. The international position of the United States has established a demand for experts in the languages, the geography, the culture, and the economy of areas which until recently were studied by only a few scholars. Thirty years ago there was no reason to wonder whether there were enough linguists, economists, historians, or anthropologists to work on problems relating to the Near East, the Soviet Union, and the Far East. The Arabic, Korean, or Russian language and area specialist represents a new kind of professional to fill a new kind of need.

The cumulative result of the nation's recent manpower experiences has been to focus attention upon its scientific and professional personnel as a whole and to encourage a search for the answers to at least two broad questions. Are the country's resources of scientific and professional manpower adequate in numbers and competence to fulfill current and future requirements? What are the significant factors which affect the development and utilization of these resources?

CHARACTERISTICS OF SCIENTIFIC AND PROFESSIONAL MANPOWER

Many criteria can be employed to distinguish one kind of manpower from another. Function, training, skill, tradition, social status, and still other considerations enter into the distinctions made among the various groups of workers in the labor force of a modern society. When the character of many jobs is changing rapidly, the large categories which once served to group workers whose occupations were reasonably similar lose much of their meaning. What formerly appeared to be distinct boundary lines between semi-skilled and unskilled workers in the United States, for example, have become quite blurred. No one would assert that all of the workers who are counted as skilled in the Census really belong in that category on the basis of any single criterion of judgment. Nor is it altogether clear how skilled workers are to be differentiated accurately from technicians.

These difficulties are encountered also in the attempt to distinguish professionals from other classes of workers. It is suggestive that the Bureau of the Census has found it wise to refrain from defining the term "profession," and that many groups have sought to acquire professional status by inducing the Census to count them as professionals. The lists of "professional occupations" used by the Census enumerators half a century ago included government clerks, as well as doctors, dentists, lawyers, ministers, and engineers. Until the last Census, on the other hand, certified public accountants were listed under "clerical and kindred workers."

Since the word "professional" was first used in something like its modern sense in the sixteenth century it has been applied to an increasing number of occupational groups. Through the eighteenth century, there were only three recognized professions: divinity, law, and medicine. Since then, many other vocations have been accorded professional status. The growth in many fields of knowledge, the continuing industrial revolution, and changes in education have all been mirrored in the appearance of new professions.

The history of the professions also reflects changes in society's evaluation of certain occupations. Thus, one might venture the surmise that, if astrology had the same function and significance today that it did in the sixteenth and seventeenth centuries, its highly skilled practitioners would be given professional status. Recognition of their importance to society, regard for the uncommon training, knowledge, and skill they require, and respect for the relatively few persons who engage in them are all involved in the acceptance of certain vocations as professions. These attitudes toward an occupation do not appear suddenly. Historically, they are largely the result of the special efforts of an occupational group to set themselves apart from others, to establish standards of training and practice, to regulate the conduct of their members, and to advance their knowledge. The professional society plays a key role in the emergence and recognition of the professional group. These societies represent their members both to the public at large and to government. Frequently, they have sought to have the status of their members distinguished and protected by licensing requirements.

Today, three features characterize the fully-developed profession. In the words of Lloyd E. Blauch of the U.S. Office of Education, these are: "(1) a specialized intellectual training on the level of higher education equivalent to at least that represented by an academic degree, (2) standards of efficiency and success that are professional rather than financial in character, and (3) associations which assume responsibility for maintaining and improving the quality of [professional] service." Although these are the essential characteristics which now differentiate professions from other vocations, others are frequently invoked in attempts to define the term profession more rigidly. Among such other features, as Mr. Blauch remarks, are "the limitation of the right to practice to those who have been adjudged competent, a sufficient remuneration to support the service provided, large individual responsibility on the part of the practitioner, and regulation in the public interest."

The preparation for both professional and scientific careers is nearly always secured today through college and post-graduate education. The nature of scientific and professional work is basically intellectual. It may be asked, therefore, whether there is any justification for making a distinction between scientific and professional personnel. Certainly, the work of both scientists and professionals rests upon their control over a body of specialized theory or knowledge which is acquired through an extended period of formal education. It is also true that scientists, to the extent that they reflect on the question at all, generally think of themselves as being members of a profession. Nevertheless, there are reasons for employing both terms instead of including scientists within the broader category of professional manpower.

In the first place, the distinguishing mark of scientific activity is the pursuit of new knowledge through research, while professional activity consists primarily in providing services made possible by the application of existing knowledge. In a formal sense, the scientist performs a research function, while the professional is a practitioner. In practice, of course, professionals also play a part in advancing the frontiers of knowledge, while many trained in both the physical and social sciences pursue careers in which research activities play little or no part. Chemists, psychologists, biologists, economists, and other physical and social scientists are found in executive, teaching, and administrative posts which involve no direct use of their research training.

It is also significant that a distinction is maintained between the scientist and the professional in popular usage. This is understandable in light of the fact that the popular idea of the professional tends to be derived from medicine and law. The sciences as distinct fields are relatively young. Until fairly recently, most persons who worked in the sciences did not think of themselves as members of a profession. Nor did they display a desire to be given professional status. The professionalization of a field of work, as has been suggested, depends heavily on the activities of organizations of those who are engaged in it. Learned or scholarly societies have not usually sought professional status for their members as have the societies in engineering, medicine, law, and other fields.

The scientists and professional persons who number about 5 million in a total working population of about 63 million in the United States can be classified in smaller groups in a number of ways. The most common classifications are based on education and function. One accepted system of classifying scientific and professional manpower uses the following ten categories:

(1) the physical and earth sciences; (2) the biological and agricultural sciences; (3) the medical and related health fields; (4) engineering; (5) psychology; (6) the social sciences; (7) the humanities and arts; (8) education; (9) business and commerce; and (10) miscellaneous other professions.

Each of these categories can be sub-divided, or combined with others to form larger divisions. The first two are frequently grouped together as the natural sciences. Psychology is sometimes classified as a biological science, sometimes as a social science. There is a lively dispute among historians over whether their discipline belongs with the social sciences, the humanities and arts, or in a separate category of its own.

All classification systems involve difficulties in placing some individuals in one category or another. There may be as much reason to place the person with a doctoral degree in engineering with the physical scientists as with the engineers. The classification of those who work in frontier or interdisciplinary fields is always highly arbitrary. Where does one place the biophysicist, the medical economist, or the foreign language and area expert? Furthermore, no classification by field of education and work can represent the particular kinds of functions performed by all the members of one group. It cannot indicate when the doctor or lawyer is an administrator or a teacher rather than a practitioner of medicine or law, or when the anthropologist is engaged in governmental service rather than research. The task of distinguishing different groups of professionals and scientists from other groups of workers and from each other contributes to the difficulties which are encountered in coming to grips with problems in the field of scientific and professional manpower.

The chapters which follow serve to place current problems relating to scientific and professional manpower within a larger historical, social, and economic setting. These problems have been sharply revealed by the emergency period which began with the Korean conflict, but they can be properly assessed only within this broader context.

CHAPTER II

The Growth of the Professions

An occupational revolution has taken place in the United States since 1870. Eight decades ago, there were less than half a million professional workers, and they represented 3 percent of the labor force. Today, there are approximately five million, and they constitute about 8 percent of the labor force. The number of professional workers increased over three and one-half times faster than the nation's population during this period and almost three times faster than the whole American labor force. The rapid growth of this group has been both a cause and a result of industrialization. Modern industry requires not only large numbers of engineers to perform technological and managerial functions, but also scientists, administrators, and other professional personnel. The dynamic expansion of the American economy since 1870 has been accompanied by striking advances in national wealth and individual and family income. These gains, in turn, have enabled the American people to consume more educational, medical, and other professional services, and to support the institutions which provide professional training.

CHANGES IN THE PROFESSIONS

An understanding of how the various professions have grown contributes to a sound assessment of their present role in American life, and to the development of wise policies which affect the competence and numbers of their members. Unfortunately, the data on scientific and professional workers in the earlier decades are inadequate. The Census statistics available for each decade since 1870 provide uniform information on only a few professional occupations. Until 1950, the chemists were the only group of scientific workers listed by the Census, and they were combined with assayers and metallurgists. The contrast between the paucity of information in previous Census reports and the data presented in the 1950 report testifies to the growing public concern with scientific and professional manpower.

Since past Censuses do not list all the scientific and professional workers who are now the subject of public concern, the description of historical trends in the growth of the professions must be based on statistics covering the groups which comprise the broad Census category, "professional, technical, and kindred workers." Some of these groups, such as artists, entertainers, and various kinds of technicians, lie outside the scope of the National Manpower Council's present study. In spite of inadequacies in the statistics, the data available do provide a broad view of the rapid growth of the whole professional field and of the changing importance of different professional groups.

Table 1 shows that the professional labor force has increased remarkably since 1870, but that its rate of growth has not been constant. The decennial figures suggest that increases in the percentage of workers employed in professional occupations are related to general economic conditions. Thus, in decades characterized by severe depressions, such as the 1890's and 1930's, the increase in the proportion of the total labor force employed in professional occupations was slight. The most rapid rises occurred during the prosperous 1920's and from 1940 to 1950.

During World War II, the number of professionals in civilian employment dropped sharply, in spite of the expansion in the total civilian labor force. Professionals who entered the armed forces could not be replaced easily, and members of such lower paid professions as teaching took better paid clerical and semi-

Table 1. Professional, Technical, and Kindred Workers in the United States, by Major Fields, 1870-1950[a]

Year	Teaching	Health	Religion and Social Welfare	Law	Arts, Letters, and Entertainment	Science and Technology	Other	Total Professional, Technical, and Kindred Workers[b]	Percent of Professional, Technical, and Kindred Workers in Total Labor Force
1870	127,265	103,197	44,035	39,242	36,797	11,855	3,209	365,600	2.8
1880	224,432	137,029	63,404	62,225	70,122	16,236	5,252	578,700	3.3
1890	342,513	176,986	86,439	84,163	154,004	53,754	11,841	909,700	3.9
1900	439,914	234,708	109,405	107,478	210,744	90,293	17,858	1,210,400	4.2
1910	611,110	354,754	131,555	114,704	301,961	185,879	31,137	1,731,100	4.6
1920	785,796	458,645	167,369	122,519	305,914	293,097	39,160	2,172,500	5.1
1930	1,106,540	660,788	210,280	160,605	435,336	450,316	92,535	3,116,400	6.4
1940	1,141,127	749,288	250,446	180,483	451,377	548,231	237,448	3,558,400	6.7
1950[c]	1,253,016	1,009,865	303,309	181,226	570,155	1,019,120	651,321	4,988,000	8.2

[a] Based on information supplied by the Bureau of the Census and the Bureau of Labor Statistics. Includes both professionals and semi-professional assistants.

[b] Figures may not add to totals because of rounding.

[c] Preliminary.

skilled jobs. In addition, many students left school before completing their training to enter the armed forces or to take nonprofessional jobs. As a result, by 1945 professional employment accounted for less than 5 percent of the labor force. The post-war years brought an increase in professional workers, and by 1950, the completion of professional training by large numbers of veterans was reflected in the occupational statistics.

While all the major professional fields have expanded, they have grown at very different rates. Figure 1 depicts the changing

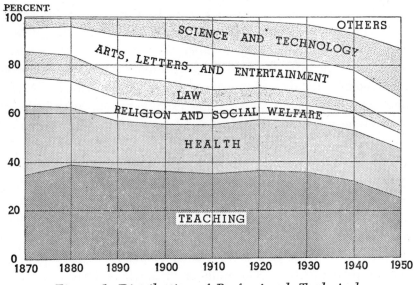

Figure 1. *Distribution of Professional, Technical, and Kindred Workers, 1870-1950*
Based on data provided by the Bureau of the Census and the Bureau of Labor Statistics

distribution of workers in professional occupations since 1870. The proportion of professional workers engaged in the traditional fields of law, health, and religion and social welfare have been declining. The teaching profession maintained its relative importance up to 1940 but has since declined. The percentage employed in scientific and technological fields has increased. The arts, letters, and entertainment group increased in importance as a field of professional employment until the first decade of the current century. Since then, the trend has reversed. The category "other professional employment," which represents a great many new or unclassified fields, has recently begun to increase. This is significant, for it calls attention to the important fact that the growth in the number of professionals represents an increase in the kinds of professions as well as continual expansion in the size of the older ones.

There is now approximately one health worker for every 150 persons in the country, compared to one for every 390 eighty years ago. The number of health personnel, nevertheless, has grown more slowly than the total number of professionals for several reasons. Since 1920, the facilities for training some of the health professionals, notably physicians, have expanded slowly. More rigorous professional standards now exclude persons with little or no training who earlier were allowed to practice and, therefore, were counted as doctors or dentists.

Developments in the health field warn against using the number of professional workers as a measure of the amount of professional service performed. The ratio of physicians to population is now about the same as it was in 1920, but each doctor can now provide more service because of improved training and techniques and the increased utilization of medical technicians both in private and hospital practice. The number of auxiliary health workers has grown very rapidly. The urbanization of the population and the improvements in transportation have enabled the doctor to spend less of his time traveling from patient to patient and more of it treating patients.

Of the groups in Figure 1, the scientific and technological workers have increased more rapidly than any other. They represented only 3 percent of all professional persons in 1870, and over 20 percent by 1950. In 1870, there was roughly one engineer for every 850 non-agricultural worker; by 1950, one for every 100. Personnel in the natural and physical sciences grew even more rapidly. Employment in these fields, excluding teachers, increased from about 1,300 in 1870, most of whom were chemists, to approximately 121,000 in 1950. The distribution among major fields in the natural and physical sciences is shown in Table 2. It should be noted that over one-fifth of all scientists are primarily teachers. The proportion who teach, however, varies from only 7 percent of the chemists to over 80 percent of the mathematicians.

Table 2. *Estimated Number of Natural and Physical Scientists, 1950*[a]

SCIENTIFIC FIELD	TOTAL	College Professors and Instructors[b]	Other
Chemists	81,676	5,929	75,747
Biologists	13,300	5,414	7,886
Physicists	10,785	3,659	7,126
Geologists and geophysicists	9,938	993	8,945
Agronomists	8,876	3,761	5,115
Psychologists	8,804	4,251	4,553
Mathematicians	6,826	5,507	1,319
Other natural and physical scientists, including medical scientists	13,752	3,448	10,304
Total	153,957	32,962	120,995

[a] Based on sample data supplied by the Bureau of the Census.
[b] College professors and instructors are included with the teaching profession in Table 1 and elsewhere in the text, unless otherwise specified.

Not all of these persons are highly trained. Most work under highly trained scientists and may have only a bachelor's degree or less, but their contribution to scientific work is, nevertheless, important. In the team operations of modern science, these persons are indispensable.

Teaching, which today accounts for about one-fourth of total professional employment, kept pace with the general growth in the professions between 1870 and 1940, but has declined in relative importance in the last decade. The number of bachelor's degrees in the field of teaching rose from 4 to 24 percent of all bachelor's degrees between 1920 and 1940. This represents an expansion of teaching as a special field of study, rather than an increase in the proportion of students preparing for teaching as a career. The colleges still employ only a small portion of all teachers. Nevertheless, since 1910, the number of college teachers has increased almost ten times, while the number of other teachers has not quite doubled.

Lawyers and clergymen have constituted a declining percentage of the total professional group. The lawyers accounted for less than 4 percent of all professionals in 1950, compared with 11 percent in 1870. Clergymen increased less rapidly than the population. The factors responsible probably include urbanization which permits larger congregations and the greater tendency of people to seek aid for their troubles from secular advisers. Thus, social workers, many of whom do counseling work, increased from a negligible number in 1910 to more than 76,000 in 1950.

The arts, letters, and entertainment increased rapidly as fields of professional employment until the first decade of the twentieth century, but have declined in relative importance since then. The development of the phonograph, motion pictures, radio, and television resulted in an absolute decline in the number of entertainers. The consolidation that has taken place in the news services curtailed the growth in the number of reporters and editors. On the other hand, the number of artists, authors, and librarians continued to increase rapidly.

Two fields of professional employment have grown very rapidly during recent decades—business administration and the social sciences. These two fields account for a major portion of the increase in "other professional workers" shown in Table 1 and Figure 1. The rapid increase in the percentage of bachelor's degrees awarded to students of business administration and social science is one of the most striking changes in higher education during the last three decades. It contrasts sharply with the relative decline in the proportion of college students preparing for the fields of medicine, law, theology, and humanities; the moderate increase in the proportion preparing for the natural and physical sciences;

and the relatively stable proportion preparing for teaching and engineering during most of the same period. One recent study found that the social sciences are replacing the humanities as the major non-vocational field of college study. (The present distribution of degrees among fields of study is shown in Table 4.) In 1950, more than 57,000 persons were working as economists, statisticians, sociologists, political scientists, and historians. Of these, about 45 percent were college teachers.

The number of undergraduate degrees awarded to students of business administration over the last thirty years has also increased rapidly. In 1952, about 50,000 students received college degrees in business fields. The growth of collegiate training for business careers is directly related to the growing size and complexity of business enterprises, which now require many kinds of specialists as well as professionally trained administrators. Aside from the specific need of business for professionally trained people, the business world has placed an increasing value on a college degree in the selection of future executives. This policy has been made possible by the great expansion of college attendance, but it has also encouraged young men who intend to pursue a business career to attend college. More rigorous licensing requirements in many states have recently made college training necessary for newly certified public accountants. Unfortunately, the Census still classifies many college-trained professional administrators, who may have extensive responsibilities in large industries, together with all other "proprietors, managers, and officials," so that it is impossible to distinguish them. In 1950, however, there were over 383,000 accountants and almost 53,000 personnel and labor relations workers listed as professionals.

HIGH SCHOOL ATTENDANCE AND GRADUATION

The colleges and universities are the main source of additions to the supply of scientific and professional personnel.

They draw their students, of course, from the graduates of the secondary schools. A veritable revolution has taken place in high school attendance and graduation during the last sixty years. In 1890, a high school education was the privilege of the few. Only 7 percent of the persons of high school age were enrolled in high schools, and only half of these eventually graduated. In 1950, over three-fourths of the age group were enrolled, and the number of graduates was almost 60 percent of the number of seventeen-year-olds.

During World War II, the proportion of young people graduating from high school fell, as the older boys and girls left school to enter the armed services or to take jobs. At the same time, the number of youths of high school age was also declining. By 1944, the number of high school graduates had fallen to one million, the lowest number since 1936. After that date, the proportion of seventeen-year-olds graduating from high school rose again, but, since the number in this age group was still smaller than before the war, the number of high school graduates in 1950 remained below the level of 1942. The estimated number graduating from high school in 1952 was about 1.2 million.

Estimates of the number of high school graduates in the future depend upon predictions of the number who will reach the appropriate age and of the percentage of that number who will graduate from high school. The number becoming seventeen years old each year through 1969 may be predicted with considerable accuracy, barring a catastrophe such as atomic war, or a major change in immigration policy. The number of seventeen-year-olds is only now beginning to increase again. Experts forecast that it will probably increase slowly until 1957, and rapidly thereafter, reaching some 2.9 million by 1960 and about 3.8 million by 1970. These developments will result from the slow increase in the birth rate after 1936 and the rapid increase after 1940.

The proportion of young people who graduate from high

school will, of course, depend on the factors which influence high school attendance. In the past, the social emphasis upon high school graduation and the rising demand for high school graduates for all levels of employment contributed to the rapid increase in the proportion graduating. Rising family income, moreover, made it financially possible for more children to forego employment in favor of education. Urbanization, improved transportation, more and better school facilities, the increasing social and recreational opportunities provided for high school students, compulsory school attendance laws, and other factors also played significant roles in increasing the percentage of young people graduating from high school.

If the proportion of young people graduating from high school remains at the current level, the number of graduates will begin to increase after 1953, and will reach 1.7 million by 1960 and 2.3 million by 1970. If the ratio increases at the same rate as it did between 1940 and 1950, there will then be 2 million graduates by 1960 and 3.1 million by 1970. It is unlikely that the ratio will rise as rapidly as it did before 1940 because of the large proportion of youths already graduating from high school. If it did, all young people of graduating age would be graduating from high school by 1960! It should be noted, however, that any great increase in the percentage of children graduating from high school would probably reflect substantial changes in high school standards and curricula.

A national picture of high school attendance and graduation hides sizable group and regional variations. Thus, 85 percent of the white children of high school age but only 60 percent of the Negro children were enrolled in high school in 1950. The percentage was even lower among Negro children in the South. Moreover, the number of days attended during the school year, the hours per day, the quality of instruction, and the content of the curriculum—all vary widely from region to region and even within the same state. This accounts for the inability of students who graduate from some high schools in the upper portion of their class to gain admission to colleges with high entrance standards.

COLLEGE GRADUATION

In the last sixty years, there has also been a revolution in college attendance and graduation. In 1890, only 3 percent of the persons of college age were enrolled, and one percent eventually graduated from college. By 1940, 15 percent of the age group were enrolled, and the number of graduates was 8 percent of the number of twenty-one-year-olds. The number of college graduates, like the number of high school graduates, declined sharply during the war. After the war, college attendance expanded to record heights as a result of the influx of veterans. By 1950, there were almost 434,000 graduates, more than double the pre-war high. This accounted, in large part, for the very rapid expansion of the professional labor force in the last two years of the decade. In 1952, when most of the World War II veterans had completed their courses, the number of graduates fell to 332,000.

It has been estimated that the number of graduates will continue to decline until 1955, and then gradually increase to about 600,000 by 1970. This estimate is based on forecasts of the number of people reaching twenty-one each year, and on the assumption that the percentage of twenty-one-year-olds graduating from college will continue to rise at about the same rate as it did between 1920 and 1940, before the effects of the war were felt. What will actually occur, however, will be influenced by a number of additional factors.

In 1870, when high school was considered primarily as a preparation for college, about 65 percent of the high school graduates graduated from college. Later, high school graduation came to be increasingly regarded as the normal terminal point for academic education. In addition, the high schools broadened their curricula to provide vocational training for students who

did not desire an academic course. Meanwhile, the development
of advanced training facilities outside the colleges for nursing,
technical, and arts training permitted many students to continue
their education without going to college. As a result, the ratio
of college graduates to high school graduates fell below 20 percent
by 1920. After a slight increase during the twenties, and sharp
fluctuations during and after the war, the ratio has now reached
about one-third.

There is reason to believe that the earlier decline will not be
resumed. The same factors which led to an increase in high
school graduation—educational requirements for employment,
increasing technological complexity, rising standards of living—
now seem to be having the same effect on college graduation.
The number of people who consider college a "normal" part of
the educational process is growing. Entrance to most state universities is open to all of the high school graduates in the state.
More young people go to college, not for professional training,
but, as has been noted, as preparation for a career in business.
If the proportion of high school graduates attending college remains stable or goes up, the rapid increases in high school graduation in recent decades will soon be reflected in substantially
larger college enrollments. Such an increase, however, may be
felt far more in the two-year rather than the four-year colleges,
as communities undertake to extend the opportunities for higher
education to as many of their citizens as possible. In the past
thirty years, enrollments in junior colleges expanded over thirty
times, compared with an increase of four and one-half times in
four-year colleges.

The number of college graduates in the future could also be
affected by short-term developments, such as another full-scale
mobilization or a change in the present policy which permits
the deferment of college students. The availability of educational
benefits to large numbers of Korean veterans will undoubtedly
stimulate college attendance during the next few years.

GRADUATE STUDY

Between 1900 and 1950, as Table 3 shows, the percentage of college graduates who went on to earn the doctoral degree remained fairly stable. The percentage who earned master's degrees fluctuated widely between 1900 and 1930, but by 1950, it was only slightly higher than in 1910. Because of the striking increase in the number of college graduates, however, almost forty times as many master's degrees and almost twenty times as many doctoral degrees were awarded in 1950 as in 1900.

Table 3. Degrees Granted in the United States, 1900-52[a]

Year	Bachelor's and First Professional Degrees[b]	Master's and Second Professional Degrees	Column 2 as % of Column 1	Doctoral Degrees	Column 4 as % of Column 1
	(1)	(2)	(3)	(4)	(5)
1900	25,324	1,583	6.3	369	1.5
1910	34,178	3,771	11.0	429	1.3
1920	48,622	4,143	8.5	690	1.4
1930	122,484	14,969	12.2	2,299	1.9
1940	186,500	26,731	14.3	3,290	1.8
1950	433,734	58,219	13.4	6,633	1.5
1952	331,924	63,471	19.1	7,683	2.3

[a] Based on data provided by the U. S. Office of Education.
[b] Includes M.D.'s, D.D.S.'s, LL.B.'s, and similar first professional degrees.

The fact that graduate degrees have approximately kept pace with college degrees is remarkable in the light of the rapid extension of college education and of the increasing tendency of young men to attend college as a preparation for business rather than for a professional career. This is especially noteworthy for 1950 because of the record high number of college graduates in that year. Those who received higher degrees in 1950 were, of course, drawn from the much smaller college graduating classes several years earlier. The large increase in advanced degrees as a percentage of first degrees between 1950 and 1952 is largely a reflection of fluctuations in college graduation because of veteran enrollments. Those who received higher degrees in 1952 were drawn from the large college graduating classes of 1950 and just before, but are compared with the smaller class of 1952. The relatively constant ratio of advanced degrees to bachelor's degrees between 1900 and 1950 is somewhat misleading. The statistics combine some professional degrees such as those awarded in medicine, dentistry, and the law with bachelor's degrees because undergraduate preparation was not a prerequisite to study in these fields when the statistics were first collected. If these professional degrees were included with the other advanced degrees, where they belong in terms of the period of study required in recent decades, the ratio of advanced degrees to bachelor's degrees would, of course, be raised for each of the years shown. The trend in advanced degrees as a percentage of bachelor's degrees, however, would decline, because the number of degrees granted in these professional fields has not increased nearly as rapidly as the number of bachelor's degrees or the number of advanced degrees in other fields.

The change in the quality of education represented by an advanced degree is as important as the increase in number. In the latter half of the nineteenth century, training for such professions as medicine, law, and dentistry was still conducted largely on an apprenticeship basis. Formal schooling in these fields was confined mainly to a few proprietary schools that had very low standards. The Johns Hopkins University, founded in 1876, was the first full-fledged graduate school in the United States. Earlier, graduate training was restricted to those who were able to study abroad, generally at German universities. As late as 1900, less than half of the theology schools required a bachelor's degree for admission, and there were no dental schools on a graduate level. Only the medical schools of Johns Hopkins and Harvard required some college training prior to admission. Other medical schools, as well as schools of veterinary medicine, law, and pharmacy, required no more than some elementary or secondary school preparation. Many schools had no educational prerequisites for admission.

During the second and third decades of this century, professional societies, associations of professional schools, and organizations such as the American Association of University Professors and the Carnegie Foundation had marked success in their efforts to raise admission requirements, lift the level of training, and standardize requirements for degrees. Together with comparable developments in undergraduate education, these changes profoundly improved the quality of education received by the scientist and professional.

Information prepared by the Office of Education in the last few years makes it possible for the first time to determine with some accuracy the distribution of degrees among different fields of study. Table 4 permits a comparison of the extent to which advanced training is pursued in different fields. It shows, for instance, that degrees in science and technology constituted about the same percentage of all degrees at the bachelor's level and the doctoral level. This comparison, however, conceals the very high percentage of natural science students who go on to receive a doctoral degree. About two-fifths of the bachelor's degrees in science and technology were received by engineering students, who accounted for only one-eighth of the doctoral degrees. On the other hand, students of the natural sciences were only one-third of the bachelor's degree group, but two-thirds of the doctoral degree group. Graduate work, apparently, has become more important as vocational preparation in the sciences than in most other fields. Moreover, many of the students who receive bachelor's degrees in the sciences continue their training in medicine or dentistry, and are therefore included under advanced degrees in health. Of the 4,200 doctoral degrees granted in the scientific and technological fields in 1952, roughly 500 were granted in engineering, 500 in psychology, 800 in the biological sciences, and 2,000 in the physical sciences. Chemistry accounted for over half of the physical science degrees, and physics and mathematics for all but a small number of the remainder.

Table 4. Percent Distribution of College and Graduate Degrees,
by Field of Study, 1952 [a]

Field of Study	Bachelor's Degrees	Master's Degrees	Doctoral Degrees
Science and technology	27	17	29
Teaching	20	33	8
Arts and humanities	16	10	6
Business	15	5	1
Social science	13	8	7
Health	4	8	45
Religion	2	2	1
Law	..	16	3
Other	3	1	..
Total	100	100	100

[a] Based on information supplied by the U.S. Office of Education.

Degrees granted in professions requiring a minimum of seven years of collegiate study (medicine) are included with the doctoral degrees; those requiring a minimum of five or six years of study (dentistry, law, optometry, osteopathy, veterinary medicine) are included with the master's degrees.

Almost half of all persons receiving doctoral degrees are physicians, who, like dentists, optometrists, and others receiving advanced degrees in the health field, generally receive their undergraduate education in the natural sciences. The relatively few bachelor's degrees in the health field are granted mainly to nurses and pharmacists. Some of this group, along with most others in the health field except physicians, terminate their education at the master's level, that is, at the end of five or six years of higher education.

Lawyers, whose college training generally requires six years, are also concentrated at the master's level. Most of them complete their undergraduate training in the humanities, social science, or business fields. Since the majority of lawyers work as practitioners, the advanced degree is obtained only by the few who intend to follow teaching or research careers. The high percentage of master's degrees in education results from the practice, followed by many school systems, of granting salary increases to teachers with higher degrees. The social sciences, the arts and humanities, and business account for a considerably smaller percentage of advanced degrees than they do of bachelor's degrees. Many students who receive their bachelor's degrees in these fields go on to advanced study in other professional fields. Those teaching and research jobs which require a doctoral degree are not abundant. Finally, women students, who less frequently pursue advanced studies, are heavily concentrated in the arts and humanities and social sciences. Among the social sciences, history, economics, political science, and sociology are most important at the bachelor's and doctoral levels. Almost a third of the master's degrees in the social sciences, however, are granted in social work where the degree is frequently a prerequisite for employment.

PROFESSIONAL EMPLOYMENT AND COLLEGE TRAINING

Although the supply of persons who have completed college or graduate education is the main source of recruitment for the professions, the relationship between trends in professional employment and trends in higher education is only approximate. Many college graduates are not employed in the field which they studied. Those who complete graduate training are more likely to work in their fields of study, but the proportion of college graduates who do not make professional use of their specialized training has probably increased with the rapid expansion in college attendance.

A major reason for the substantial number who do not work in the field studied is that the percentage of women among college graduates has been rising. In 1920, only about one-third of the college students were women, compared with over two-fifths by 1940. During World War II, of course, more than half the students were women. In the post-war years, enrollment of veterans reversed this trend. With girls constituting the majority of high school graduates in recent decades, however, it is expected that the proportion of women graduates will again rise until it reaches nearly half of the total. Because many women give up careers in favor of marriage shortly after graduation, they will form an increasingly large reservoir of unutilized professional training in coming decades.

Many persons still work in professional fields for which they never completed formal training. Except in such fields as medicine and dentistry, where license requirements include the completion of a prescribed amount of formal training, individuals have been able to qualify for employment through experience, partial training, or self-study. Thus, almost 20 percent of those employed as engineers today never graduated from engineering school. The increasingly rigid, though informal, organization of many professional fields, the increase in legal licensing requirements, the rising educational standards of employers, and the rapidly growing number of college graduates, however, are making it increasingly difficult for those who are not formally trained to obtain professional employment.

The changing age composition of the population will have an important influence upon the future course of professional training and employment. Because the twenty-one-year-old age group will be smaller in the next few years, the number of college graduates will probably continue to decline from the abnormally high point reached in 1950 until about 1955. The 1950 level may not be regained until 1964 or 1965. This trend is the basis for many of the current predictions of future shortages in the supply of professionally trained persons. From a reduced supply of college graduates it will be necessary to meet demands for men for the armed forces for business and industry, for advanced professional training, and for professional employment. Attainment of doctoral, M.D., or other advanced professional degrees normally requires from three to nine years after college graduation. Several years of experience are necessary, moreover, before a responsible position can be occupied. This means that the effects of the contraction in the supply of college graduates will be felt during most of the next two decades.

SEPARATIONS FROM PROFESSIONAL EMPLOYMENT

The need to replace people who leave professional employment represents the minimum occupational demand to which estimates of additional demands for personnel in each field must be added in any analysis of future requirements for professionals. Death; retirement because of age, disability, or, in the case of women, marriage and family responsibility; and transfer to other work are responsible for the termination of employment in a professional field.

The age at which professional workers generally retire varies in different occupations. Independent practitioners, such as doctors and lawyers, may continue to work as long as they choose. In other fields, where most professionals are salaried employees, the influence of compulsory retirement policies is becoming increasingly important. In fields such as teaching or nursing, in which women are a large part of the total labor force, great difficulty is encountered in maintaining the supply as a result of early retirement for marriage and motherhood. It is estimated that about 30 percent of all professionals working in 1950 will die, retire, or leave their profession for other reasons by 1960, but that over half the nurses and nearly 70 percent of the teachers will no longer be employed in their fields.

Many scientists and professionals assume administrative functions for which their training and knowledge prepare them, but which may require relatively little use of their highly specialized capacities. A chemist may become a college president, or an engineer a business executive. Shifts from professional to nonprofessional work, as well as to a different professional field, also occur, especially when war or depression cause rapid changes in employment opportunities. An extended period of inflation will cause professionals whose salaries are inflexible, such as teachers and other government workers, to change their jobs. A depression may force some professionals to seek clerical and sales positions. A long-term decline in the relative compensation and attractiveness of employment in a particular field may cause shifts to other fields.

As the size of the professional group increases, the problem of finding replacements for those who leave, merely to maintain the existing supply, becomes increasingly important. The rapid increase in the number of older people in our population will intensify the problem. The Bureau of Labor Statistics estimates that 1.6 million professionals will die or retire between 1950 and 1960. This is greater than the total number of professionals in 1900.

CHAPTER III

Training and Occupational Distribution

At the same time that deaths, retirements, and transfers to other fields of employment cut into the number of scientists and professionals actually available for work, the educational system continually provides a new supply. The size of each of the groups which comprise the total supply of scientists and professionals depends, in the first instance, on decisions made by individuals to train for and to choose employment in particular fields. Broadly speaking, the decisions to go to college, to specialize in a field, and, on the completion of training, to seek a particular kind of employment determine the size and the distribution of the total supply of scientific and professional manpower.

The decisions that individuals make with respect to their training occur within the context of a continuing process of personal development and education. Decisions about schooling and work made at one period of time will have an influence on and may even determine decisions at a later date. A boy who fails to pursue an academic course in high school will find it difficult to obtain admission to college.

The number of students in college at any time is limited by the size of the population of college age who have completed high school, which, in turn, is a function of the number of births some sixteen to twenty years previously. The extent of college attendance also depends heavily upon prevailing attitudes towards the value of education, which are neither quickly nor easily modified. One measure of society's regard for formal schooling appears in the fact that high school attendance, once viewed as preparation for college, is now characteristic of three-fourths of the population in the appropriate age group. The democratic belief in equality of opportunity, as well as the demands of a technological and urbanized culture, have encouraged attitudes that favor more education for more people. Compulsory school attendance laws and larger educational budgets are tangible expression of the strength of these attitudes.

What were once "upper-" or "middle-class" aspirations for college study are now found in all social groups. The desire to improve one's status and to provide greater advantages for one's children is the natural legacy of a nation of immigrants. Increasing numbers of parents are willing to make sacrifices so that their children can secure the kind of education which will help them to have a better life.

ECONOMIC FACTORS AFFECTING COLLEGE EDUCATION

In addition to the birth rate and social attitudes towards education, three other factors are crucial in determining how many people actually seek a college education. These are the economic incentives in the society, the costs of education to the individual and his family, and the availability of educational and training facilities.

The economic incentives involve the difference between the anticipated earnings of people who are college-educated and of those who are not. The promise of higher earnings for college graduates acts as a magnet to pull people into the colleges. The costs of education—that is, the price one must pay to become educated—obviously limit the number of people who can afford a college education. The availability of training facilities affects not only the number who are college-educated, but also the numbers in different fields.

Education is an investment in the sense that money and effort must be spent to acquire it, and the decision about whether to make the investment depends on how people estimate the returns. Since the preparation for certain kinds of work which are well rewarded is largely made through college training, the college graduate is likely to occupy a preferred economic status. The available studies do in fact show that the incomes of college graduates in each age group are considerably above those of non-graduates, but this gap may reflect differences in the ability and opportunities of the two groups. Since income and social position tend to be closely related, college graduates are likely to have higher social status.

In recent decades, colleges have been the training grounds not only for scientific and professional work, but also for a growing range of positions in the business world. Today business strongly prefers the college graduate to the person with less formal education. The college graduate may or may not perform better in business than the non-graduate, but the presumption is that he will. Even if there has been no notable difference in performance, once the practice of employing college men is established, it is likely to be continued. Because of the preference for college graduates, the young person with ambition is better armed in competing for advancement to managerial and executive jobs if he has a degree. Unemployment during the depression of the 1930's made it possible for the business community to set higher standards for employment, including higher educational attainment. Those who aspired to better industrial employment were quick to realize the desirability of college training. During World War II, the armed forces also played a part in the formation of attitudes favorable to college education. Education was a factor in granting direct commissions, in selection for officer candidate schools, and in promotion to responsible posts. A sample survey conducted in 1944, for example, revealed that over two-thirds of all army officers had attended or graduated from college.

This emphasis upon college education has been questioned on

several counts. In *The Market for College Graduates*, Seymour Harris of Harvard University argues that, while the average income for college graduates is higher than that for other groups, the differential has been declining in recent decades. Ascribing this decline in large part to the great expansion in the number of college graduates, he warns of a potential oversupply of graduates in relation to employment opportunities. However, the economic incentive for college education need not be significantly weakened by a reduction in income differentials. As the number of college graduates rises, a college or even a post-graduate degree becomes more, rather than less, essential for high-salaried employment. Moreover, for those who seek economic and social advancement through education, the aim seems to be relative improvement over the status of their parents, rather than absolute increases. For the individual who achieves a relatively better economic and social status through college graduation rather than by some other path, his education, in spite of its cost, will probably prove worthwhile.

The second factor which influences the number who go to college is the cost of education, which includes living expenses and tuition. This is borne in the main by the individual student or his family directly, and in part by the community through taxes and private endowments. Moreover, earnings from work are foregone wholly or in part during the period of study, a major consideration for lower-income groups. The ability of individuals or families to finance education has increased markedly. The real average per capita income after taxes, for example, increased 42 percent between 1929 and 1951. At the same time, education has acquired a higher priority in the pattern of expenditures of more people. In recent decades, a large percentage of college graduates have been educated in state-supported institutions. The extension of free municipal colleges and the development of community junior colleges, which enable students to live at home, and expanded scholarship aid have also made it possible for more persons to afford college.

About $25 million in scholarship grants is available each year, and an estimated $50 million is available in the form of loans or payment for work. Scholarships vary widely in the amount of assistance they provide and are unevenly distributed over the various fields of study. More scholarships are available for the study of music than for any other subject. Ancestry, the accident of birth in a particular community, or other irrelevant factors often determine who are eligible to receive scholarships. Needy students may be deflected from the field in which they are most competent to fields in which scholarships are available.

Living expenses account for the largest part of the cost of education. The fact that college enrollment did not fall during the depression of the 1930's, in spite of the decline in national income, is accounted for in part by a decline in the cost of living. The increasing competition for jobs, the lack of job openings, and increased government and university aid programs also helped to keep enrollments up. The striking increase in enrollments when the G.I. Bill went into effect after World War II was due in part to the fact that college attendance had been postponed for most males who would normally enroll. It also illustrates the important influence of educational costs on the number of persons who attend college. About 20 percent of the veterans entering college in 1946 would not have enrolled if the G.I. benefits had not been available. Educational benefits for Korean veterans may also be expected to have a significant effect in expanding college attendance among young men who normally could not afford to go to college.

In addition to raising the living costs which students must bear, inflation has compelled colleges and universities to raise their tuition charges. These higher costs make it more difficult for some qualified students, who would otherwise go to college, to attend. Increases in tuition have not freed the colleges from financial difficulties. The Commission on Financing Higher Education has estimated that the colleges and universities of the nation need an additional $250 million, or 15 percent a year more than they now receive, to meet current operating costs.

The third major factor bearing on the supply of students is the availability of educational and training facilities, including the buildings, libraries, laboratories, and especially the faculties. These facilities do not grow in direct response to the demand for education. Since receipts from student fees never meet even the current operating expenses of colleges, the expansion of facilities depends upon the availability of public or private funds. Originally facilities were provided by private grants, supplemented by some direct and many indirect state aids, such as tax exemptions. More recently, Federal, state, and municipal funds have been used directly and in large amounts to support institutions of higher education. In 1950, the income provided by state and local governments to public colleges and universities came to $493 million, according to the Report of the Commission on Financing Higher Education, with the state governments accounting for about nine-tenths of this sum.

Substantial Federal contributions began as early as 1862 with the passage of the Morrill Act, which made possible the creation or expansion of state universities, primarily to train specialists in agriculture and "the mechanic arts." The Commission report shows that by 1950 the Federal government was contributing $468 million annually to institutions of higher education in the form of payments to students to help them attend a college or university; of payments to institutions for services; of grants and gifts for improving their physical facilities; and of grants supporting specific teaching and research activities. Federal, state, and local governments provide almost three-fifths of the total annual income of institutions of higher education.

Although the facilities available ordinarily set an upper limit on the number of students enrolled in colleges and universities, the existing facilities do have some flexibility. After World War II, the colleges handled unprecedentedly large numbers by utilizing faculties and physical facilities more intensively, and by adding staff members. The problem of facilities, however, has a qualitative as well as a quantitative aspect, and it cannot be taken for granted that the ability of institutions to absorb a heavier student load does not affect the quality of the education they provide.

CHOICE OF FIELD OF STUDY

The choices which students make among fields of study determine the number of new entrants into each field of professional and scientific employment. Some young men and women who attend college as preparation for a professional career have decided upon their field of study and their subsequent career before they enter college. The majority, however, probably make their final choice only after they are enrolled in college. Home influences and individual interests and capabilities incline them to pick one field rather than another. With greater maturity and better knowledge about the content of alternative fields of study and employment opportunities, earlier uncertainties are reduced and final commitments to a field of study and a career are made. In the case of some professions, particularly engineering, the commitment must be made early, because the student frequently enters professional training immediately on graduation from high school. This situation may force a premature choice of career, since the young man may not have had adequate opportunity to learn about himself and the world of work. When a student goes from high school to a liberal arts college, the field of major study may not be decided upon until the second or third year. This later choice will be made with greater awareness of the opportunities for a meaningful career in the physical or social sciences that are not within the horizon of the average high school student.

One factor which enters into the individual's choice among broad fields of study is his ability. The same individual may have widely different capacities for such activities as solving mathematical problems, perceiving spatial relationships, verbalizing, and getting along with people. Some people think more readily about human problems, others about physical problems. These differences contribute to many of the choices that people make between such major areas as the humanities and the physical sciences. The origin of these differences is obscure, but it is certain that they are deeply imbedded. Particular abilities cannot be readily modified by efforts made late in high school or in college.

Since many individuals are as well equipped for study in one broad field as in another, a large part of the decision-making process turns on factors other than ability. In reaching a final choice, the individual weighs not only his abilities, but, as will be seen, the availability and costs of particular kinds of education and the anticipated money rewards of a particular career. He also takes into account non-economic considerations, which are frequently of major importance. The weight assigned to each of these considerations depends primarily upon the values and goals of the individual. Some students develop a consummate intellectual interest in a given field which dominates all other considerations. Frequently, this is the result of stimulation by an especially able teacher. The way of life which is part of a given professional career may be the key influence in another individual's choice. Thus, a student may become a biologist rather than a doctor because the scientist need not contend with suffering, the responsibility for life-or-death decisions, or the constant demands upon his time which confront the doctor. The decision to work in most scientific fields, particularly in research, is likely to be associated with intellectual values which are not generally shared by a society which assigns great weight to monetary rewards.

The same economic considerations which influence college attendance also play a role in the choice of field of study. One of these is the probable financial reward of a career in a given field. The desire to maximize earnings is not the dominant motive of most students contemplating a professional or scientific career. While the average earnings of professionals and scientists are well above the earnings of the population as a whole, few fortunes are made in these fields. Like other Americans, however, those who prepare for the professions prefer a large income to a small one and a field with abundant job openings to one in which job opportunities are scarce. Some closely related fields offer widely different economic rewards. A large number of industrial jobs with good beginning salaries and good chances for advancement are open to industrial chemists, while the research-minded biochemist may find only a few posts open to him in colleges or universities, most of them at relatively low salaries. The student who prefers to enter a relatively low-paying field obviously places less value upon money rewards than upon non-economic considerations.

The role of economic incentives in determining most choices made by individuals among professional fields is not clear-cut. The capable student can expect to earn a substantial income in all the fields which offer good opportunities for industrial employment or private practice, such as engineering, chemistry, law, medicine, or dentistry. Although average earnings differ among these fields, the earnings of the individual depend at least as much on his ability and energy as on the field itself. This is likely to be more true in the case of the independent practitioner, such as the doctor or dentist, than it is for the salaried employee. In most scientific and professional fields the range of income from the lowest to the highest is enormous. For teachers and government employees, however, the range is much smaller.

The second economic factor which strongly influences the choice of field of study is the cost of acquiring advanced training in different fields. Medical training, for example, requires at least five years after college. The demands of medical training are so heavy that the student can seldom work part-time. The law also forbids him to practice before his training is completed. If he elects to specialize, he must forego the major portion of his potential earnings for several more years. By contrast, the graduate student of the sciences can frequently earn part of his expenses by teaching, serving as an assistant, or doing other work. Moreover, he can usually interrupt his graduate work at any point to start working and earning in his field, but at less desirable jobs than he could secure had he completed his advanced training.

Medicine is probably the only field in which the number of capable applicants far exceeds the number who can be trained in existing facilities. For every field, however, the concentration of facilities in certain areas and local variations in the quality of facilities have a strong influence on the choices made by individuals. For example, first-rate advanced training in physics is available at a relatively small number of universities. The cost of an advanced degree in physics is raised for most students because they must seek a large university and cannot live at home. On the other hand, the student who finds himself at Cornell or Iowa State may specialize in agricultural science because their facilities and faculties in this field are outstanding. In every college, moreover, some departments are better than others, and this accounts in part for the choices made by many students among different fields of study.

To improve the educational facilities for any field of study it is necessary to strengthen at least the faculty and the library. In the case of the laboratory sciences, new buildings and equipment are also essential. First-rate medical schools cannot be developed except in conjunction with good hospitals. Only a few universities can afford outstanding facilities and faculties in a wide variety of fields, and the high cost of teaching some subjects, such as medicine, dictates their concentration in a few centers of study. An attempt to expand the number of fields in which a college has good facilities may result in uneconomical duplication of the facilities and faculties of other nearby institutions. Yet, where funds are available, the attempt may be justified on the ground that it produces a more balanced and educationally richer institution.

EMPLOYMENT MARKETS FOR SCIENTISTS AND PROFESSIONALS

There are three basic employment markets in which the nation's scientists and professionals are employed. Two are commercial markets: independent professional practice and employment by private industry. The third is non-commercial:

employment in non-profit institutions such as schools and colleges, government, libraries, foundations, and most hospitals.

The distribution of professionals among these markets is affected by income differences. Generally speaking, the independent practitioner earns more than the industrial employee, and the latter more than the employee of a non-profit institution. Salaries are not the only consideration influencing distribution. The young person who has just completed his professional training is more free to search for a job in a high-paying market than the person who is already established in a job. For the latter, a change of employment may mean a sacrifice of security, pension rights, relations with colleagues, and community ties. Many will be unwilling to sacrifice these for a moderate salary increase. A spirit of public service or the attractions of an academic life hold many professionals in government or education, where they earn less than they could in industry.

In most professions, employment immediately after the completion of formal education is usually a period of continued training. The new graduate may take a relatively low-paying job, either because he wants additional training or because he is unable, without further experience, to enter better-paying employment. The medical school graduate serves an internship and frequently a residency in a hospital before he enters private practice. Most law graduates work at relatively low salaries for law firms, and many young scientists teach in order to continue their education. Industrial employers are becoming increasingly aware of their role as trainers as well as users of manpower. The opportunity for additional training, therefore, may also be an important consideration in the choice of an industrial job.

Most doctors and dentists, many lawyers and accountants, and smaller numbers in several other fields work as independent practitioners. The demand for their services and, consequently, their earnings, fluctuate with consumers' expenditures. Normally, and particularly in recent prosperous years, the average income of independent practitioners has been higher than that of professionals in other types of employment. The pension rights and greater security of some salaried personnel may counterbalance the higher earnings of independent practice. Nevertheless, higher incomes from independent practice may induce appropriately trained and licensed professionals to shift from the other markets to independent practice.

The services of practitioners are distributed among consumers by means of prices, but not in precisely the same way as commodities are. Physicians, dentists, and other professionals sometimes adjust their charges to the consumers' ability to pay. In recent years, as the demand for professional services has risen, charges have risen, with the result that groups at the bottom of the income scale may either restrict use of professional services to periods of emergency or depend upon free services, such as medical clinics and legal aid societies. In the case of medical service, various community plans, such as Blue Cross, have helped many consumers to meet the financial burden involved. Shortages of practitioners do not appear in the form of unfilled job openings. They exist only in terms of a social criterion of the level of medical services that is considered desirable.

In the second type of market, scientists and professionals are employed by industry in engineering, research, or managerial positions. Scientists and professionals employed by industry have increased more rapidly than the industrial labor force as a whole because of such long-term trends as increasing complexity of organization and processes, greater investment in product research and development, and the emergence of personnel management, marketing research, industrial training, and other specialized functions within business management.

The distribution of scientists and professionals among commercial employers is determined largely by the availability of jobs in depressed economic periods, and by income differentials in periods of full employment. Income differentials have more effect on the distribution of recent graduates than they do on the movement of older persons who have established positions with a particular company.

Since industry employs a large proportion of the engineers, chemists, and other scientific specialists, the number undertaking training in these fields is likely to respond to changes in technology and economic conditions, which influence trends in job opportunities and earning levels.

Schools, hospitals, universities, and government are the primary employers in the third market for professionals and scientists. Most employers in this market usually make services available to consumers below cost. These institutions seldom provide salaries matching those in the commercial markets. The salaries of non-commercial employers, moreover, are much more inflexible than those of commercial employers. Non-commercial institutions tend, in consequence, to lose employees to industry and private practice in periods of full employment and inflation. There are instances where industry secures scientists, not because of salary differentials, but because they cannot make the grade in the academic world. During periods of deflation and depression, on the other hand, the relative position of those employed by non-commercial institutions improves, since their salaries do not fall as rapidly or as much as the cost of living.

There are important economic differences among employers in the non-commercial market. Hospitals and universities have much in common. They both derive their income from the sale of their services, from gifts, and usually from government appropriations which reach them directly or indirectly. Few hospitals or universities are able to meet operating expenses solely from income from the sale of services. Since the real value of endowments has fallen, they have encountered serious difficulties in increasing income proportionately to rising costs.

According to Dr. Clarence Long ("Nothing to Lose but Its Brains," *The Johns Hopkins Magazine,* June, 1952), the average full professor at Johns Hopkins in 1952 had one-fourth less purchasing power than in 1940, even before higher income taxes are taken into account. In contrast, manual workers and most other professionals earned between one-third and one-half more in real dollars, after income taxes, than they did before World War II. The persistence of such a situation will reduce the number of able young persons who undertake graduate work in the professions and encourage established teachers to seek employment outside of the academic world or compel them to undertake supplementary work.

Public schools derive their income entirely from taxes or appropriations. Although other tax sources have become increasingly important, most school systems still rely heavily on income from local real estate taxes. Since real estate taxes are relatively inflexible, school income and teachers' salaries have also fallen behind the general rise in salaries in other fields.

The Federal government employs large numbers of scientists, engineers, economists, and other professionals. In recent decades it has paid them better starting salaries than most other non-commercial employers, and has therefore been able to recruit younger professionals during inflationary periods. A Civil Service position is frequently a good way for a young graduate to gain experience without sacrificing income. On the other hand, government salaries are also relatively inflexible, although they are less rigid than those of colleges and universities. The government is at a disadvantage in competing with industry and private practice for more experienced personnel, for the top salary levels in the Civil Service scale do not compare with the earnings of competent professionals in industry or private practice. Consequently, government tends to lose its better employees when they are able to step into higher paying positions in the commercial world.

ARTIFICIAL BARRIERS

The preceding discussion of the factors which influence college attendance and choice of field of study and of employment has ignored the role of artificial barriers resulting from deeply imbedded social attitudes. Although discriminatory barriers against racial and ethnic groups and against women have been greatly reduced in recent decades, they still severely limit the number of Negroes and women in scientific and professional work.

Relatively few Negroes attend and graduate from college, chiefly because the primary and secondary education which many of them receive does not qualify them for or interest them in college education. Most of them leave school before receiving a secondary diploma. These factors, in turn, reflect the fact that the Negro population is concentrated in areas where income is low and where many communities neglect Negro education.

The scarcity of scientific and professional employment openings for Negroes also discourages them from undertaking advanced education and influences their choice of field of study. Apart from teaching and nursing positions, and these mainly in Negro schools and hospitals, there are very restricted career opportunities in the professions for all but the most unusually gifted. The barriers against Negroes in professional life are an extreme form of the discrimination still felt in lesser degrees by other ethnic groups, especially by Spanish-speaking Americans.

The barriers against women are of somewhat different form. Women receive the same early schooling as men, and nearly as many attend college. Yet relatively few are employed in scientific or professional fields other than teaching and nursing. In part, this underrepresentation reflects the fact that few women expect to pursue professional or scientific careers in other fields. On the other hand, the unwillingness of many employers to hire women discourages them from preparing for certain fields such as engineering and the physical sciences. The problem is complicated because the prejudice of some employers is reinforced by the general knowledge that a young woman hired for a responsible position may well leave within a short time to marry and raise children.

CHAPTER IV

The Potential for Higher Education

A CONCERN WITH the numbers and competence of the nation's scientists and professional persons raises important questions about the proportion of the population which has the high ability required for advanced training. Far more is known about the country's reserves of natural resources than about its reserves of intellectual resources. The possibility that reserves of essential materials such as oil and timber might be depleted has long been recognized, and means have been sought to guard against such an eventuality. Only recently, however, has an awareness developed that the nation's reserve of men and women capable of advanced training is also limited.

How large is this reserve? A precise numerical answer cannot be ventured until research develops the answers to a large number of problems about human resources. However, a beginning can be made in estimating the size of the reserve.

Today, most of the young people who enter scientific and professional occupations are college graduates or, at the very least, have completed part of a college education. A good deal is known about the distribution of mental ability among those entering and graduating from college and among the population as a whole. Consequently, one way of estimating the size of the reserve of individuals of high ability is to compare the number in the population who are capable of successfully pursuing a college education with the number who actually enter and graduate from college.

IDENTIFICATION OF COLLEGE ABILITY

Colleges conventionally use two methods for judging whether an individual has the mental ability to complete college. One is based on high school grades, which are highly correlated with scholastic performance in college. There are, however, great variations in the standards of high schools. This method, therefore, would not be useful for estimating the number in the nation as a whole capable of completing college, even if adequate data on grades were available. Colleges can employ high school grades as an aid in selecting freshman students only when they can judge from experience how the grades earned in a particular school are reflected in the scholastic performance of its graduates in college.

The second method relies on a variety of scholastic aptitude tests, the scores on which are also closely related to scholastic success in college. Moreover, the scores of individuals from different schools can be compared. These tests are similar to the Army General Classification Test (AGCT). While the AGCT measures approximately the same abilities as the college aptitude tests, it has not been used to predict success in college. Since the AGCT was given to many millions of young men during World War II, however, it provides a convenient tool for estimating the proportion of the college-age population with the mental ability to graduate from college. The AGCT is also closely related to intelligence tests, but its score is not the same as the much better known IQ.

Figure 2 shows the distribution of AGCT scores for the population as a whole. The average score is 100, and most people achieve scores somewhere near this average. Sixty-eight percent of the population score between 80 and 120.

In order to estimate the number of people able to graduate from college, it is necessary to draw a line at some point in this distribution separating those deemed able to complete college from those who are not. Wherever this line is drawn, it will not distinguish with any high degree of accuracy those who will fail to graduate from college from those who will succeed. There is no sure way of predicting on any basis whether an individual will do well or poorly in college.

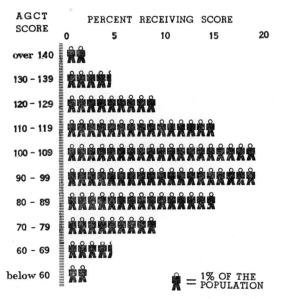

Figure 2. Distribution of Population by AGCT Score

Some people who score fairly low on the AGCT succeed in graduating from college and go on to perform well in professional or scientific work. On the other hand, every college has repeated experience with individuals who despite high aptitude for college work fail to pass. The assertion that individuals who achieve a certain score are capable of completing college, therefore, only means that they are more likely to have the ability required for graduation than persons with lower scores.

An AGCT score of 120 is certainly high enough to justify using it as a minimum for estimating the number of individuals capable of college work. This score was used during World War II in deciding who should go to college under the Army Specialized Training Program. Scholastic aptitude equivalent to an AGCT score of 120 is now one of the criteria for determining whether a college student should be considered for deferment. A lower score (110) was used in selecting students for Officer Candidate Schools during World War II. It is known, moreover, that over 60 percent of those who enter college and half of those who graduate achieve scores on scholastic aptitude tests which are the equivalent of an AGCT score of less than 120. The facts indicate that a score of 120 on the AGCT is a high standard for determining how many persons are capable of graduating from college, and that its use will underestimate, rather than overestimate, the number with the requisite intellectual ability to pursue a college education with success.

THE RESERVE CAPABLE OF COLLEGE AND POST-GRADUATE EDUCATION

The distribution of AGCT scores (Figure 2) shows that about 16 percent of the population of college age has the mental ability needed to score 120 or higher. Figure 3 shows the percentages of the population of college age and of the high school graduates now completing various stages of higher education. In recent years, the attendance of large numbers of veterans has caused college enrollment and graduation to fluctuate widely. When the figures are adjusted to eliminate this effect, it appears that about one out of five of the college-age group now starts college and about one out of nine graduates. If almost 12 percent graduates from college and 16 percent of the population scores 120 or above on the AGCT, it would appear that the reserve able to complete college but not doing so is about 4 percent of the population of college age. This figure, however, errs on the side of safety, for it substantially underestimates the size of the reserve. It has been seen that the majority of those entering college, as well as half of the graduates, have less ability than is represented by a score of 120 on the AGCT.

Extent of Higher Education of High School Graduates of College Age, 1951-52.

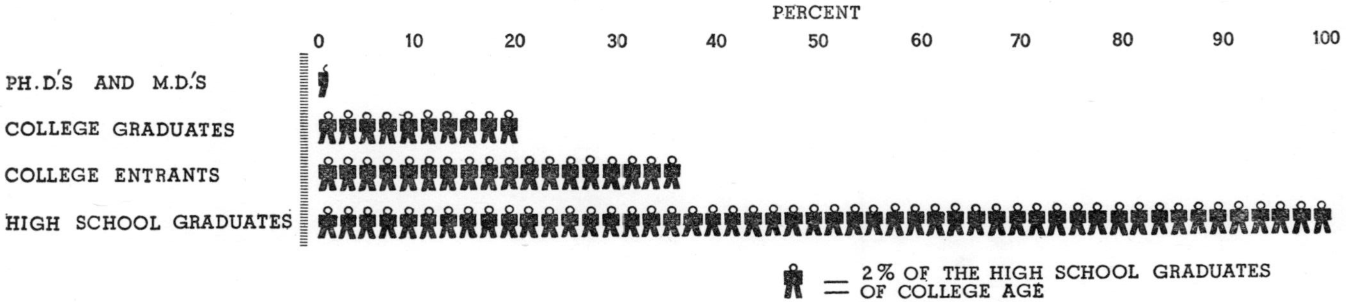

PERCENT

0	10	20	30	40	50	60	70	80	90	100

PH.D.'S AND M.D.'S

COLLEGE GRADUATES

COLLEGE ENTRANTS

HIGH SCHOOL GRADUATES

figure = 2% OF THE HIGH SCHOOL GRADUATES
OF COLLEGE AGE

Extent of Higher Education of Population of College Age, 1951-52.

PERCENT

0	10	20	30	40	50	60	70	80	90	100

PH.D.'S AND M.D.'S

COLLEGE GRADUATES

COLLEGE ENTRANTS

HIGH SCHOOL GRADUATES

COLLEGE AGE POPULATION

figure = 2% OF THE POPULATION
OF COLLEGE AGE

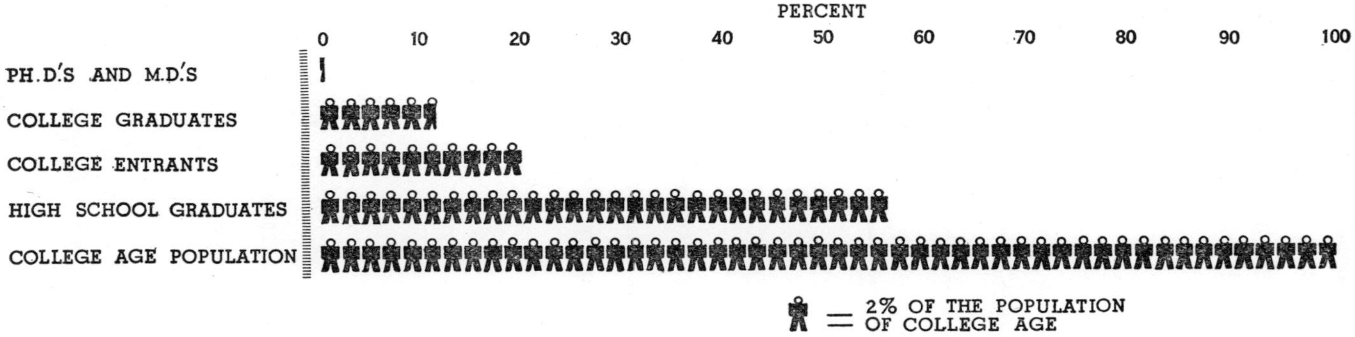

Figure 3. Higher Education in the Population of College Age, 1951-52

Based on data provided by The Commission on Human Resources and Advanced Training

A better estimate of the size of the reserve can be developed from the data summarized in Figure 4 which shows the percentage of persons not entering college, entering college but not graduating, and graduating from college for three ranges of scholas-

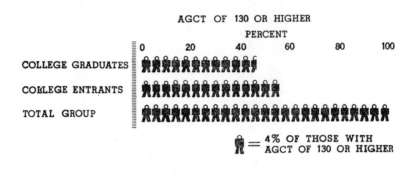

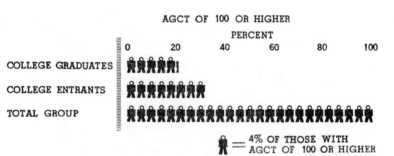

Figure 4. Extent of Higher Education in the Population of College Age by AGCT Score, 1951-52

Based on data provided by The Commission on Human Resources and Advanced Training

tic ability. These figures indicate that the higher the mental ability of the group, the more likely are its members to graduate from college if they enter. While about two-thirds of those with an AGCT of 100 or higher who enter college finally graduate, almost 84 percent of those with an AGCT of 130 or higher who enter college graduate. The higher the mental ability of the group, moreover, the greater is the percentage of persons entering college. Yet, half of the persons with an AGCT of 120 or higher do not enter college and only about one-third of them graduate. The remaining two-thirds are the reserve of persons with the necessary ability to graduate from college. Of the more than eight million people of college age, about 800,000, or 10 percent, have the ability to complete college but will not, under current conditions, graduate. Most of them will not even enter college.

Many professional and scientific careers call for further formal training after graduation from college, as in the case of medicine and research careers in physics, chemistry, and the social sciences. In scientific and scholarly fields a doctoral degree (usually the Ph.D.) has come to symbolize the completion of advanced formal training. As the next step in estimating the reserve capable of undertaking higher education it is necessary to compare the number in the population deemed to have the required intellectual ability with the number that actually acquire postgraduate degrees. Again it is necessary to select an AGCT score representative of the ability necessary to obtain these degrees. Tests of mental ability indicate that an AGCT score of 130 is about average for persons who now receive doctoral degrees, including the M.D. This score, therefore, may safely be used to determine how many of the college-age population have the ability required for these degrees. The use of 130 will result in an underestimation of the reserve for graduate education, but makes it very likely that those in the estimated reserve possess the required mental ability. Since it is the average score, it matches the severe standard of 120 used above to estimate the reserve of undergraduate ability. Between 6 and 7 percent of the total population, as Figure 2 shows, have scholastic ability equivalent to an AGCT score of 130 or higher.

About 2 percent of the college graduates actually go on to earn doctoral degrees other than the M.D. About the same number receive the M.D. Since only about 12 percent of all young people graduate from college, the number earning these degrees is less than half of one percent of the college-age population. The difference between the number who have the ability and the number who now acquire such advanced education is great, and points to a sizable reserve of individuals with high intellectual ability who are not receiving post-graduate training.

HIDDEN POTENTIAL

The reserve capable of graduating from college or obtaining advanced degrees consists of persons identified on the basis of standard tests. That reserve has been estimated very conservatively, for the AGCT scores of 120 and 130 which have been used represent relatively high standards. There is another reason for regarding the estimate of the reserve as conservative rather than optimistic. Scores on tests of mental ability do not measure inborn potential. They reflect differences in education and cultural opportunity. It is pointed out in *The Uneducated,* published in 1953, that "it is difficult, perhaps impossible, to devise a test which takes proper account of the cultural and environmental factors in the individual's background so that his response to questions reflects his intellectual ability and not his specific knowledge of certain words and circumstances." If more children attended school regularly, if they attended school longer, and if the schools they attended were better, then more than 16 percent would develop learning ability equivalent to a score of 120 or more on the present AGCT and more than 6 or 7 percent would be capable of scoring 130. There is, thus, a hidden reserve of persons whose intellectual potential for advanced training has not been adequately developed.

Obviously, those who comprise this hidden reserve are not

using their ability in acquiring the education needed for scientific and professional work. Their capacities, moreover, have not been developed to the point where they would be revealed by national survey or testing programs. No one can say with confidence how significant an addition to the number of persons capable of undertaking college training could be obtained by developing this hidden reserve. There are indications, however, that it may be very great. This judgment is supported by recent studies of the performance of Negroes on scholastic aptitude tests. Most social scientists now believe that there are no inborn differences in intellectual potential between Negroes and the rest of the population, or that such differences, if they exist, are very small. Yet, a study made a few years ago of college freshmen showed that the average freshman in a Negro college scored only a little higher on aptitude tests than the lowest-ranking freshman in the average college. This finding testifies both to the sensitivity of the test to prior educational experience and to the great differences between the educational opportunities of Negroes and whites.

Because this hidden reserve is not revealed by the usual scholastic aptitude tests, it has sometimes been contended that the tests are grossly unfair. This conclusion, however, misconceives the purpose of the tests, for they undertake to measure ability to do well in college, in Officer Candidate Schools, or in some other learning situation. They claim to measure not the amount of intellectual potential with which an individual is born, but the immediate readiness of individuals for advanced education. Individuals who have been educationally deprived and who do not perform well on these tests would not perform well in college either. Aided by intensive pre-college work they could probably better their test scores and improve their later college performance.

The improvement of elementary and secondary education, which would raise the percentage of the population with college ability, would not necessarily result in an increase in the percentage attending college. If applicants for admission had greater ability, colleges might raise their standards and thus keep the college population relatively stable. Even the mental tests might not reveal that the college ability of the population had risen, for ability tests are periodically revised and restandardized. The average score remains at some arbitrary figure, such as 100 AGCT. Scores on such tests reveal how an individual performs compared to others, and not how he measures up to some absolute standard. For these and other reasons, the tangible results of improvements in pre-college education, which would have the effect of increasing the mental ability of the population, might be obscured.

GROUP AND REGIONAL DIFFERENCES

The failure of a great many people of high mental ability to undertake or complete higher education is due to various economic and motivational factors which have already been discussed in Chapter III. The members of different socio-economic groups in the population vary, not only in financial ability to secure higher education, but also in the interest they have in doing so. The lack of motivation among some groups is to some extent economically determined. Thus, the young man who has grown up in a home where making ends meet had been difficult may be determined to achieve economic independence early, even when his family is in a position to send him to college. Many who do not attend college because of economic reasons would be capable college students. Studies of veterans who would not have been able to go to college without the aid of the G.I. Bill show that they did at least as well as other students.

There are striking differences among states in the proportion of young people entering college, as Table 5 shows. The statistics upon which it is based are not completely reliable, but they adequately demonstrate the existence of great state variations. From all the Southern states except Florida the percentage enrolling in college in the fall of 1948 was below the national average. On the other hand, the percentage was very high in most of the Far Western states. South Carolina had the lowest percentage, under 10 percent, while Utah, with almost half of its young people entering college, had the highest. (The national average, shown in the Table as 24.6 percent, includes veterans and is, therefore, higher than the 20 percent figure previously used.)

These differences are accounted for in part by the proportion of the population completing high school and in part by the proportion of high school graduates entering college in the different states and regions, both of which are, in turn, closely related to variations in economic conditions. The percentage of young people graduating from high school in 1948 was below the national average in all but two of the Southern and Southwestern states. This was due in part to low average per capita income in these states, which, in spite of substantial increases since 1929, remained well below the national average. The high percentage of Negroes in the population of most of these states was also a significant factor. Even in Maryland and the District of Columbia, where per capita income was above the national average, high school graduation was low because of the pattern of Negro education.

It is significant that the percentage of high school graduates who went on to college was above average in several states, including Georgia, Louisiana, and Tennessee, which ranked near the bottom both in per capita income and percentage of population graduating from high school. The explanation lies in the fact that high school graduation was far more the privilege of a small minority who expected to enter college in these states than it was elsewhere.

Eighteen states were above the national average both in percentage of population completing high school and percentage of high school graduates entering college. All but five of these states were above the national average in per capita income in 1948. These prosperous and well-educated states were not concentrated in any region, nor were they all highly urbanized. Among them were New York, Illinois, Wyoming, and California.

Economic considerations do not explain all the differences among the states. Utah, with the highest proportion of population entering college of any state, was below average in per capita income. Several other Western states also had a higher proportion entering college than one might anticipate solely from income data. The opposite was true of a number of states, especially Pennsylvania, where per capita income was high but the number entering college was low.

Table 5. College Entrants as a Percentage of Eighteen-Year-Olds, 1948 [a]

Alabama	14.6	Nebraska	29.5
Arizona	25.4	Nevada	28.4
Arkansas	19.5	New Hampshire	24.7
California	32.8	New Jersey	28.8
Colorado	33.8	New Mexico	20.1
Connecticut	32.8	New York	33.7
Delaware	22.2	North Carolina	15.7
Dist. of Columbia	30.6	North Dakota	32.7
Florida	25.5	Ohio	24.8
Georgia	17.8	Oklahoma	31.4
Idaho	39.1	Oregon	34.9
Illinois	37.2	Pennsylvania	19.4
Indiana	25.7	Rhode Island	24.9
Iowa	28.5	South Carolina	9.7
Kansas	33.5	South Dakota	30.5
Kentucky	15.1	Tennessee	18.3
Louisiana	19.6	Texas	23.7
Maine	18.6	Utah	48.4
Maryland	23.3	Vermont	27.8
Massachusetts	28.4	Virginia	19.2
Michigan	22.3	Washington	34.3
Minnesota	29.7	West Virginia	17.8
Mississippi	18.5	Wisconsin	22.8
Missouri	26.8	Wyoming	29.4
Montana	32.5	U.S. Average	24.6

[a] Based on U.S. Census Reports and publications of the U.S. Office of Education. The figures represent the residents of each state entering college in any state.

In short, much of the difference among states in college enrollment can be explained in terms of the ability to pay for higher education and of employment opportunities for college graduates.

But this is not the whole story, for variations in the value placed upon education in different areas are also important. The same situation is found with respect to elementary and secondary schooling. Counties and states with approximately the same per capita income frequently differ widely in the quality of their school systems and the proportions of children enrolled in them.

PROBLEMS IN MAKING USE OF THE RESERVE

The conclusion that the United States has a large reserve of persons capable of graduating from college and of securing advanced degrees must be qualified in several important respects. Mental ability, as determined by a score on a test, has been used as the sole criterion of ability to pursue higher education, but it is clearly not the only factor which influences success in college or in later life. There may be other abilities not highly related to general scholastic aptitude which are vital for success in certain fields. Relatively little is known about such abilities or how to measure them, but that does not mean that they are insignificant. The important role of motivational factors has already been indicated. It is known that high scholastic aptitude cannot lead to college success and outstanding performance in later professional work unless the individual wants to succeed.

Even if it is assumed that all persons with a specified level of scholastic aptitude are capable of earning a particular degree, not every individual in the group can be counted on to secure it. As stated previously, although about 6 percent of the population possesses the mental ability assumed to be necessary, less than one-half of one percent now secures a doctoral degree or an M.D. This suggests a reserve of about 5½ percent of the population, half male and half female, that could be drawn upon to increase the numbers now obtaining these degrees. Actually, far more than half of this theoretical reserve is made up of women, because only a small fraction of the doctoral and M.D. degrees are currently granted to women. About 10 percent of the doctoral degrees given in the sciences, which account for about half of all doctoral degrees, for example, are received by women. The comparatively small number of women who receive doctoral degrees is obviously not due to any failure in the public school systems since more girls than boys graduate. Nor is it due to a lack of qualified women college graduates, for over 40 percent of non-veteran college students are women. The small number of women who secure doctoral degrees reflects their role in society. Parents and teachers are not as likely to encourage girls to continue their education past college as they are to encourage young men. Neither are the girls themselves likely to be as strongly motivated. Most of them intend to marry and have children. They do not contemplate an active professional or scientific life. Traditional barriers to admission into many professional and scientific fields also play a part in discouraging women from seeking advanced degrees.

Still other considerations impede the training of all of those who are apparently able to complete post-graduate education. Males with the mental ability represented by an AGCT score of 130 amount to about 3 percent of the total population. The entire 3 percent cannot, however, be considered as likely candidates for the doctoral or M.D. degrees, for some do not enter college, others do not graduate from college, and some of the graduates do not do well enough in college to warrant their continuing their studies.

Approximately one-fifth of all the male college graduates who have the ability do now receive either doctoral or M.D. degrees. The four-fifths who do not go on with their education past the bachelor's or the master's degree may be estimated at about 40,000 college graduates a year. The significance of this figure can be appreciated when it is contrasted with the record high number of almost 14,000 students, counting women and veterans, who received doctoral degrees and M.D.'s in 1952.

It cannot be concluded, however, that all of this reserve of 40,000 persons should receive doctoral degrees. Many in this reserve now enter employment which demands a high order of intelligence, but does not require an advanced degree. It is essential to draw upon the most intelligent 6 percent of the population for many occupations, both professional and non-professional. In short, unless the total number of college graduates were also increased, any substantial increase in the numbers acquiring doctoral or M.D. degrees might be made only at the expense of reducing the number of high potential people entering other fields. A substantial increase in the number of college graduates who would go on to secure a doctoral degree would be difficult to achieve without expanding significantly the number of persons of high ability who enter and graduate from college.

The number of persons of high ability who graduate from college and who earn higher degrees has, in fact, been continually increasing as a result of long-term occupational and social changes, such as rising national income, changing attitudes toward education, and the reduction of religious and racial inequalities in educational opportunity. It may be argued that these changes, even if accelerated, operate slowly, and if an appreciable addition to the number of scientists and professionals is desired, more direct measures to increase the number trained must be developed.

To proceed with confidence toward increasing the number of college graduates who receive higher degrees, firmer knowledge is essential in at least two areas. First, one must know what would happen to the work that high potential people without advanced degrees now engage in. At present, there is little information available on the occupational distribution of able college graduates who do not complete post-graduate education. It is also necessary to know more about the reasons why such high potential persons terminate their formal education with a bachelor's degree. The failure of many to go on to graduate study or professional school is due, not to economic barriers, but to lack of motivation for further education. It is not known what incentives would be effective in inducing additional students to complete their studies and continue in the field for which they were trained. If these additional students were not strongly motivated to study and to work in particular fields, later occupational performance would be disappointing, among other reasons because many would probably leave the professional field for which they prepared themselves.

Another approach to the problem of stimulating an increase in the numbers securing advanced training is to raise the proportion of able persons who graduate from college. It has been pointed out that less than half of those whose AGCT score is 120 or over enter college, and that the majority of college students are below this standard. These facts have led certain experts to argue that it would be desirable to "exchange" college students with relatively low mental ability for abler people who do not now enter college. They contend that the quality of professional and scientific workers could be raised by concentrating educational efforts on the abler people rather than dissipating them on the less promising. Why should the doltish sons of the rich enter college while the brilliant but less affluent high school graduate works at the filling station?

If those who achieve low scores were exchanged for those who achieve high scores on a national test of scholastic aptitude, the results would be quite different from those intended. Because the score on such a test depends heavily on the quality of prior educational experience, the children in deprived groups, who now manage to get into college, would be the first to suffer from this reshuffling of the college population. It has been noted that students in Negro colleges do relatively poorly on scholastic aptitude tests. If college entrance were limited to those attaining high scores on a college aptitude test, the enrollment of Negroes would be greatly reduced. The same would be true, but to a lesser extent, of Southern whites as compared to Northern whites, rural residents as opposed to those who live in large cities, and children from poor families compared to the children of the well-to-do.

This, in turn, would impede the processes through which the position of such groups is being raised. Thus, teachers for the schools of the depressed rural areas are not recruited from among the well-prepared high school graduates in New York, Chicago, or Los Angeles who score high on tests of college ability. They come, rather, from the areas in which they teach and consequently, on the whole, score poorly on tests of scholastic aptitude.

There need be no fear that the nation is short of young persons with sufficient ability to complete advanced training. All of the approaches to the problem of increasing the number of persons who secure such training, however, will involve major difficulties.

CHAPTER V

Research and Development

AMERICANS ARE JUST becoming aware of the fact that significant scientific and technological advances depend upon the availability of competent scientists and research engineers. Not all of the work of scientists and engineers, however, contributes directly to scientific and technological advance. Many scientists spend much of their time teaching. Most engineers work as executives or supervisors in some part of the production process. That part of the work of scientists and engineers which does contribute to new knowledge and new products is commonly described as "research and development." Scholars in all fields, including the social sciences, the arts, and the humanities, may also be engaged in research. This chapter is primarily concerned, however, with research which leads, or may lead, to the development of new products, and with that development itself. In terms of people, therefore, it is concerned primarily with physical scientists and research engineers.

Even with these limits, the term research and development is very broad. At one extreme is an Einstein working with paper and pencil on the fundamentals of physical theory. At the other extreme is the development engineer in an automobile company, making a minor change in design in order to enhance the sales of a new model. There is little point to so broad a definition, except that it helps to distinguish those whose work is directed to current output from those engaged in work directed toward developing new or improved products for the future. The scientist frequently has no concern himself with the production of goods but only with the development of new ideas.

THE MEANING OF RESEARCH AND DEVELOPMENT

Because the category of research and development is so broad and includes many different types of work and workers, the relations of those in the field with each other and with those outside require additional clarification. It is comparatively simple to recognize the difference between the theoretician engaged in basic research and the development engineer who is but a step away from current production. Yet, under certain conditions, even the most theoretical scientist may shift, at least for a time, the focus of his work. This is what occurred during World War II when the nation made a major effort to increase its military strength in the shortest possible time. The important point is that while the scientist may be converted into a technologist, the reverse is rarely true. The Nobel Prize winner in physics may be able to turn his genius to the solution of a pressing technological problem, but the industrial chemist or engineer will not usually be able to unravel theoretical difficulties that stand in the way of further progress. As far as applied research is concerned, however, the team approach is coming increasingly into use, which makes it possible for men of different backgrounds to contribute their different skills to various stages of the solution of a problem.

The distinction between development and production personnel is as difficult to maintain as the distinction between research and development personnel. Engineers are frequently transferred from development to production and back again. To further complicate the problem of definition, a substantial amount of governmental and industrial work which is called research and development does not justify the term, even broadly used. In *Management Controls in Industrial Research Organizations* (1952), Professor Robert N. Anthony wrote about industrial research laboratories: "Some of them do no research. Most of them do quality control work, or product testing, or installation work, or trouble-shooting of various kinds, or sales promotion, or design and engineering, in addition to what is commonly thought of as research and development work."

The difficulties of defining clearly the field of research and development distinctly indicate the need for caution in any analysis based upon quantitative data. Inadequacies in the data available on research and development expenditures and personnel reinforce this need.

THE SCALE OF RESEARCH AND DEVELOPMENT

Expenditures for research and development by government, industry, and the universities, provide the best measure of the past and present scale of the nation's research and development program. The best available data, which are summarized in Tables 6 and 7, have been prepared by the staff of the Research and Development Board of the Department of Defense. The staff is now revising its earlier estimates, but new figures are available only for 1952. Table 6 shows the scale of expenditures for research and development in 1952.

*Table 6. Research and Development Expenditures,
in Millions of Dollars, 1952* [a]

	Expenditures	Performance
Industry	1,300	2,300
Government	2,100	800
Colleges, universities and other non-profit institutions	100	400
Total	3,500	3,500

[a] Source: data provided by the Research and Development Board, Department of Defense. "Expenditures" indicates who pays for the work; "performance," who does it.

These figures are a rough approximation of the amount of money allocated directly for research and development purposes. They are derived in large part by multiplying the estimated number of research and development personnel by the expenditures per person as indicated by sample studies. Neither set of figures can be regarded as accurate. In addition, the estimate does not include all the overhead expenses that can properly be charged against research and development. It should also be noted that the figures cover funds allocated for research in all fields, including the biological and social sciences, psychology, and the arts and humanities. The great bulk of research and development funds, however, are spent in the fields of physical science and engineering with which this chapter is primarily concerned.

Whatever their limitations, the data do indicate clearly that only a small part of the total national income is invested in research and development. The gross national product of the American economy in 1952 was just under $350 billion. Since, as Table 6 shows, total expenditures for research and development in 1952 are estimated at about $3.5 billion, one dollar was spent on research and development for every hundred dollars of goods and services produced.

The research and development effort also engages a very small proportion of the nation's trained personnel. The best current estimate suggests that in 1952 about 160,000 out of the approximate total of 700,000 scientists and engineers were engaged primarily in research and development. Even this relatively small figure of 160,000 overstates the number of scientists and engineers whose work is likely to lead to significant progress.

There is no reliable way of differentiating among the nation's scientists and engineers in terms of qualitative characteristics, but two methods are suggestive. Individuals are listed in *American Men of Science* on the recommendations of experts in their respective fields. Inclusion of a man's name in this volume suggests that his contribution has been considerably above the average. In 1948, approximately 50,000 scientists and engineers were listed. A second approach to a qualitative differentiation is through the number who have acquired doctoral degrees. Although it is not essential to hold a doctoral degree in order to perform at a high level of competence, there is no question that most of the major scientific advances in recent years have been made by men who have earned a doctorate. In engineering, however, it has been the exception rather than the rule for even the research-minded person to study for the doctorate. In 1950, 34,000 scientists and engineers held this advanced degree.

There is no point in elaborating on methods of distinguishing between the average scientist and engineer and the man whose aptitude and training are superior. The important point is that only 160,000 scientists and engineers devote themselves primarily to research and development. This last figure, moreover, includes many young persons who have not yet acquired much advanced training or experience, and many others who have been at work long enough to suggest that while they can do certain things competently, they will never make a major contribution to scientific or technological advance. It has been estimated that less than 15,000 are engaged in the basic research which produces fundamental new scientific knowledge.

THE GROWTH OF RESEARCH AND DEVELOPMENT

Research and development is paid for and performed by government, industry, and the universities. As early as 1789, the Congress of the United States made funds available to the Navy for the purpose of improving its guns and its ships. In spite of the rapid industrialization of the country during the second half of the nineteenth century, it was not until 1900 that General Electric established the first major industrial laboratory. Until then, industry had depended upon the independent inventor who came to it with an improvement, or upon the ideas of men who were engaged primarily in production. After that, it sought to accelerate the process of invention through the establishment of its own laboratories. Industrial research grew slowly between the beginning of the century and World War I, at which time there were approximately one hundred industrial laboratories.

World War I provided a major impetus, particularly in the field of chemistry, and industrial research continued to grow throughout the 1920's. During this decade such important laboratories as those of Bell Telephone, du Pont, and Westinghouse were established. By 1930, there were 1,600 industrial laboratories, whose annual expenditures were about $116 million. This amounted to 70 percent of the total expenditures in the United States on research and development by industry, government, and the universities. The rapid expansion of industrial research and development was slowed for a few years by the depression which began in 1929, but by 1939 expenditures for industrial research and development were approximately twice those at the beginning of the decade.

Since the beginning of World War II, the pattern of research and development expenditures has been revolutionized. Before the war, by far the largest part of all research and development work was financed by industry. The accelerated expansion since 1940, however, was financed primarily by Federal funds. The changes are summarized in Table 7. In 1941, total expenditures by government, industry, and educational institutions for research and development amounted to $800 million. By the end of the war, annual expenditures were estimated at $1.3 billion; at the outbreak of hostilities in Korea, $2.2 billion; and in 1952, the preliminary estimate was $2.9 billion. As has been noted, the 1952 estimate has recently been revised to $3.5 billion. Since revised figures for the earlier years are not yet available, the smaller figure must be used for comparative purposes. The unrevised data probably reflect major trends with reasonable accuracy. On this basis, total research and development expenditures increased 266 percent between 1941 and 1952. When allowance is made for the inflationary trend during these twelve years, expenditures increased by 95 percent.

During this period, while research and development expenditures almost doubled in terms of dollars of equal purchasing power, the gross national product increased by approximately 44 percent. Hence, expenditures for research and development, which amounted to six-tenths of one percent of gross national product in 1941, increased to about one percent in 1952.

Table 7. Research and Development Expenditures, in Millions of Dollars, 1941-52 [a]

EXPENDITURES

YEAR	TOTAL	Government	Industry	Colleges and Universities
1941	800	240	510	50
1942	930	340	540	20
1943	1,050	630	400	20
1944	1,200	770	410	20
1945	1,300	880	410	10
1946	1,490	660	800	30
1947	1,810	790	950	70
1948	2,060	920	1,030	110
1949	2,080	1,050	920	110
1950	2,240	1,040	1,080	120
1951	2,590	1,310	1,170	110
1952[b]	2,930	1,640	1,190	100

PERFORMANCE

YEAR	TOTAL	Government	Industry	Colleges and Universities
1941	800	200	520	80
1942	930	240	600	90
1943	1,050	300	650	100
1944	1,200	390	700	110
1945	1,300	430	750	120
1946	1,490	470	890	130
1947	1,810	520	1,120	170
1948	2,060	570	1,290	200
1949	2,080	550	1,310	220
1950	2,240	570	1,430	240
1951	2,590	700	1,630	260
1952[b]	2,930	830	1,820	280

[a] Source: data provided by the Research and Development Board, Department of Defense. "Expenditures" indicates who pays for the work; "performance," who does it.
[b] See Table 6 for revised 1952 estimates.

By far the largest contributor to the total increase was the Federal government, whose expenditures grew seven-fold, while industry's expenditures more than doubled and the universities' just doubled. In terms of performance, industry continued to carry the largest part of the load although the research work performed in government and university laboratories increased substantially. During World War II and again in recent years most of the research and development bill has been paid by government. When governmental expenditures declined immediately after the war, however, there was apparently no difficulty in finding sufficient industrial support to maintain the rapid expansion of the total research and development effort.

It has been estimated that the number of research engineers and scientists approximately doubled between 1941 and 1952. Just under 60 percent of the total of about 160,000 are employed by industry, with the remainder distributed almost equally between government and the universities. For the same number of dollars devoted to research and development the universities employ a much higher number of research and development personnel, primarily because pilot models and other more costly projects are usually undertaken by industrial or governmental laboratories.

Since 1941, the major use of increased funds for research and development has been the employment of more scientists and engineers. The additional funds were also used to hire technical and clerical assistants, purchase more expensive equipment, and for such activities as travel and the purchase of books and periodicals.

At present, expenditures average about $22,000 annually for each of the 160,000 scientists and engineers engaged in research and development. There is, of course, wide variation among laboratories and projects in expenditures per scientist or engineer. Some of these variations have been analyzed in *Industrial Research and Development,* recently published by the Bureau of Labor Statistics and the Research and Development Board of the Department of Defense. Among industrial laboratories, average annual expenditures per scientist or engineer range from $14,500 for those specializing in basic or medical science to $34,000 for those engaged in ordnance research and development.

INDUSTRIAL RESEARCH AND DEVELOPMENT

There are striking differences among industries in the costs of research and development as a percentage of sales. Research and development performed by food and primary metals industries amounts to less than half of 1 percent of their sales. In contrast, the cost in the electrical machinery industry equals more than 6 percent of sales, and in the aircraft industry almost 13 percent. The average for all manufacturing is 2 percent. The electrical machinery, aircraft, and chemical industries accounted for over half of the total cost of research and development work performed by industry as a whole in 1951, which totaled, according to the latest figures, almost $2 billion. These figures do not indicate how much of its own funds each industry spends on research and development, since they are based on the total cost of work performed, including work paid for by the Federal government. In 1951, the government paid for 85 percent of the research and development performed by the aircraft industry and almost three-fifths of that performed by the electrical machinery industry. By contrast, the food industry paid for over 95 percent of its research work from its own funds. In terms of expenditures from their own funds, no industry spends as much as 3 percent of sales. The leading industries are electrical machinery, which spends almost 3 percent, and professional and scientific equipment, chemical, and aircraft, each of which spends about 2 percent.

The amount of money which an industry or a company spends on research and development is determined by several considerations, including the amount of support available from the government. The decision about how much of its own funds a company should spend depends essentially on an estimate of the added income likely to result from the investment. To forecast the profitability of a new research project is a complex task. Every research project involves a risk. For every important discovery, there are likely to be many unimportant improvements and more false starts which produce no useful results. The directors of the company must consider the availability of capital to produce and market a new item, and the possibility that after allowance has been made for the costs of changing over the production lines and advertising and marketing the new item the anticipated profits might never appear. Since the better industrial research laboratories offer their scientists much the same kind of employment security as universities and government, even though it is not always explicit, additions to the research and development staff represent an important long-term cost to the concern. Moreover, each new scientist must have proper laboratory facilities, which may cost $10,000 or more per scientist. Thus, the industrial requirement for research and developmental personnel is limited by the fact that industry must balance the costs of expanding this effort against the returns likely to accrue from it. Frequently, past experience may be of little help because it may be impossible to say how much of a given profit increase is the result of the research program.

A recent survey of industrial research laboratories which employ over 44,000 professional personnel sought to estimate their demand for additional scientists and engineers for research and development work between March, 1952, and the end of the year. The survey indicated that the laboratories might desire to add almost 10,000 scientists and engineers to their staffs within that period. The larger laboratories indicated a desire to increase their staffs by about 13 percent, while the smaller ones indicated an additional requirement of almost 30 percent. (*A Study of Team or Group Research*, David B. Hertz, September, 1952.) The results of this survey, however, cannot be accepted uncritically. There is always a tendency to overstate future requirements for scarce resources. In part, the estimated requirements may have reflected nothing more than the hope of the smaller companies to secure additional research and development contracts from the government. Moreover these estimated requirements are also open to suspicion because they are so much greater than the actual expansion in personnel which has taken place since Korea.

THE GOVERNMENT'S RESEARCH AND DEVELOPMENT PROGRAM

It has been seen that the scale of the research and development program in industry is determined mainly by anticipated profits from the laboratory as compared to profits from possible alternative uses of company funds. Governmental expenditures, however, are not determined by profit considerations. Since about 90 percent of the government funds for research and development are directly under the control of the Department of Defense, the Atomic Energy Commission, and the National Advisory Committee for Aeronautics, it is obvious that the primary consideration is the security of the nation. The remaining 10 percent is spent by other Federal agencies on projects more directly related to welfare than to defense, although frequently the two cannot be separated.

By comparison with total defense expenditures which are now over $40 billion a year, total expenditures of the Federal government for research and development, about $2 billion, are relatively modest. Why does the government not increase its efforts to improve weapons and military equipment through research and development and thereby provide the nation with greater security? Improved defenses are the best protection against the outbreak of hostilities and, in the event of hostilities, the best insurance of victory. There is no single answer to this complex problem.

A part of the explanation lies in the fact that the country is in a period of partial rather than full mobilization. Although the Federal government has induced private industry to make available about half of its industrial research facilities for work on problems of high concern to the military, it has encountered some resistance in seeking to increase further the scale of government research and development contracts. This is not difficult to understand since every company wants to continue enough of its own work to safeguard its competitive position in the future. Moreover, the inability or disinclination of the Federal government to tie in research and development contracts with contracts for production has further reduced the willingness of private industry to convert more of its research facilities to government work. Industry looks to its laboratories as an important source of future profits. There are no significant profits possible in a research and development contract; for profits, production contracts are needed.

There are further reasons which limit the amount of research and development work performed for the government by industry. Some companies have succeeded in maintaining their competitive position largely by virtue of patents on new products developed by their laboratories. Since there are many complications involved in securing and protecting patents on products developed with the aid of Federal funds, some concerns in high tax brackets prefer to spend their own money on research and development.

To some degree the government has purposely limited research and development contracts. Government experts are increasingly reluctant to make additional funds available to industry for certain types of work since competent scientific and engineering personnel are simply not available. Shortages of highly trained manpower are an important factor, therefore, in limiting the amount of governmental work performed by industry.

Since these factors limit the extent to which the government can utilize research and development facilities of private industry for defense work, why does it not expand its own facilities so that it can do more itself? The amount of work performed in government facilities has increased considerably over the past few years from $570 million in 1950 to $830 million in 1952. It is doubtful that the government should in fact do much more to expand its own facilities. The senior members of industrial research laboratories, as well as university personnel, have tenure in their present positions. Some may be willing to sacrifice this for special opportunities with the government. But much is unattractive about government employment, including security clearances and the uncertainties of Congressional appropriations. Although the Federal government has been able to obtain some individuals from the ranks of industrial and academic employment, they have been mostly junior personnel or individuals who have entered government service as consultants or for a limited period on a leave of absence from their employers. Moreover, rather liberal government contracts have enabled industry to attract away some of the government's senior civilian personnel through the offer of higher salaries. Thus, the shortage of mature, highly competent research personnel also limits the amount of research and development carried out in government laboratories.

THE GOALS OF THE GOVERNMENT'S RESEARCH AND DEVELOPMENT PROGRAM

Although there are many parallels between research and development work in industry and the problems faced by the government when it expands its research and development program for defense, there are also significant differences. For the most part, industrial research and development is directed toward the improvement of existing products and processes or the development of new approaches that are likely to add to the profits of a specific company. Although all research and development has an element of uncertainty in it, industrial laboratories, with some notable exceptions, try to avoid assuming too large a risk.

The military establishment, of course, needs research and development aimed at product improvement, but its primary goal must always be to gain a big lead in strategic and tactical potential. Hence, it must be concerned with the complicated problem of how best to develop a whole new array of weapons and merge them into an effective new weapons system. Today, this problem includes such difficult tasks as the perfection of guided missiles and their integration into an effective air defense system, and the development of atomic weapons for the use of the ground forces. To accomplish such aims requires the assumption of substantial risks.

The goals of a military research and development program are also different during a prolonged period of partial mobilization than they are during full mobilization. The development of the atomic bomb during World War II demonstrated that once a fundamental theory is developed, problems involving its application can be solved in a relatively short time. The only requirements are a willingness to direct sufficient scientific resources to work on the solution and to disregard questions of cost.

It may well be that the country learned too well the lesson of what the lavish expenditure of money and human resources can accomplish. In a period of partial mobilization, the country cannot afford to concentrate the work of its laboratories on the solution of one or two specific problems. The security of the nation cannot be guaranteed by any single new weapon, even if it is as revolutionary as the atomic bomb. Soviet Russia has also developed the atomic bomb. Because progress is required over a very broad front, personnel and money must be allocated to a variety of research projects. There is not enough of either to duplicate, or even approximate, the intensive effort that led to the atomic bomb. Money and trained manpower are always needed, but without bold new ideas they will prove insufficient.

Today, the country requires ideas which will meet not one, but a whole range of military needs, and the most useful ideas are those which will lead to important advances in spite of limited funds and limited research personnel. If possible, therefore, the nation is even more dependent than it was during World War II on men with a high order of competence.

Because of the complexity of the problem of research and development for defense in a period of partial mobilization, the effectiveness of the government's program depends very heavily on the quality of the planning that goes into it, the quality of control that is exercised over it, and the quality of the evaluation to which it is submitted, as well as on the creative ideas of the scientists who participate in it. For every one of these tasks mature and experienced men are required. Moreover, much of the current developmental work is team work, which depends for its success to a large degree on the competence and maturity of the team leader, qualities which can be developed only with time and experience.

The shortage of creative scientists and of senior scientific administrators has made it difficult to plan and supervise effectively the large-scale program now under way. A considerable part of the military effort in research and development today is directed toward small improvements in existing equipment which can readily be undertaken by the personnel available. The full implications of a large-scale program which is concentrated primarily on the improvement of individual products have not been appreciated. The experience of private industry indicates that many laboratory discoveries are not put into production because they would be too expensive to manufacture and market. One of the important questions that businessmen face is whether there will be enough time to recover the costs of introducing a new product before new production facilities become obsolete.

In short, the effectiveness of development work cannot be measured in terms of technical improvements achieved, without reference to the economic implications of utilizing the advances. It is necessary to consider the costs of producing the improved product and of operating and maintaining it, including the mental and physical demands upon operating and maintenance personnel. In spite of recently expanded research in "human engineering," insufficient consideration has been given to the human factors involved in the production and use of new military equipment. Even less attention has been paid to the economics of the problem. When expensive apparatus is already in use, with large stocks of spare parts and training and maintenance manuals on hand, changing over to a new model can be justified only if it represents a major advance, especially if radical changes in the weapons system loom on the horizon.

THE UNIVERSITIES AND RESEARCH AND DEVELOPMENT

The quality of the research and development work currently being carried on by the Federal government could probably be raised considerably if the country's top scientists increased their participation in it. The difficulties which the government has encountered in seeking to attract more senior scientists into its own laboratories, particularly from industry, and in seeking to have more of its research and development work performed by industrial laboratories, have already been described. The participation of the nation's senior scientists in the government's program could be increased substantially only by transferring scientists from university to government employment, or by placing more research and development contracts with universities. This, however, would only add in the long run to the manpower shortages that are already serious, because the teaching of advanced students in the universities would suffer.

The best protection against future shortages of scientists in new and rapidly expanding fields is to broaden and deepen the training of young men while they are still studying at the universities. There are other useful measures. The Atomic Energy Commission, for instance, has sought to relieve the shortage of nuclear physicists by encouraging its major contractors to train engineers in the principles of nuclear reactors. Nevertheless, the basic remedy lies in university training which will enable scientists to cope more easily with new fields of knowledge. The importance of breadth and depth in training is only now coming to be generally appreciated. The fellowship program of the National Science Foundation and the slow but steady expansion of industry-sponsored fellowships are directed largely to this goal, but a broadened teaching program would be far more difficult to achieve if additional university personnel were deflected to current developmental or administrative work for the government.

The implications of the government research and development program for the universities, and therefore for the future quality of the nation's scientific manpower, go far beyond the dangers of depleting the faculties or deflecting them from teaching. Until World War II the universities carried the principal responsibility for the discovery of new knowledge and the training of young scientists while industrial research laboratories were making a growing contribution to applied research and to the development of competent research investigators. Except for relatively specialized fields, the Federal government played a minor role. Today, however, Federal expenditures for research and development amount to more than $2 billion annually and account for 60 percent of the total national expenditures for research and development. In 1952, the universities spent approximately $100 million of their own funds on research and development while their total performance amounted to about $400 million. The difference between these two figures represents work performed under governmental contracts and, to a lesser extent, industrial contracts for research and development.

The long-run implications of turning so much of the effort of academic institutions to projects connected with the current rearmament effort have not been adequately considered. To a substantial degree, many scientific faculties have been converted into commercial development establishments. Professor George B. Kistiakowsky of Harvard University has warned against the dangers of hiring young graduate students to work on rather narrow developmental projects in which their major duties are to carry out instructions and to follow in the footsteps of others. This is the time in their careers when they should be exploring on their own with only the guidance of a professor. With many of the teaching staff occupied with the administration and supervision of projects, and many graduate students working on narrow assignments on narrow projects, there is a real danger that today's development work is being accomplished at an exorbitantly high cost in terms of the future quality of the nation's scientific manpower and the advancement of basic knowledge.

The 1952 report of the National Science Foundation presents figures about Federal obligations for scientific research and development at non-profit institutions (mostly universities) which reinforce these fears. The report shows that out of total obligations to non-profit institutions of $341 million, only $71 million, or 20 percent, are for basic research. Four out of every five dollars are being spent for applied research and development work. These large-scale expenditures by the government do contribute, of course, to the training of younger scientists, especially in those fields where very expensive equipment and materials are required. This, together with the fact that government contracts make it possible for the universities to expand their staffs, probably explains why most universities have been so eager to secure large government contracts. The precarious financial position of most universities also helps to explain why they are willing to take these serious risks.

The determination of the proper balance between the growth of new knowledge and the exploitation of old knowledge, between broad training for young scientists and the utilization of available scientific resources to meet currently pressing demands, is dependent on a wise evaluation of the dangers which face the nation. If the country is in imminent danger of attack, then current developmental needs are preeminent; if the cold war should continue for years or decades, then basic knowledge and depth of training are paramount. If both contingencies are more or less equally probable, a delicate balance must be maintained between immediate improvements and long- term gains of greater potential significance. There is reason to fear, however, that immediate needs have been overemphasized. Because of the limited understanding of these exceedingly complex issues, Congress tends to favor projects which promise quick, visible results, and is hesitant to make investments which may produce far more important results but only after years have elapsed.

After many delays the National Science Foundation was established by Congress in 1950 to develop a policy for the promotion and support of basic research and education in the sciences, to award graduate fellowships, and to foster the interchange of scientific information. In its budget request for the fiscal year 1952-53 the National Science Foundation asked for $15 million. The Committee on Appropriations of the House of Representatives recommended that it receive only $3.5 million. The Committee declared that it "is aware of the importance of this activity and the program which it sponsors, and it is reluctant to retard development of it. However, it is a new activity which is unlikely to provide assistance to the country in an immediate emergency. The Committee feels, therefore, that expansion to the full amount of the authorization ($15 million) should be deferred until the financial condition of the Treasury has improved."

The House Appropriations Committee recently took much the same attitude toward appropriations for the Atomic Energy Commission. During the last four fiscal years (1949-52) the Atomic Energy Commission received total appropriations of just under $5 billion. In considering the budget request for $1.3 billion in 1952-53, the House Committee recommended a reduction of about $25 million from a request of $341 million for use in connection with "source and fissionable materials." It stated that "this reduction has been applied to items other than those involving the acquisition of fissionable materials . . . such items as exploration work . . . processing and development work, and experimental work in connection with the operation of producing plants." The Committee concluded that a reduction aimed at exploration, development, and experiment was relatively safe, since it did not affect the immediate acquisition of fissionable materials.

This attitude toward immediate results, of course, is not held by Congress alone. As has been seen, it is paralleled by the concentration of the military research and development program on product improvement. Moreover, many scientists in industry and the universities are disinclined to tackle basic problems of great difficulty when easier and less risky issues are awaiting solution.

RESEARCH AND DEVELOPMENT IN THE FUTURE

The size and character of the research and development program are the major determinants of the demand for scientists and research engineers. The striking increase in the number of scientific and technological workers, especially since World War I, has been stimulated in large part by new opportunities for employment in the expanding industrial research laboratories of the country. Although this expansion was interrupted during the major depression of 1929-33, it continued once business improved. There is every reason to believe that industrial research will continue to expand even though it may again suffer a temporary setback in the event of a depression.

While industrial research has expanded consistently, the part played by the Federal government in the financing of research and development has fluctuated considerably. From a very low level at the beginning of World War II the government rapidly increased its share in the financing of the total research and development effort. With the end of the war, government funds were somewhat reduced but with the deterioration of the international situation, particularly after the beginning of hostilities in Korea, government expenditures again increased rapidly.

Governmental expenditures will almost certainly continue on a scale substantially greater than prevailed before the outbreak of World War II, and will probably remain above the $700 million a year level of the immediate post-war years. It is not clear, however, whether, or for how long, they will continue at the present level of about $2 billion per year. The future scale of governmental financing of research and development will depend in the first instance upon the government's estimate of Soviet intentions and of the rate of progress in Soviet Russia in perfecting the instruments of war, since most of the governmental expenditures are directed toward defense. It is exceedingly difficult to obtain firm knowledge about the rate of scientific and technological progress in Soviet Russia, but the abilities of

Russian scientists and engineers must not be underestimated. Nor can it be assumed that the totalitarian environment is stifling creative research entirely.

The American Association for the Advancement of Science recently held a symposium on "Soviet Science," during which the following evaluation was made of the present state of Soviet physics and chemistry: "It is however evident to any observer that Soviet chemistry and physics is a well organized body of well trained scientists carrying out creditable work in many branches of their subjects in the best traditions of the West." Another expert commented, "I would like to describe Soviet mathematics as a most active and fruitful activity where fundamental results are being obtained and where there is no evidence of thought control." There was a strong suggestion throughout the symposium that Soviet science is borrowing what it can from Western science in terms of basic concepts and important technological advances and is directing its own research program largely "toward life, toward practice, toward the defense needs of the country and of the national economy." To the extent that this evaluation is correct, the opportunity of the United States to gain a big strategic lead through imaginative basic research is so much the greater.

It may well be that the current efforts of the United States, particularly in the application of atomic energy to defense, will provide it with a sizable lead in the armaments race in the relatively near future. If this should occur, there might be an inclination to reduce the scale of future governmental research and development expenditures.

Another consideration that might lead to some reduction in future expenditures is the increasingly effective evaluation of the current program. Every year younger men gain in experience and the older men who serve the government in a consulting capacity become more expert in discerning the shortcomings of the program. These developments may result in the conclusion that too much effort is now being put into minor improvements of equipment while the major need is the development of more radical approaches which take more advantage of the potentialities of contemporary science and technology.

To redirect the whole research and development program for defense in this way would be no easy task. The primary difficulty is the limited number of scientists and engineers capable of producing new and important ideas. If the nation were engaged in a major war, it would have to risk handicapping future industrial and academic progress by devoting almost all available talent to the solution of major military problems. This is what happened during World War II, but since no one knows how long the current period of tension will continue, the nation cannot now disregard the consequences of present action upon its future strength.

There is a distinct relationship between a nation's sense of urgency about the danger which confronts it and the way it utilizes its top scientific personnel. The British, apparently less concerned about the early outbreak of war, continue to work for the most part on long-range problems. It is possible that American scientists, under the promptings of Washington, are too heavily engaged in relatively unimportant defense projects. There is a growing tendency among educational institutions to reappraise and reduce the scale of their government contract work.

There is also mounting discontent and overt criticism among scientific leaders about the large flow of Federal funds into support of applied research, particularly in the universities. The main criticism is that these funds are resulting in too narrow utilization of senior personnel and too narrow training for younger men. To the extent that younger men are being encouraged into the narrow confines of limited projects and directed away from the broad and unknown frontiers where alone they can gain the experience needed for growth, the future of American science is being placed in jeopardy.

If it is determined that the country will need a larger research and development program in the future than in the past, it will become necessary to approach the problem, not in terms of the annual appropriations of the Congress, but in terms of a strengthened and expanded base in universities, industrial research laboratories, and in the government's own installations. The most serious shortcoming of the approach which has been followed since the end of World War II is its emphasis upon rather limited projects and its neglect of the base. Before the nation can develop a larger number of well-trained and highly competent scientists and research engineers, conditions must be established and maintained which will draw and keep the right kind of men interested in the right kind of work.

The American people have been blind to the fact that their progress depends to a very great extent on the work of less than 15,000 men who are spending their lives in fundamental scientific research, most of them at universities. Great care must be taken to insure that the universities can continue to meet their major responsibilities of discovering new knowledge and training tomorrow's scientists and scholars. Only if this is done will the nation be able to reap the full benefits of science and technology for defense and for its expanding welfare.

CHAPTER VI

The Armed Forces
and Highly Trained Manpower

THE ARMED FORCES are the largest employer of manpower in the country. Together their military and civilian personnel comprise almost eight percent of the labor force. There are now over 3.6 million persons in uniform, or almost the number established as essential to meet the present world-wide military commitments of the United States. In addition, the Department of Defense employs about 1.3 million civilians in domestic and foreign assignments.

More than three-quarters of the civilian employees are directly engaged in producing or repairing military equipment, including aircraft and ships, and in maintaining stations or supplying arms and equipment for the field forces. In addition to those employed directly by the military establishment, many thousands of others are engaged on a contractual basis in the research and development programs of each of the major services. Many millions more, of course, are employed by industry in the manufacture of arms, equipment, and supplies for the military forces of the United States and its allies.

Partly because of increased defense production goals, the demand of civilian employers for professional and scientific workers is larger than ever before. At the same time, because of the increasingly technical nature of modern warfare, the armed forces also require larger numbers of highly trained specialists, including engineers and scientists as well as numerous technicians. Consequently, the withdrawal of such persons from civilian employment for service in the military is a major concern of the industries and educational institutions which lose them.

In the present period of partial mobilization, the relationship between the military establishment and the rest of the nation with respect to manpower is extremely complex. The large direct and indirect manpower requirements of the military create major problems for both the armed forces and the civilian economy. Because the period of partial mobilization may continue for decades, the armed forces must attempt to avoid practices which, in the long run, might impair the nation's scientific and professional manpower resources.

The military services have been criticized for absorbing people in short supply and even more for underutilizing them. Some of this criticism, however, reflects the memory of World War II improvisations and outright mistakes in manpower classification and utilization. After the war, the armed forces did little to apply the lessons of their wartime experiences with respect to the handling of highly trained personnel. Much legitimate criticism is based on the emergency recall of reservists after the outbreak of hostilities in Korea, which disrupted some vital defense production and led to the gross misassignment of many recalled reservists. The partial mobilization initiated at that time indicated not only that the armed forces reserve policy was wholly inadequate, but also that the military services had not progressed very far in improving the utilization of their available manpower resources.

Effective utilization of manpower by the armed forces has been a subject of inquiry and debate by the Congress, by professional societies, and by the press. Since 1950, the armed forces have adopted policies which constitute a real advance toward better utilization of highly trained manpower. At present, practice still lags behind policy, and to the extent that intent and performance do not agree, there is room for improvement. The necessity for a constant, critical assessment of how policy is being carried out, therefore, cannot be stressed too strongly.

There is, for example, some indication that opportunities for receiving a commission are not as great for men in professional assignments as for men in combat arms. The traditional association of rank with command functions may be the barrier here. An ameliorative step might be the more extended use of the warrant officer category to provide higher pay for professional personnel and at the same time relieve them from the routine "details" required of enlisted men.

There have also been criticisms to the effect that it is difficult for an individual to obtain assignment as a scientist or professional because of the high standards which the services set for such specialized assignments. These standards reflect the fact that the mission of the military is not primarily the effective employment of scientific personnel. Its mission is a military one. To the extent that its military mission requires the services normally performed by specialized personnel, however, it is reasonable to expect that every effort will be made to assure a close correspondence between the competences of the personnel taken into service and the positions to which they are assigned.

Actually, however, most of the men entering enlisted ranks today are too young to qualify as scientists or professional persons, or even as skilled technicians. Fewer still can be directly utilized by the military services without special training. The Air Force, which has not had to resort to Selective Service to fill its ranks since World War II, and which actively recruits specialized personnel, finds that less than 10 percent of its enlistees can be used immediately for technical military duties. These men, called "by-passed specialists," move immediately to military jobs for which their civilian experience qualifies them.

Most of the men now entering military service must be trained, not only in basic military matters, but in technical fields as well. The maintenance of adequate numbers of trained specialists in the armed forces is complicated by the fact that most men now in service will serve for only two to four years. The armed forces are too large to hope to fill more than a small part of their manpower needs from among those men who will make military service a career. Although there is some evidence that military careers are increasing in attractiveness, very few draftees enlist in the regular Army when their two years of service are up, and less than half of the volunteers for the Army, Navy, or Air Force reenlist after their first four-year period of service. Consequently, the armed forces lose trained specialists rapidly. Obviously, their ability to meet their needs depends on the development of programs which provide the necessary training quickly and effectively, and which make efficient use of specialized knowledge, whether acquired in service or in civilian life.

Because most of the men now in service will remain for no more than four years, the armed forces may be regarded as the temporary custodians of an important part of the nation's manpower resources. In this role, they are engaged in training their personnel in skills and knowledge which, to a large degree, are common to military and to civilian life. For the majority of the young men entering military service, the two, three, or four years spent in uniform contribute to their knowledge or skills. Since most of the men trained do not remain in service, the full benefit of their training is received, not by the armed forces, but by the civilian economy. Thus, the military training programs improve the quality of the labor force. Moreover, if the armed forces make effective use of highly trained personnel, and if such personnel take full advantage of the opportunities afforded, technical competence will be increased through fruitful experience. If trained personnel are not utilized in their fields, skills and knowledge will deteriorate through disuse. To some extent, such deterioration is inevitable since the military services must use a man where they need him most.

THE ARMED FORCES IN A TECHNOLOGICAL ERA

Modern warfare has not outmoded the basic foot soldier using relatively simple arms to fight in limited engagements. Within each of the services there are also many routine jobs which can be performed by men with little or no training. Yet, technological changes affect the armed forces as they do modern industry. Advances in electronics, engineering, mechanics, and many other fields have been reflected in larger, more complex weapons and equipment in all the military services.

The electronic equipment alone on an Air Force fighter plane today costs more than an entire fighter plane during the last war. Personnel competent to use and service such equipment is an obvious necessity. The Army's extensive ground communications network requires the services of electronic experts and a wide variety of technicians skilled in signal work. Its engineers construct and maintain railroads and highways, and it employs physicists to develop guided missiles. Mortar squads at the front lines now rely upon radar teams to spot the location of enemy mortar units.

The official list of suggested assignments for scientists and other professional persons entering the Army furnishes a summary of the many specialized activities carried out. A graduate electrical engineer who scores high on certain aptitude tests is supposed to be assigned as an electrical-electronic assistant. If he cannot be used specifically in this assignment, he may be assigned to any one of thirty-nine related jobs in three general fields, all of which call for men with this type of training. Language teachers may be assigned as interrogators, translators, or interpreters; geologists and geophysicists as terrain intelligence analysts; communications engineers as microwave radio repairmen or radio teletypewriter repairmen.

As this listing indicates, the military establishment contains a wide variety of jobs which are related to civilian occupations, but others are unique to military service. The transformation of civilian skills, training, and experience into the appropriate military occupational specialties constitutes the most basic classification and training problem of the military services.

The total number of fully qualified scientists and professionals in the armed forces is small. Of all enlisted men entering the Army since 1948, only 10,800 met the Army's requirements for classification as scientists or professionals. The number of enlisted personnel given assignments as technicians is far larger. It is not so much the actual operation of the more complex weapons and equipment as their maintenance and repair which creates the military requirements for specialized personnel. One piece of naval underwater detecting equipment, for example, is so complex that it cannot be completely checked while aboard ship. Because it is not practical to carry the required testing apparatus and technicians, overhaul has to await the ship's entry into drydock. Generally, however, the scientists and technicians must be available wherever the equipment is used. Some of the newer jet aircraft, for example, have extremely thin wings and a narrow fuselage which are structurally sound aloft but which must be handled carefully on the ground. Should one of these aircraft be disabled and have to be removed from the airstrip for repairs it could be destroyed by a crane operator's mistake. To prevent such costly errors, an aviation structural engineer frequently supervises such operations.

Technological developments are not the only reason for the high military demand for professionals, scientists, and skilled technicians. Americans generally expect that soldiers will receive many of the services which are available to civilians. Thus, the armed forces require social workers, dietitians, lawyers, clergymen, nurses, doctors, entertainers, writers, and other professionals who are either not used by the armed forces of most other nations, or are used in much smaller numbers. The development of psychological warfare and the expanded scope of military intelligence have created the need for psychologists and social scientists.

American military policies conceive of the armed forces primarily as mobile striking units, and seek to limit casualties through the lavish use of equipment. These policies complicate the problems of logistics and maintenance and add to the number of highly trained specialists needed. In short, most of the factors which have led to the rapidly increasing employment of professionals and scientists in civilian life also operate within the military establishment.

THE TRAINING AND UTILIZATION OF SPECIALISTS

Two separate but related aspects of military policy with respect to specialized personnel are of crucial importance. One is the military utilization of trained scientists, professionals, and skilled specialists who, through induction, voluntary enlistment, the Reserve Officers Training Corps programs, or other routes, become members of the military establishment. The second is the extent and range of specialized training given in the military services.

Partial mobilization creates special problems in training and utilizing specialized personnel. These problems, moreover, are not the same for all the services. The enlisted personnel of the Navy and Air Force still consists primarily of volunteers for four or more years of service. The Army, however, has had to rely heavily on men inducted through Selective Service, and on recalled reservists, who serve for two years or less. Because the Navy and Air Force have been able to rely on volunteers, in addition to some recalled reservists, they have somewhat greater control over the kinds of personnel they receive. They direct special recruiting efforts towards attracting the kinds of men they need and want. The Army does, too, but it must select most of its personnel from among the men made available by the Selective Service System. Since May, 1951, the "Qualitative Distribution" policy of the Department of Defense has improved the Army's position somewhat by limiting the number of volunteers of high intelligence which the other services may accept. This assures that each of the services will receive a roughly equal share of the more intelligent men entering service. Nevertheless, the Army, unlike the other services, must still rely mainly on men drafted for two years of service. The Army, moreover, must use many two-year draftees to replace casualties and men "rotated" from combat in Korea. For the Navy and Air Force, Korea creates a much smaller casualty and rotation problem.

Because of these circumstances, the Navy and Air Force have been able to preserve their "career programs" which represent a special effort to place each individual in the career field and even in the specific job for which he is best fitted by ability, training, and interest. The career programs also provide advanced training to fit qualified men for promotion up an established career ladder. Since their first-time enlistees can be counted on for at least four years of service, the Navy and Air Force provide the same initial specialized training for men who intend to leave after their enlistment period as for those who intend to make the service their career.

Primarily because it has to maintain large forces overseas, the Army has been compelled to suspend indefinitely its career program for enlisted men. Draftees are usually assigned only to the shorter technical courses for which they qualify. Even then the Army can count on little more than a year's overseas service from a draftee who has completed a short technical course. Admission to the specialist courses of sixteen weeks or more is limited to Regular Army personnel insofar as practicable. Because of the preponderance of Selective Service personnel in the Army, however, all openings cannot be filled by career personnel. Consequently, some two-year draftees must be trained in the longer courses. For example, in the fiscal year 1953, about 12,000 Selective Service draftees will be enrolled in courses at least sixteen weeks in length, largely because qualified long-term enlistees are not available.

THE IDENTIFICATION AND UTILIZATION OF SPECIALISTS

None of the services guarantees that specialized personnel will perform military duties completely or exclusively in line with their background and training. To require this would, in effect, place the services in a strait jacket. The Army, recognizing the problem no less clearly than its critics, specifically warns those individuals whom it classifies as scientists or professionals that they may not be used in the specialty for which they are classified. The information sheet given every soldier identified as being in one of the scientific and professional areas, states:

> In addition to your principal duties of a scientific, professional, or technical nature you will be required to perform additional duties, appropriate to your grade, the "details" normally required of all enlisted men. . . . Your assignment to one of [the higher pay] grades will depend upon your performance of duty and Army-wide grade authorizations. . . . Although the Army will make an effort to assign you to a duty position in which your special qualifications will be well utilized, the nature of many Army job requirements will not always make possible full utilization of all your background. Because Army duties do not precisely match civilian areas of specialization, the Army will consider you properly utilized if only a part of your special qualifications are directly used or if most of your background is indirectly required by the job. For example, an astronomer or astro-physicist may be best utilized computing firing data in connection with guided missile research.

Some of the jobs to which men with scientific or other professional training are assigned could be performed by men with less extensive education, provided they were given specialized training. The Army, however, is faced with the problem of getting the greatest amount of useful service from its two-year draftees, with the least investment in training time. Some "down-grading," therefore, is inevitable. Present Army policy states in essence that an individual will be used at his highest level of competence if military requirements call for it. Otherwise, he will be used in the job which most closely calls upon his background.

The military establishment cannot be operated like an industrial plant or a research laboratory. In addition to performing their scientific or professional duties, all service men must learn to work and live as soldiers, sailors, or airmen. An effort is made to keep these duties at the minimum necessary to operate a military post and to educate the men in military life. Generally, they do not occupy more than 20 percent of the time of specialized personnel. Obviously, however, a still further reduction of time required for non-professional tasks would contribute to a more effective utilization of scarce skills and competence.

It has been noted that since World War II, each of the armed forces has made significant progress in using the scarce skills and abilities of men entering service. Because there is no exact military counterpart for many civilian occupations, and because the armed forces have less flexibility in the selection and separation of personnel, the problems faced are far different from those in civilian life. Military manpower policy now insists that men with scientific or professional competence be identified early and placed in those jobs which most fully draw upon their particular skills. Air Force policy for officer assignment states: "Effective manning of Air Force activities requires the fullest utilization of those skills which are in limited resource. . . . Accordingly, officers who possess a limited resource specialty will be utilized in that specialty or in another in the same occupational field."

In its Special Regulations covering the utilization of enlisted scientific and professional personnel, the Army declares:

> In the interest of the national welfare and the need to conserve our human resources, the Army recognizes the advantages of utilizing to the fullest extent possible special abilities . . . acquired through long years of education and experience. These abilities represent a national resource which should be effectively utilized for national defense. . . . Those . . . coming into the Army constitute a pool of highly trained manpower the size of which varies from time to time. The Army will endeavor to utilize this manpower pool in selected scientific and professional areas, to the fullest possible extent consistent with its combat mission.

In January, and again in August, 1952, the Army rewrote its regulations governing the identification, classification and utilization of enlisted scientific and professional personnel. Under the revised regulations, college-trained draftees or enlistees in twenty-six specialized fields are required to take only eight weeks of basic training instead of the customary sixteen. Men who have a bachelor's degree, and, in some cases, a master's degree, or one or two years of actual work or research in these fields, and who achieve sufficiently high scores on aptitude tests are identified as scientific and professional personnel. The Adjutant General's Office in Washington makes and records the assignment of every soldier so identified. While the soldier is in basic training, his qualifications are checked against the Army's requirements for professional and scientific personnel. If a man with his particular qualifications is needed when he completes basic training, he is assigned immediately to that position. If not, he is assigned to the next most appropriate duty or training program. In the latter case, if a need later arises for men of his exact qualifications, the Adjutant General's Office will direct his reassignment.

Periodic checks are made on the actual assignment of every individual designated as a scientific or professional specialist. The Army has even broken with tradition to suggest that the man himself may inform the Adjutant General's Office, through regular channels, whenever he believes that he has not been properly assigned. One recent check by the Army of some five thousand enlisted personnel identified as scientists or professionals found less than 4 percent improperly assigned. Orders directing new assignments were immediately issued. The provision for a check of the actual work assignments of 10 percent of all enlisted scientific and professional personnel each month is another forward step.

Air Force and Navy practice has not been so formalized or centralized, but the same general policy applies. In the Air Force, for example, enlisted men with college degrees in the natural sciences, engineering, psychology, sociology, or mathematics are reported to Air Force Headquarters for assignment where needed if their specialties cannot be used within their own units. Moreover, the actual assignment of each of these men is checked against his educational and occupational background at least once every six months by the Air Inspector.

Not all the scientists and professionals enter the armed forces as enlisted personnel. Many enter with a commission or are commissioned through an Officer Candidate School soon after entry. College graduates are encouraged to apply for officer training, but, since this nearly always entails at least a few months additional military service for the successful graduate, many enlisted men refuse the opportunity. Still others refuse because their proposed commission would not be in the field of their technical competence; for example, an engineer might refuse an opportunity for a commission in the Infantry.

The largest single source of college-trained officers for the Army is the Reserve Officers Training Corps program. Between 1952 and 1955, the Army hopes to produce about 60,000 commissioned officers through its ROTC program. In the past, all college students being trained in ROTC units as officers were appointed in a particular branch of the Army, such as Infantry or Field Artillery. Except for a few whose applications for transfer were approved, they were commissioned upon graduation in the branch which maintained the ROTC unit at their particular school, regardless of their field of study in college. To correct this, the newly instituted Army ROTC units and some of the older units are no longer associated with a particular branch of service. The newly commissioned officer of these "branch immaterial" schools may now be assigned as nearly in accordance with his specialized background as current military requirements permit. Because the Army requires more combat leaders than the other services, however, some men who are considered to possess high leadership ability must be assigned to combat arms (Artillery, Armor, and Infantry), regardless of their professional backgrounds.

The relatively heavy concentration of ROTC units in the nation's engineering and technical colleges has been regarded by some as a serious danger to the nation's scientific manpower resources. It has been feared that if the ROTC programs are further expanded, a high proportion of engineering graduates would be prevented from entering the labor force or undertaking graduate study until after completing their tour of military duty. Precisely how many engineering students are now ROTC members is not known. A reliable estimate of the number in the senior class of 1952 is 16 percent. The percentage in the other three college classes is larger, but not all those presently enrolled will remain in the program and graduate with commissions. Because a declining number of engineering graduates over the next two years will coincide with some increase in the number who are ROTC graduates, the percentage of engineering graduates being commissioned in the military services will increase sharply.

Although the number of students enrolled in the ROTC programs of the armed forces has increased during the current partial mobilization, only about one-eighth of all men graduating from college are ROTC graduates. Each service permits limited numbers of qualified ROTC graduates to continue with graduate study before beginning active duty. Since Korea, for example, the Army has postponed active duty for some seven hundred ROTC graduates, in some cases for as long as three years. The ROTC programs, however, will have an increasing effect in future years. Because most ROTC members are advised to increase their knowledge of mathematics, the sciences, and engineering, the impact of an expanded ROTC program on college curricula should be a matter of continuing concern to all educators. A further concentration of engineering and technical students in the ROTC programs may also lead to assigning many of them to areas other than their professional fields while at the same time reducing the opportunities for qualified individuals from other fields, particularly the social sciences, to secure commissions.

The Air Force considers its ROTC program a valuable source

of technical officers. In 1952, as in 1951, it brought the top 10 percent of its ROTC graduates from engineering schools directly into its research and development program.

All the services offer direct commissions to some specialists on the grounds that their professional practice within the military is essentially the same as in civil life. Most of these direct commissions are given in the health field—to doctors, dentists, nurses, and veterinarians. Except for these the number commissioned directly from civilian life on the basis of professional skills is not large. Most of the remainder are lawyers and clergymen, commissioned to serve as Judge Advocates or Chaplains.

The kinds of measures now being taken to assure efficient utilization of officers possessing critical scientific and professional skills are indicated by the Air Force program for research and development personnel. Beginning in December, 1951, the professional qualifications of all officers on active duty with the Air Force were thoroughly reviewed. About 6,000 officers were identified as fully or partially qualified for research and development work. A review board was established to determine whether each individual would be more useful in research and development work or in some other capacity. Air Force policy with regard to their assignment is clear:

> Air Force assignment policies as they relate to Research and Development officers will be directed toward the advancement of professional competence, maximum utilization consistent with Research and Development objectives, wide latitude in individual career development, and the stabilization of personnel. Methods will be established at all echelons to provide for positive and continuous examination of assignments to insure maximum effective use of personnel talent and to promote scientific advancement.

TRAINING SPECIALISTS IN THE ARMED FORCES

The procedures for identifying and utilizing men possessing scarce skills are designed to conserve and make efficient use of existing skills and abilities. The extensive training programs of the armed forces, on the other hand, are aimed at improving the military effectiveness of individuals by teaching new skills and knowledge and enhancing their competence. These training programs, in consequence, make a significant contribution to the quality of the labor force.

The scope of the military training programs is enormous. The Navy claims to have a training program for every skill that it uses. About 40 percent of those who enlisted in the Navy during 1952 were sent through formal training school courses. Except in times of emergency expansion, the Navy prefers to use formal school courses only to give the necessary technical background data and theoretical understanding. Practical knowledge and skills are taught through on-the-job training.

The Army maintains over thirty-five different kinds of schools which offer more than 500 different courses of instruction, ranging in length from a few weeks to longer than a year. They provide formal training by means of the usual classroom techniques together with supervised practice. In addition to the formal school courses, specialist courses are taught at training divisions and replacement training centers. Many of the courses in the thirty-two fields in which enlisted and officer specialist courses are given are relevant to civilian as well as military occupations. These include Army Aircraft, Automotive Maintenance, Communications, Electronic Maintenance, Engineer Equipment Maintenance, Engineering and Construction, Finance, Machine Accounting, Mapping and Reproduction, Marine Operations, Medical, Military Police, Motor Transport, Personnel and Administration, Photography, Quartermaster Maintenance, Railway, Scientific Services, Supply, Wire Maintenance.

Many courses in these fields are intended to provide training at the skilled worker level but some are technical and semi-professional in nature. Thus, in the Scientific Services field, there is a twenty-one-week course for enlisted men in petroleum products analysis which provides training in the principles and procedures of laboratory analysis and testing. The course covers petroleum products specifications, refining methods, laboratory analysis, operation of mobile laboratories, testing machines, etc. To enter this course the enlisted man must achieve a certain score on aptitude tests and have credit for high school courses in chemistry or physics. A forty-week course in Armed Service Medical Equipment Maintenance is given in the Electronics Maintenance field to train officers and enlisted personnel in the installation, inspection, and maintenance of electromechanical medical equipment. These examples of the many which could be cited are drawn deliberately from the training program of the Army, the service generally thought of as far less technical than the Air Force or Navy.

A mistake commonly made during World War II was to narrow excessively the scope of specialist training courses. While this reduced the training time for each course, it necessitated a great deal of re-training as the demands for different kinds of specialists shifted during the war. Today, the trend is to broaden training courses as far as practical, and to leave details to on-the-job training. This is especially true for the Navy, although all three services follow this practice. After training is completed, however, the Army usually classifies a man in a narrow occupational specialty, which tends to create assignment problems as personnel requirements change. The Air Force, on the other hand, by classifying an airman in one of forty-four career fields in eight occupational areas, maintains a more flexible assignment system.

The Air Force offers a good illustration of the kinds of military and specialist training provided for officers. General training and education in military subjects and in the relationships between the military establishment and other sectors of society are provided in the Air Force service schools—the Air University, the Air War College—and in the armed forces schools—the National War College, Industrial College, and the Armed Forces Staff College. Technical training is provided by the Air Training Command through three subordinate commands—the Technical Training Air Force, the Flying Training Air Force, and the Crew Training Air Force. The Technical Training Air Force conducts hundreds of specialized courses in every field in which the Air Force requires specialists—electronics, engineering, aircraft mechanics, radar, radio, communications, etc. Most of this training, of course, is designed to produce competent technicians and not qualified scientists or professionals.

The Air Force, like the Navy and Army, sends many officers each year to civilian educational institutions for completion of undergraduate and graduate degree requirements. The Air Force now has about 1,000 officers at various colleges, about 80 percent of whom are studying engineering or science. The Navy has about 350 and the Army about 700 officers in civilian colleges. Reserve officers on active duty may participate in these programs if they agree to stay on active duty after completing training, generally for three years.

The rapid expansion of the Air Force and technological developments have led to a need for officers trained, not only in engineering and electronics, but also in industrial procurement, production management, research and development, and supply and maintenance. To meet these needs and to improve and maintain the scientific, technical, and professional competence of its officers is the primary mission of the United States Air Force Institute of Technology at Wright-Patterson Air Force Base, Ohio. It offers a two-year program at undergraduate college level in engineering sciences with aero-mechanical and electronics options. Graduate level courses are offered in advanced engineering management, aeronautical engineering, engineering administration, armament and automatic control engineering, electronics, and industrial administration.

These examples, drawn from each of the military services, point up two noteworthy aspects of the training conducted by or under the auspices of the armed forces. One is the great number of people trained. Depending on the particular service, from 35 to 65 percent of all enlisted men receive technical training of one kind or another. Virtually all officers who do not already possess scientific, professional, or technical abilities useful to the military are required to attend some military training school or course. The other noteworthy aspect is that the range of subjects taught goes far beyond strictly military affairs and, in fact, closely parallels the technical training given in civilian institutions. A substantial number of officers receive advanced scientific and professional training. Each of the services seeks to provide proper assignments for the specialists it trains as well as for those who were trained in civilian life. Regulations provide that each graduate of a specialist course must be assigned to a position which utilizes his training.

Under conditions of partial mobilization, the utilization of personnel by the military is profoundly affected by the fact that most men pass through the services within a definite, short period of time. Most of those beginning service have not received any specialized training at all, or have had little experience in the fields in which they are trained. When they leave, two to four years later, the majority of them have received training and experience related to civilian work.

All the services use aptitude tests, together with an evaluation of prior training and experience, as aids in determining the training and assignment of each man. Undoubtedly, some men are guided into lines of work closer to their abilities than are the fields they would have chosen for themselves. Others, who would not have continued in school as civilians, receive valuable technical training. Most of those who were trained as specialists before entering service gain useful experience in their fields. These early adult years, of course, would also have been used by many as a period of training and professional development had they remained in civilian life. Nevertheless, by serving effectively their own needs for specialists, the armed forces do make a valuable contribution to the quality of the nation's manpower resources.

DEFERMENT OF SPECIALISTS AND STUDENTS

Both the civilian economy and the military training and utilization of specialists, as well as the relationship between them, are affected by a number of broader military manpower policies. Chief among these are the policies affecting deferment, rotation, the reserve forces, and employment of civilians.

The compulsory induction of men through the Selective Service System was established to maintain the armed forces at their prescribed strength and at present is intended to require eventual military service of all acceptable men reaching the age of eighteen and a half. Except for clergymen, no one is exempted from service because of his occupation. Nor, except for doctors and dentists, is anyone compelled to serve because of his occupation.

In order that essential civilian and defense activities not be disrupted, however, individuals employed in critical fields may be granted temporary deferments from military service. One major purpose of these deferments is to provide employers with time to find adequate replacements for such personnel. It may prove difficult if not impossible, however, to replace some key scientists and professionals engaged in critical research and development activities. The number of men actually deferred as essential to the nation's activities is not large: on March 1, 1953, about 29,000 in industrial occupations and another 87,000 in agriculture were deferred. Only a fraction of this total of 116,000 are scientists and professionals.

In addition to persons actually engaged in activities deemed essential to the nation, others are in training for similar activities. Current Selective Service practice is to defer students who meet certain prescribed standards of performance in school and apprentices enrolled in approved training programs. On March 1, 1953, 216,000 college students and 5,000 apprentices were deferred. Deferment always rests upon considerations of national interest, not of personal interest. Students and apprentices are deferred because of the desirability of continuing the flow of highly skilled, scientific, and professional persons into the labor force.

Unlike Great Britain, the United States has not provided an administrative link between deferment of apprentices and their subsequent military assignments. In Britain, apprentices who are deferred are assured that when they enter military service after completion of their training, they will receive an assignment in line with the civilian training for which they were deferred. In the United States, this outcome does not always result.

The idea that special categories of men should be permanently exempted from military service because of their competence in occupations of great importance to the nation runs counter to American ideas of equity and fairness and has consistently been rejected. Nevertheless, it is frequently urged that some members of certain critical professions be allowed to perform "equivalent civilian service" in lieu of military service. The idea behind the proposal is that these persons could serve the national interest better by remaining in their civilian jobs. To provide the armed forces with specialists from these groups would require special procedures independent of the normal operation of the Selective Service System. The chief danger of such a policy lies in creating special groups within a democratic society which are relieved of obligations imposed upon others.

A policy of exempting persons in certain occupations would be difficult to administer. The selection of specialist groups for preferential treatment would be an especially difficult problem, which would have to be reviewed periodically as certain groups of occupations became more or less important to the national interest. The selection of some members of the specialist group to serve in uniform while others remained in civil life would be no less difficult. For these and allied reasons the policy of providing no permanent exemptions from military service because of occupation has been established as national policy.

The importance of maintaining certain essential civilian activities has been recognized through temporary deferment of key individuals. The decision to defer an individual is not based solely upon his profession or occupation. It is based upon a consideration of the national need for military manpower, of the national interest in continuing certain essential activities, and of the individual's own contribution to those activities. All deferments are reviewed periodically to determine whether the deferment should be ended because of a change in any one of these factors.

The selection process is carried out by local boards which try to take into account the civilian need for scarce categories of specialized personnel. Today, as during World War II, critical skills and essential activities are identified by national Selective Service Headquarters on the basis of the Department of Labor's list of critical occupations and the Department of Commerce's list of essential activities. Local boards take into account both national and local requirements for men who possess these skills or are engaged in these activities in deciding whether they should be deferred or inducted. The decentralized operation of Selective Service has contributed greatly to the strength and flexibility of the selection process.

ROTATION

Whenever the military services are actually engaged in fighting, they face the difficult problem of reconciling equity to individuals with effective training and utilization of specialists. Fairness would seem to require every soldier, sailor, and airman to take his turn at overseas duty. Because the same kinds of personnel are not required for manning the front lines as for logistical support at home stations, strict rotation is not possible without gross malassignment of some men.

Rotation is not viewed as a difficult problem by the Air Force or the Navy. The variety of duties performed aboard ship and ashore permit ready reassignment from one to the other. Reassignment within the Navy is also facilitated by the fact that the Navy, more than the other services, seeks to train personnel to perform a variety of functions. The Air Force uses the same kinds of personnel for operations overseas as for operations in the United States. Rotation, therefore, is fairly simple. The Air Force, however, makes no attempt to assure equal overseas duty for everyone when strict application of such policy would result in malassignments. For some airmen, including those in the Strategic Air Command, the primary defense mission lies in the United States. The Air Force specifically forbids the assignment outside the research and development field of all officers qualified for this work, except to broaden their experience and increase their value to the research and development program. The vast majority of research and development activities, of course, is carried on in the United States.

The Army's problem is more complex. For both humanitarian and operational reasons, troops actually engaged in combat should be rotated. The need to place combat troops in the field as replacements complicates the Army's programs for training specialized personnel. Primary attention has to be given to the specialists needed for direct support of combat operations. Less attention can be given to developing other skills, including those required in an integrated reserve force. The problem is made more difficult by the two-year period of service of Selective Service inductees. Operational necessity frequently dictates the assignment of two-year men to duties other than those for which they show the greatest aptitude.

RESERVES

Under the Universal Military Training and Service Act of 1951, as amended, men between the ages of eighteen and one-half and twenty-six years have a total military obligation of eight years. If inducted for a period of two years, they must serve an additional six years as members of a reserve component; if enlisted for four years, their reserve obligation is four years. Within a few years, the majority of all young men in the labor force will be in one of the reserve components of the military services.

The Armed Forces Reserve Act of 1952 makes a distinction between the "ready" and the "standby" reserve. Generally speaking, a man must serve a total of five years on active duty and with the ready reserve before being eligible for transfer to the standby reserve for the remainder of his reserve obligation. The ready reserve may be called out in time of war or when a national emergency is declared by either the Congress or the President. Members of the standby reserve can be called only in time of war or national emergency proclaimed by the Congress, and only if adequate numbers of qualified ready reserves are not available. Although the Act limits the number of men in the ready reserve of all the services to 1.5 million, men currently serving in a status comparable to the ready reserve already exceed this ceiling, and in most instances do not meet the criteria for transfer to the standby reserve.

If an emergency is declared, the authority to recall reservists rests with the military. No means of providing selective recall independent of the policies of the military services have yet been developed. Thus, the commanding general of an Army area is ultimately responsible for acting upon all requests by Army reservists for a delay in reporting for active duty. He is guided by Army Regulations which specify the categories of men who are eligible for delay. The criteria for delay are quite similar to Selective Service criteria for deferment. An Army area commander may authorize delay for individuals employed in critical occupations or essential activities as defined by the Departments of Labor and Commerce; for individuals occupying key managerial positions in industry or government; and for individuals enrolled in educational institutions or engaged in technical research or scientific activities.

It may be questioned whether final action in the recall of all reservists possessing skills and competences of national importance should be left solely to the military establishment. In the event of war or full mobilization, men possessing critically needed skills could be taken by the armed forces before a civilian evaluation of where they could best serve the national interest could be made. Obviously a portion of the reserve must be available for immediate recall to active duty by the military services. But the fact that the majority of young men in the labor force will be subject to recall as reservists makes the reserve problem a national rather than purely a military problem.

Maintenance of the professional or technical competence of reservists is a difficult problem for the military services. Most of the men who receive technical training in the armed forces return to civil life within a few years. The Air Force estimates that 85 percent of its reserve officers, mostly ROTC men, who receive scientific and professional training while on active duty will leave active duty status within a few years after completing training. How to prevent the abilities and knowledge acquired in service from being lost is a problem not yet satisfactorily solved. The freedom of the reservist to pursue a career of his own choice cannot be abridged. Nor can the armed forces afford technical refresher courses for men who do not plan to return to active duty.

The Army has a program to preserve and develop the competence of reservists qualified for research and development activities. There are now nearly 100 training units solely for research and development reservists, with a membership of approximately 2,500 professionals. Some are just beginning research and development activities while others are distinguished scientists. Members of the units report their accomplishments in their own fields, work on research and development problems or materiel assigned them by the Army, provide assistance in editing technical manuals, and engage in similar activities. They provide the nucleus around which the technical services will expand their professional staffs in the event of full mobilization. The Navy has a similar program.

CIVILIAN PERSONNEL

The armed forces employ civilians in a great variety of jobs. Some are permanent employees. Others are consultants hired for specific assignments. Still others work indirectly for the armed forces as employees of civilian organizations which have contracted to undertake projects for the services. All the services are now using civilian scientists in their research and development programs. Other specialists are employed by each of the services as teachers in service training programs.

Through still greater use of civilians in such capacities, the requirements of the armed forces for scientists, professionals, and technicians in uniform might possibly be reduced substantially. No matter how effective the military forces are in assigning and utilizing specialized personnel in uniform, some of the time of such persons is necessarily occupied with military duties which do not require their special skills. Nevertheless, merely using a civilian scientist or professional in place of one in uniform would not save manpower. The function to be performed would remain the same. The civilian, too, can lose time in non-professional activities associated with the job. The use of civilians in lieu of military personnel would reduce the magnitude of the problems created for the services by the necessity of training and using for professional and scientific assignments men who are in service for only a short period. On the other hand, it would also create some additional problems, such as maintaining the morale of military personnel who receive less pay, have less free time, and are subject to stricter discipline than civilians doing similar work.

The Army has recently established a civilian career development program to secure the best utilization of the skills, knowledge, and experience of their civilian employees over a long period of time. A substantial increase in the number of very capable career employees depends largely on the attractiveness of employment opportunities. This, in turn, depends on such factors as pay, job security, opportunities for advancement and for further training, and freedom to work on assignments within the employee's main field of interest. An increase in the amount of work performed by civilian organizations under contract to the services depends mainly on the contract terms offered.

UNIVERSAL MILITARY TRAINING

The discussion in this chapter has been based on the assumption that the present state of partial mobilization will continue. Either full mobilization or a reduction in the size of the armed forces accompanied by a Universal Military Training program would raise a host of different problems regarding specialized personnel and the armed forces. Universal Military Training, for instance, would require consideration of the following questions: How could the armed forces provide adequate technical training to UMT personnel who would be in training only four or six months? How would the armed forces secure the required numbers of specialists if all men were brought into service at the age of eighteen? What procedures should be adopted to secure fair and effective selection of men for active duty with the standing forces if there were insufficient volunteers? A discussion of these problems and many others that would arise is beyond the scope of this chapter.

These brief analyses of military policy toward such manpower problems as deferment, rotation, the reserve components, and civilian employees of the services illustrate the complexity of the relationship between the military establishment and the civilian economy during a period of partial mobilization. The essential characteristic of military manpower utilization during a period of partial mobilization is the steady flow of men through the services in a short period of time. Consequently, partial mobilization adds to the problems of training and using specialized personnel, who require a relatively long period of training. It would be naive to assume that these problems have been solved, that all scientists and professionals in the services are now effectively employed, or that continuing efforts to improve the military utilization of specialists are not warranted. On the other hand, because relatively few service men remain in service for more than four years, the extensive training programs of the services are contributing to the size and quality of the professional, scientific, and technical labor force in the civilian economy.

CHAPTER VII

The Nature of Manpower Shortages

AFTER THE OUTBREAK of hostilities in Korea, it was widely believed that the country could not increase significantly its production for defense without running into serious shortages of resources, particularly human resources. Unlike the manpower situation in 1941, there were no large reserves of unemployed workers. Although some of the anticipated shortages did appear after large-scale defense contracts were let in 1951, they affected relatively few sectors of the economy. Toward the end of 1952, the Director of the Office of Defense Mobilization stated that the manpower needs of the current emergency "have been met to date without great strain—except for persistent shortages of engineers, scientists, and other professional personnel. . . ."

EVIDENCES OF SHORTAGES

What does it mean to say that there is, or is not, a manpower shortage? The answer may seem obvious; yet consideration of the nature of manpower shortages indicates that the answer is not obvious at all, and even a brief analysis of the causes and results of different shortages and of their possible remedies indicates that a single, useful definition is impossible.

There are, nevertheless, clear evidences of shortages. The most obvious evidence of the shortage of engineers, for example, is that employers, in spite of intense efforts, are finding it impossible to hire as many engineers as they want. One sign of a shortage then is the existence of a large number of unfilled jobs.

Almost every newspaper in the country has been carrying columns of want ads, directed particularly toward engineers and scientists of every level of competence, from the recent graduate to the mature person with wide experience. The columns of the professional journals duplicate this. The employment services of a number of professional societies have far more requests for men, especially in physics and chemistry, than they have men available. They report that poorly trained men who in former years would have had great difficulty in finding employment in their fields are now hired immediately at salaries far above those of a few years ago. Many employers have compromised their standards to get more personnel.

College campuses have been overrun during the last two years by company representatives seeking employees, not only in May and June—the traditional period for industrial recruitment—but throughout the year. Each concern is trying to reach young men scheduled to graduate at the end of the term before some other corporation hires them. Thus, the primary evidence of a shortage of engineers, scientists, and certain other professional personnel is the desire of employers to hire far more of them, at or above the current salary rates, than are available.

If one turns from engineers and scientists to physicians, the signs of shortage are quite different. The President's Commission on the Health Needs of the Nation reported in December, 1952, that there were demonstrable shortages of physicians. The evidence cited by the Commission included the inability of many local and state health departments and mental hospitals to fill budgeted positions. On the surface, these signs of shortage seem to be the same as for engineers, that is, an abundance of unfilled jobs. The salaries offered for most of these unfilled jobs, however, are well below the earnings possible in private practice. The scarcity of doctors for salaried positions in health departments and mental hospitals, therefore, does not necessarily indicate anything about the adequacy of the total number of doctors. It may indicate merely that doctors, like other people, are seldom willing to work for less when they can readily earn more. Since most doctors are independent practitioners, a shortage of doctors is recognized, not by the numbers of unfilled jobs, but by comparison of the supply with some standard of the number of doctors required to insure that the essential health needs of the population can be met.

The identification of a shortage of teachers presents still a different problem. It is generally agreed that there is a nation-wide shortage of elementary school teachers. Yet, even though teachers are salaried employees, this shortage is not manifested by a large number of unfilled jobs. Very few classrooms have been closed because a teacher is unavailable. When a teacher with the desired qualifications is not available, someone with lesser qualifications is hired. Thus, a shortage of teachers is manifested by the inability of schools to secure teachers who meet established qualifications.

There are still other signs of manpower shortages. One, which has the sanction of economic theory, is a sharp and disproportionate increase in salaries or earnings. But the earnings of teachers and nurses, for instance, have barely kept pace with or have lagged behind the general increase in wages, salaries, and prices in recent years, although shortages of these professionals have been regarded as serious.

These illustrations suggest that the word "shortage" is a conventional term applied to a variety of consequences which follow from an imbalance between the supply of and demand for scientific or professional manpower. A shortage is recognized by and is important because of its consequences. These may be the output of a lesser quantity or a poorer quality of certain social services than is deemed to be desirable by one standard or another. Unfilled jobs appear to provide a more objective criterion of the existence of a shortage, but this is illusory. The manufacturing industries, which employ the great majority of the nation's engineers, for example, are less concerned with hiring a specific number of engineers than with obtaining engineering services which will enable them to operate at a higher rate of output and profit. The earnings of any particular company, however, are of no concern, *per se,* to the public at large. The public is concerned when, as a result of shortages of engineers, a rise in its standard of living or the defense production effort is retarded. Thus, a conclusion about the existence of a shortage, from the standpoint of social policy and action, always involves the application of some standard of what is desirable for the society.

Nevertheless, except in the case of physicians and other professionals who generally work as independent practitioners, a wide gap between the number of jobs and the number of qualified applicants does provide reliable evidence that a shortage exists. In such a situation, a larger volume of goods or services could theoretically be produced if more trained personnel were available. But the production of most goods and services can be increased by several means other than increasing the number of professional or scientific workers. Moreover, the production of all goods and services always requires the utilization of scarce resources, whether human or material. Consequently, the evaluation of a manpower shortage requires a series of judgments about alternative ways of raising production of one type of goods or services, about the costs and difficulties of each alternative, and about the need for other types of goods or services.

SHORTAGES IN THE PAST

In the past, government agencies and private groups have frequently acted to increase the numbers in certain professional groups. Harvard College was founded primarily to insure that there would be an adequate number of well-trained Congregational clergymen. West Point and Annapolis were established by the Federal government to provide the nation with professionally trained military and naval leaders. Congress passed the Morrill Act during the Civil War in an effort to insure that the number of technologically trained persons would be adequate to meet the demands of an expanding agriculture and industry. When Congress decided to restrict immigration in the 1920's, it made special provision to permit the entry of professional workers.

As the frontier moved westward, every new community experienced shortages of professional and skilled workers. Constant efforts were made to entice school teachers, judges, doctors, and others to move from the East. These efforts to increase the supply of professional and scientific manpower are signs of the kind of shortages which are inevitable in an expanding, mobile society. As the population grows and becomes wealthier, as new communities and new business enterprises are established, the demands for professional and scientific services multiply. The supply also grows, but frequently not as rapidly. Education has never been a self-supporting enterprise, responding to profit opportunities. Building new schools and enlarging old ones is a slow process which depends upon the concerted efforts of communities, private groups, and government agencies. Even when facilities are available, the training of a professional takes years. Consequently, shortages of one kind of professional personnel or another in one part of the country or another mark the development of a free and dynamic society.

During World War I and World War II, quite different kinds of manpower shortages appeared. In both wars, the nation sought to build up its armed forces and to produce the maximum number of guns, ships, planes and ammunition. More than 4 million men were mobilized in World War I; more than 15 million in World War II. In both, a major effort was made to turn the economy from peace to war production as rapidly as possible, but in World War I hostilities ended before these efforts had gone very far. During World War II, they progressed much further. Although many things that were not strictly essential were still being produced for civilian consumption in 1944, a very large part of the country's resources had been redirected to war needs before that date.

The effort to produce very large quantities of products which had previously not been produced at all or only in much smaller quantities led inevitably to serious manpower shortages, particularly since millions of men were withdrawn from the civilian economy for military service. These shortages, caused by sudden, large increases in demand for many kinds of personnel, differed from those the country had earlier experienced. Because it would have taken too long, relief for the shortages which developed during World War II could not be obtained by increasing the number of highly trained personnel. Consequently, scarce scientific and professional personnel were directed into high priority work through controls over men subject to compulsory military service, the conversion of industry to war production, and the cooperation of professional societies.

One serious consequence of the shortage of certain kinds of professionals during the War, such as aeronautical engineers, was the loss of time in the designing and production of military aircraft. Quite different consequences followed from the shortage of physicians. The amount of care which many in the civilian population were accustomed to receiving was greatly reduced. To conserve their time, physicians stopped making house calls except for major emergencies. Many persons, aware of the tremendous pressure on their doctors, took care of their own minor illnesses, and limited their demands on the physician, when possible, to a telephone conversation.

The most striking result of wartime manpower shortages was the elimination of many types of production and services characteristic of the peacetime economy. Only by this most radical of all adjustments—the cessation of previous types of work—was it possible to find the numbers of people and the specific skills required for war demands. The shutting down of the automobile assembly lines freed engineers, technicians, and skilled workers for the production of aircraft and tanks. The fact that young men entered the services rather than the colleges released teachers for specialized war work, primarily in governmental service.

But these measures—the lowering of standards of service, and the reduction of goods and services for civilian consumption—did not suffice. Additional adjustments were required to meet the swollen manpower requirements. Three major steps were taken. Large numbers of persons previously not in the labor force— young men, old men, and women—took jobs which required little training. Those with aptitude, interest, or experience were given an opportunity to acquire additional training in order to work at a higher level of skill. Finally, work was redesigned to make the maximum use of those with the scarcest skills. Only in this manner was it possible to meet the tremendous military and civilian goals which had been set.

Little attention could be paid to the long-run consequences of the manpower adjustments necessary to win the war. These included the impairment of the future supply of trained persons which resulted from sharply reducing the number of young men attending college during the war, and the sacrifice of basic scientific research to the immediate need for applied research and development.

THE CHALLENGE OF PARTIAL MOBILIZATION

The problem of manpower shortages is more complex in the present period of partial mobilization than in times of either peace or full mobilization. Persistent shortages of various types of highly trained personnel, resulting from the failure of the supply to keep up with the growing demands of an expanding society, are compounded by the sudden new manpower demands of defense production and the armed forces. In this respect, current problems are much like those of World War II, though on a smaller scale. The country, however, is also committed to maintaining, and, if possible, to raising, its standard of living. The pressing demands of World War II for various types of scarce manpower were met only through a substantial reduction in the production of goods for civilian consumption and by lowering the standards for various types of civilian services. The motivation for sacrifice produced by full-scale war does not now exist, and there is no disposition to curtail the civilian consumption of goods and services.

During the three and a half years of World War II, the country had no choice but to devote most of its resources to the immediate build-up of military strength, regardless of the long-run consequences. At present, the security of the nation does not depend so overwhelmingly on the immediate build-up of military strength. And particularly because the present emergency is likely to continue for a decade or more, it is essential, not only to avoid weakening the nation's resources of scientific and professional manpower, but to improve them.

After Korea, a number of restrictions were placed on the civilian economy in order to accelerate defense production. The manufacture of certain consumer products was temporarily limited by rationing scarce raw materials. At most, however, these measures released only a handful of scientific and professional personnel for defense work. The only significant parallel between the present period and World War II in the shifting of personnel lies in the area of research and development. Recognizing the danger which faces the country, industry and the universities have been willing to deflect many of their research personnel from problems of their own choosing to work which has a high defense priority.

There is no question that present shortages of engineers and scientists have had serious consequences. These include loss of valuable time in strengthening our defenses, the failure to exploit certain potentialities for enhanced security such as an improved system of air defense, and the production of poor products as, for instance, in the case of radar equipment. Less clear is the primary cause of current shortages of scientific and professional manpower. Are they the result of imposing a large defense program upon an economy already operating near full capacity? Or are they the result of long-run imbalance between the supply of and demand for professional personnel which arises primarily from the expanding needs of American industry and the rising standard of living of the American people?

Current shortages of scientific and engineering manpower, although unquestionably precipitated by developments since Korea, are, in the opinion of many students, likely to continue for some time. It is argued that if the international situation remains threatening, expenditures for defense, including large-scale expenditures for research and development, are certain to create a continuing high demand for scientific and engineering manpower. Even if the prospects for peace should improve, a steady rise in the demand for scientific and professional personnel would still be probable. In the past, the expansion of the population, rising per-capita income, increasing mechanization of production, the spread of education, and many other factors have contributed to a constant increase in the demand for professionals. Unless these trends are halted, the demand for professionals and scientists will surely continue to rise.

ECONOMIC ANALYSIS AND THE PROBLEM OF SHORTAGES

The term "shortage" denotes a demand greater than supply. Since economic theory has concentrated on problems of supply and demand for more than a century and a half, it is appropriate to make use of the tools of economic analysis in a discussion of manpower shortages. Yet, it is important to note that economic analyses of supply and demand have focused almost entirely on commodities. The aim of commodity trade is profits. The aim of a young person who decides to pursue a scientific or professional career, however, is to provide for himself a particular way of life. Clearly, the factors subsumed under the terms "supply" and "demand" are quite different in the case of commodities than in the case of professional manpower.

An imbalance between the demand for and the supply of a commodity is reflected in the movement of its price. Normally, when there is a shortage of a commodity, its price will increase, with the result that some persons will restrict their consumption and thereby reduce the demand. The rise in price will stimulate producers in search of greater profits to increase supply. Increases in the supply will act to reduce the price, thereby tending to restore the balance between supply and demand. The supply of most commodities can be increased quite readily. An increase in the output of wheat can usually be secured within the course of a single growing season. If copper is short, it can be increased just as rapidly as it is possible to attract more miners or to install additional machinery.

The factors which come into play when an imbalance develops between the demand for and the supply of some group of scientists or professionals are different in many respects. In the first place, the "price" of specialized manpower does not respond as readily to changes in supply and demand. Employers are understandably reluctant to raise the salaries of one group to a point where they are far out of line with established salary patterns for other employees. Some employers, such as schools, colleges, hospitals, and other non-commercial institutions, are frequently unable to raise salaries substantially.

Quite apart from these considerations, the supply of professionals and scientists cannot be increased rapidly to meet changes in demand. Scientists and professionals come from the relatively small group in the population who are intellectually and financially able to graduate from college and motivated to do so. This group would have to be substantially expanded before a significant increase in the total number of scientists and professionals could take place. Educational facilities would also have to be expanded.

The decision to become a scientist or professional is not made in a moment or in response to the opportunities existing at one point in time. It is made over a period of years, and it depends upon how the individual wants to spend the rest of his life. The education and training of the professional is a long process. It takes a minimum of nine years after high school for a young man to secure his license to practice medicine. If he expects to specialize he must look forward to a training period of at least twelve to fourteen years. Eight years of college and graduate work are generally required for a doctoral degree in the sciences.

Thus one major difference between commodities and professional manpower with respect to supply and demand is the much greater difficulty of increasing the supply of the latter to meet increases in demand. There is an even more fundamental difference. Since "shortage" is essentially an arithmetic concept, it is strictly applicable only to units which, because they are roughly equivalent, can be added and subtracted. Individuals, like commodities, can be classified, counted, added, and subtracted. But the tremendous differences in ability, training, and competence among individuals warn that the results of arithmetic computations do not have the same validity for manpower as they do for commodities. Subtracting an Einstein from a group of ten physicists signifies a great deal more than a 10 percent reduction in the effectiveness of the group.

In the sense that they are capable of making unique contributions to society, men like Einstein, Toscanini, or General Marshall are always in short supply. They must be excluded from any consideration of shortages of normal men. To exclude them, however, does not solve the difficulty, for the presence of a great creative genius in the supply of any group of professionals or scientists can completely alter the character of the demand by changing the nature of the problems with which the group is concerned.

Regardless of considerations of genius, qualitative differences of a lesser order make quantitative analysis of supply and demand extremely difficult. In several scientific fields, the major unmet demand is for individuals of very high competence and great experience. "In the whole range of scientific and technological activities," Dr. James B. Conant has remarked, "there is no substitute for the first-rate man. Ten second-rate men cannot replace him." One large Eastern university did not make a permanent appointment in the field of theoretical physics for many years, because it was unable to acquire a first-rate man, and did not want to appoint a second-rate person.

The analysis of professional manpower in terms of supply and demand is also complicated by the fact that many professional services must be rendered at the point of need. It is a relatively easy matter to ship commodities from one end of the country to the other, but the very large number of doctors in relation to the population in New York is of no use to farmers in New Mexico, who may not be able to secure medical attention when they need it. The demand for school teachers in rural areas cannot be filled by the much larger supply of teachers in urban communities. Teachers and physicians, of course, can be induced to move, but people do not respond solely to monetary incentives in choosing their homes any more than they do in choosing their professions.

The values of a free society lead to different attitudes toward the solution of commodity and manpower shortages. In time of national emergency, there is a readiness to ration or allocate commodities so that they are devoted to the most critical needs. Only under very critical circumstances, however, is there a willingness to allocate and ration men.

This brief discussion indicates that a shortage of commodities is quite different from a shortage of scientific and professional manpower. However, the economic analysis of the supply of and demand for commodities does contain one basic lesson for the student of manpower. Whether or not a shortage of one resource exists cannot be determined without reference to other relevant resources. This is true of all resources, physical or human. The availability of all relevant resources must be evaluated before it can be determined that there is a meaningful shortage of any one specific resource. How much point is there in saying, for example, that there is a shortage of research scientists, unless there are adequate capital funds and enough design and development engineers available to exploit the new products which are discovered in the laboratories? Britain today is short of scientific and particularly engineering manpower in that it has fewer than it requires to achieve its industrial and defense objectives. Its highly trained persons are a much smaller proportion of the total labor force than in the United States. But Britain is also critically short of capital funds. In this situation, it is not very meaningful to say that it is suffering from a shortage of scientific and engineering manpower, since output could not be raised greatly merely by increasing this one resource.

SHORT-RUN AND LONG-RUN SHORTAGES

The United States, it has been seen, has experienced two quite different kinds of shortages of highly trained manpower in the past. One represents a long-run imbalance between an increasing demand and a more slowly increasing supply. Shortages of this kind are generally felt in certain regions or professional fields. The second type of shortage is experienced when there is a sudden expansion of demand, such as during wartime, which results in nation-wide shortages in most fields and which disappears, for the most part, with the end of hostilities. In the current shortages of professionals and scientists both long-run and short-run imbalances are present. It is necessary to determine for each field whether the shortage is the product of long-run or short-run causes in order to appraise its consequences and to determine possible remedies.

Because the supply of scientific and professional personnel cannot possibly be increased rapidly enough to meet the demands of a sudden temporary emergency, the remedy for such shortages must be found in various means of stretching the available supply. In times of full-scale war, of course, drastic methods involving government controls may be used which are not practical at other times. At all times, however, employers may seek to improve the utilization of manpower. Indeed, the extent of any shortage can be estimated by the efforts that are made to do just this.

One means of stretching the available supply is to waive compulsory retirement, or to raise the age of retirement. During recent decades, industry, government, and many voluntary organizations have adopted compulsory retirement programs. Although some persons cease to function effectively even before they are retired, it is also true that many are forced to retire who are capable of additional years of useful work. A second way of increasing the effectiveness of the existing supply is by providing additional specialized training for those already working at a professional or sub-professional level who have the potential for work at a still higher level. The readjustment of existing patterns of work so that professionals and scientists spend more of their time at work which makes full use of their knowledge and specialized skills is still another way of stretching the existing supply. This usually requires the employment of additional auxiliary workers to relieve professional personnel of less demanding work.

Perhaps the greatest opportunity for raising the effectiveness of the available supply is in the shifting of individuals from less essential work to work of higher priority. But this is never easy. Even in wartime, the United States has been reluctant to impose direct occupational controls. Indirect controls through curtailment of "non-essential" production serve the same purpose, but they have not been used to any great extent since World War II. Short of these controls, salary differentials are the major mechanism available to direct and redirect physical and human resources. Scientists and professional persons, however, make their occupational choices in terms of a lifetime career. They are committed to their work and to the conditions surrounding both their work and life. They are not, therefore, particularly sensitive to small monetary incentives. One authority has pointed out that even at the end of World War II, a considerable number of scientists in industry were still working on problems which had little or no significance for the war effort, for the simple reason that there had been no sufficiently strong mechanisms in operation to effect their transfer to work of importance.

The possibility of stretching the available supply through

changes in utilization suggests further limitations to the application of the market concept of shortages to shortages of professional and scientific manpower. Whether or not a shortage of a particular type of manpower exists depends, not only on the criterion employed and the availability of other resources necessary for increasing output, but, since more effective utilization increases the available supply, on the way in which the supply is used. To say that defense production has been slowed by the shortage of engineers may be true in that with more engineers certain production goals could have been met earlier. But it is also true that the same end might have been achieved by increasing the number of technicians to release engineers for higher-level work, or by deflecting engineers from the design of new automobile models to the design of new aircraft models.

Since the effective supply of manpower is partly a function of its utilization, it is important that inefficient utilization is encouraged by several characteristics of partial mobilization. Periods of inflation and high income always result in increases in the demand for scientific and professional manpower. One of the typical consequences of a period of inflation is a scramble for scarce or potentially scarce resources, on the theory that it is better to pay a little more today than to be without tomorrow. Such a scramble for engineers and scientists was manifested by industry after the outbreak of hostilities in Korea and a certain amount of hoarding of valuable manpower resulted.

The fact that the Federal government pays for much of the current work of research engineers and scientists in industry and in the universities through cost-plus contracts further contributes to inefficient use of manpower by making employers careless about keeping manpower costs down. In addition, the current tax structure has encouraged concerns with high profits to expand their research activities since, if their profits are not spent on such activities, most of them would go to the government in taxes.

The methods which can be used in an attempt to remedy

persistent shortages of groups of scientists and professionals are quite different from those which are required to meet a sudden, temporary imbalance between supply and demand. A persistent shortage cannot generally be relieved without efforts to increase the supply. Nevertheless, it is also impossible to remedy some persistent shortages solely or even primarily through increases in the supply. The number of college graduates who meet most if not all of the requirements for teaching is much greater than the number of teachers. As long as teaching remains a relatively unattractive career, especially for men, there is no reason to expect that the training of more teachers will overcome the persistent shortages which have characterized the profession since early in World War II.

Because most persistent shortages cannot be relieved without increasing the supply, the adequacy of the nation's educational and training facilities becomes an important consideration in this connection. Today, a career in most scientific and professional fields requires the completion of formal training at institutions of higher learning. Because colleges and universities are established and run, not to make money, but to provide important social services, they are not expanded in direct response to shortages of personnel whom they help to train. Even when abundant facilities are available, the problem of speeding up an increase in the supply of professionals presents difficulties. To expand substantially the numbers completing each level of education would require changes in the motivations and financial resources of many students. Moreover, although the number of persons potentially capable of completing advanced training is undoubtedly far larger than the number who do, it is not unlimited. It is not even certain that the number securing advanced degrees could be substantially increased without a prior expansion of the number who graduate from college.

Still another factor is that some professional groups have established standards which may seriously interfere with the willingness of individuals to choose a career in those professions.

It may well be that a considerable number of young people who might otherwise enter the field of psychiatry decide not to because the requirements include the completion, not only of medical school and internship, but also of a residency in psychiatry and, for many students, a training psychoanalysis. The fact that so many individuals are entering the field of psychotherapy through "lay analysis," clinical psychology, or social work, suggests an imbalance between the community's demand for this type of service and the number who are able or willing to complete full psychiatric training.

Discriminatory practices in education or employment can likewise impede the development of an adequate supply of professional personnel. The difficulties encountered by Negroes, particularly in the South, when they seek admission to institutions of higher learning in order to prepare themselves for professional careers is only one facet of a more complex pattern of discrimination. Many do not study for a professional field, not because they cannot obtain the needed education, but because they recognize the discrimination which will face them when they look for work. Still others cannot meet the entrance standards of colleges and universities because their earlier education was inadequate.

One other important aspect of persistent shortages of scientists and professionals is the constant development of new fields and the constant changes which take place in old fields. Some shortages are inevitable until training catches up with new requirements, and in the interval, the only remedy is to adapt the existing supply to meet changing needs. The extent to which this adaptation can succeed depends largely on the breadth and depth of the training already received by scientists and professionals. A narrowly specialized education is less expensive than one which is directed toward preparing a person for a wide range of responsibilities. Moreover, the rapid development of new knowledge has narrowed the area in which one person can be fully competent, and has resulted in greater specialization. Yet, a sensible balance must be established between the need to provide intensive training at a reasonable cost and the need for broad training which imparts flexibility and permits the individual to cope with the changing demands that he will encounter.

MANPOWER SHORTAGES IN FOUR FIELDS

To analyze the specific as well as the general factors responsible for current shortages of scientific and professional manpower, four fields have been selected for detailed appraisal in the following chapters.

Engineers are the largest single group of trained technological manpower in the nation. Partly because their activities are crucial for the defense effort, a large part of the current discussion about shortages of professional manpower is focused on them. In contrast to the other groups, the great majority of engineers are employed by industry. The demand for engineers differs from the demand for the other three groups in that they are much more frequently employed to perform managerial functions.

Physicists represent the scientists. In contrast to the half million engineers, most of whom have bachelor's degrees, research physicists number only a few thousand, many of whom have completed a very high level of training. The physicists illustrate a group facing the problems of adjusting to sudden and revolutionary advances in knowledge. Finally, this group provides an example of the difficulties of increasing supply, even in the long run, when requirements for effective performance are unusually high.

Elementary and secondary school teachers represent by far the largest single group of professional personnel, over one million. Teachers differ from the other groups in several important respects. Most of them are women. The great majority are public employees whose salaries are relatively low and inflexible. A large part of the problem of teacher shortages springs from the fact that, because of the nature of their services, the location as well as the size of the supply is a crucial consideration.

Because most physicians work as independent practitioners,

demand for them cannot be measured in terms of job openings. Some standard of need must be invoked. The length and high cost of their training introduce still another important set of considerations. Finally, medicine represents the only important profession where the number of qualified applicants is considerably in excess of the available training facilities.

The four case studies supplement this consideration of shortages of scientific and professional manpower by providing concrete and detailed analyses. They emphasize that problems of manpower shortages are far more complex than problems of commodity shortages. They call attention, finally, to the fact that the contribution which any group of scientists or professionals can make to society depends as much on their quality as on their number.

CHAPTER VIII

The Engineering Profession

THE OPERATION of a complex technology depends to a significant degree on a supply of well-trained engineers. The growth in the number of engineers attests their importance to the American economy. In 1890, the Census counted about 30,000 engineers; by 1940, the figure had risen to 261,000, and by 1950, to over 530,000. About four-fifths of those employed as engineers are in private industry, primarily in manufacturing. The ratio of engineers to other workers in industry increased almost fivefold in this period. In 1890, there was one engineer for every 290 workers in manufacturing, construction, utilities, and transportation. In 1950, there was one engineer for every 65 workers in these fields.

Since the beginning of hostilities in Korea, shortages of engineers have frequently been reported by employers, the Bureau of Labor Statistics, the Office of Defense Mobilization, the National Security Resources Board, the Engineering Manpower Commission of Engineers Joint Council, and other groups. The Council is made up of eight societies, representing the basic branches of engineering. The Engineering Manpower Commission has investigated employment levels, enrollment in engineering schools, and other problems relating to the demand for and the supply and utilization of engineers. The information which it has made available is of great value in studying the profession. Studies by the National Society of Professional Engineers have also provided useful data.

In its *Newsletter* of June 28, 1951, the Engineering Manpower Commission reported that its annual survey showed an estimated immediate demand for 80,000 new engineering graduates and a supply of only 38,000. The survey also estimated that some 15,000 engineers would be absorbed by the armed forces during the following year. About half of the new graduates were eligible for the draft or were in the reserves and, therefore, subject to call. On the basis of these data, the Commission estimated a shortage of 57,000 engineers. The Commission's 1952 survey showed a demand for at least 40,000 additional new engineering graduates compared with a supply of 30,000. At least 6,000 of the new graduates, however, were expected to enter military service immediately as commissioned graduates of Reserve Officers Training Corps programs, while many others were expected to enlist or be called by Selective Service. The available data pointed to an estimated shortage at the close of 1952 of approximately 25,000 engineers. The Engineering Manpower Commission estimates the demand for engineers by asking a sample of leading industrial and governmental employers, who account for the employment of roughly one-third of all the engineers in the nation, how many young men with engineering training they would like to hire at the existing salary level.

In the case of engineers, as of other professionals, however, simple numerical estimates of supply and demand may be misleading because they take no account of important qualitative factors. There are different kinds of engineers; they are used in different kinds of jobs; and the professional competence of individual engineers varies greatly. The first step toward an evaluation of the problem of shortages, therefore, is a closer examination of the profession.

CHARACTERISTICS OF THE PROFESSION

One basis for sub-dividing the members of the engineering profession is the specialized branch of engineering in which they are employed. This usually reflects the type of college training the engineer has received. The 1950 Census showed about 24 percent in civil engineering; 21 percent in mechanical; 20 percent in electrical; 6 percent in chemical; 4 percent in mining and metallurgical; 3 percent in aeronautical; and 22 percent in other branches. Each of these branches may be further divided into a hundred or more sub-branches.

Table 8. Estimated Number of Male Engineers, by Field of Employment, 1950 [a]

Manufacturing: durable goods	176,000	
Manufacturing: non-durable goods	55,000	
Total in manufacturing		231,000
Trade, finance, and service industries	44,000	
Professional service fields	31,000	
Total in trade and service		75,000
Construction	45,000	
Utilities	25,000	
Communication	16,000	
Mining	12,000	
Transportation	11,000	
Agriculture, forestry, and fishing	1,000	
Total in private industry		416,000
Federal government	51,000	
State and local government	42,000	
Total in government		93,000
Professors and instructors	8,000	
Others in education	5,000	
Total in education		13,000
Grand Total		522,000

[a] Based on 1950 Census sample. Excludes about 7,000 women, and others who were retired or not employed for other reasons at the time of the survey. The Engineering Manpower Commission estimates that there were 450,000 engineers in 1952 on the basis of its correction of Census data.

Another basis of classification is the field of employment. The vast majority of engineers, as Table 8 shows, are employed by private industry. In 1950, however, over 90,000 were employed by government agencies ranging from the Atomic Energy Commission to the sewage and road departments of local governments. The table does not, of course, indicate changes in the employment pattern since Korea, but it does reflect a decline in the proportion of engineers employed in manufacturing and government after World War II.

The distribution by branch of engineering among the major employers is shown for 1950 in Table 9. The great majority of mechanical, chemical, and aeronautical engineers were employed in manufacturing in 1950. Over two-fifths of the civil engineers were employed by government, primarily on the state and local level in road building and maintenance, sanitation, and similar functions. Electrical engineers were distributed more evenly among the different kinds of employers, but the largest number, over one-third of the total, was in manufacturing.

Table 9. Percentage Distribution of Engineers in Selected Branches of Engineering, by Field of Employment, 1950 [a]

EMPLOYMENT	ENGINEERING BRANCH				
	Aero-nautical	*Mechanical*	*Civil*	*Electrical*	*Chemical*
Manufacturing	80.0	62.3	9.2	35.1	76.4
Utilities	.2	3.9	4.6	15.5	2.2
Communication	.2	.8	.5	12.1	.3
Construction	.7	7.4	23.4	5.2	2.6
Transportation	3.0	2.5	3.7	2.0	.2
Mining	. .	1.3	1.1	.9	2.5
Other industries	3.2	16.4	14.1	20.7	12.5
Government	12.7	5.4	43.4	8.5	3.3
Total	100.0	100.0	100.0	100.0	100.0

[a] Based on 1950 Census sample.

Engineers are a mobile group. Over 30 percent of them moved from one state to another during World War II. Because most engineers are employed by manufacturers, over half of them

live in the heavily industrialized Middle Atlantic and East
North Central states. Their movement during the war did not
significantly alter the overall geographical distribution. During
the same period at least one-quarter of all engineers moved from
one industry to another. Many also moved from one branch of
engineering to another. Between 8 and 14 percent of those who
were in each of five major branches of the profession in 1939
were in another branch by 1946. In that year, more than one-
fifth of all engineers were working in a branch other than the one
for which they had been educated.

THE DEMAND FOR ENGINEERS

There are two particularly important characteristics of the
demand for engineers. First, it is a demand for men to perform
a wide range of different functions from top management to
routine testing. Second, the demand is subject to wide fluctuations. The overall demand varies with business conditions while
the demand for specific types of engineers also varies with such
developments as the growth of new industries or processes.

The range of functions for which engineers are employed was
illustrated in the Engineers Joint Council's 1946 study, *The
Engineering Profession in Transition*. About two-fifths of the
engineers questioned were employed in administrative or managerial positions, including the supervision of construction projects. Over one-fourth were in design, development, and applied
research positions. Eight percent worked as consultants, 5 percent
as teachers, and 4 percent in the sales field. Another 5 percent
were employed in drafting, testing and analysis, estimating, and
inspection. Under one percent were engaged in fundamental
research. The remaining 10 percent were employed in a wide
variety of occupations.

The nature of the position held and the salary earned depended
largely on the education and experience of the engineer. Generally
speaking, the more formal training he had had, the more likely
it was that he would work at design, development, research, or

teaching. A third of the engineers with degrees, but only a fifth of the non-graduates, worked at design, development, or applied research. One-fourth of those with doctoral degrees and 15 percent of those with master's degrees were college teachers. The total number engaged in basic scientific research was very small, but the proportion was higher among those with advanced degrees. Engineers with the least training were likely to work at selling or at one of the routine positions such as drafting, testing and analysis, estimating, or inspection. Half of those without an engineering degree were in administrative posts. One reason for this is that management positions are generally held by older men, who entered the profession when formal educational requirements were lower. Engineers with bachelor's degrees were as likely to hold sales positions as were non-graduate engineers— 6 percent of each—but those with advanced degrees were much less frequently salesmen.

In short, engineers are not only employed in purely technological capacities for which engineering training is generally essential. They are also employed in managerial or administrative jobs for which engineering training is very useful, and in occupations such as sales or supervision requiring some technological knowledge. That the completion of formal education is not absolutely necessary for many jobs is indicated by the substantial number of engineers who do not hold engineering degrees. In 1946, the proportion in each of the major branches who did not have a bachelor's degree ranged from almost 6 percent in chemical engineering to over one-fifth in civil engineering. From one to 5 percent of the engineers in each of the different fields had no college training at all. Opportunities for engineering employment for men without degrees declined during the 1930's, however, and during the following decade a very small proportion of those entering the field were not engineering graduates. As a result, the number of persons employed in engineering without degrees declined from 27 percent in 1930 to less than 20 percent by 1950.

The salaries of engineers are closely related to their formal training, their experience, and to the function they perform. Earnings are highest for engineers in administration and management who are usually men with considerable experience. Average salaries are progressively lower in development, applied research, testing, and drafting.

In many cases, the functions performed by a person classified as an engineer cannot be distinguished from those of a technician, who is usually trained on the job or in two-year courses after high school. The higher the demand for graduate engineers, the less likely they are to be employed on jobs which do not require professional training. At the other end of the industrial hierarchy, the functions of the engineer and of business and industrial executives frequently overlap. Consequently, a shortage, in quantitative or qualitative terms, of either technicians or of executives for management or sales positions will increase the demand for engineers. Thus, if the supply of technicians is inadequate, young engineers may be employed for longer than an initial training period in routine tasks. If the supply of administrative or sales personnel from other sources is inadequate, men trained as engineers may be taken out of technological work and used in executive or sales posts.

Industry's increasing preference for engineers for managerial functions accounts for some of the expansion of the profession, This preference reflects the growth of an increasingly complex technology, but other factors have also contributed. The managerial performance of men trained as engineers has probably justified their employment in preference to other groups, even at somewhat higher starting salaries. Moreover, the managerial group has come to consist increasingly of engineers, who prefer to hire other engineers for a number of reasons, including pride in the profession and a desire for easy communication with fellow-executives. The prestige which engineering training enjoys as preparation for a management career is suggested by one of the findings of Ernest Havemann and Patricia West's study of college graduates (*They Went to College*). One-third of the business administration graduates reported they wished they had majored in some other field. The field most frequently mentioned was engineering.

Within the long upward trend in the demand for engineers, the demand at any one time depends largely on current business conditions because most engineers are employed by private industry. The effect of a large-scale depression on employment in engineering can be read in the history of the 1930's. Between 1929 and 1932, the median annual income of engineers with less than one year's experience fell from $1,300 to $600, where it remained through 1934. Unemployment among engineers increased from one percent to 10 percent, and many previously in engineering secured other jobs, while many new graduates did not enter the field.

A great many factors other than business conditions also affect the demand for engineers. The development of new industries, processes, or products creates a heavy demand for engineers. So does the rapid expansion of old industries. The investment which management decides to make in research and development depends on competitive pressures, profit levels, tax policies, and other considerations. Some industries require a higher ratio of engineers to workers than others. Consequently, unequal changes in employment levels in different industries change the demand for engineers. Between 1939 and 1950, the output of manufacturing industry doubled. Output in such industries as machinery, transportation equipment, chemicals, and iron and steel, however, increased three or four times. These industries are among the most important employers of engineers, and their size, rapid rate of expansion, and technology all contribute to their requirements for engineers.

SHORTAGES

There is no doubt that since Korea there has been a shortage of engineers in the sense that employers want to hire more engineers than they are able to. The supply of new engineering graduates has not been large enough to meet the great and sudden expansion in demand since the summer of 1950. It is significant that even with the relatively high employment and production levels of the immediate post-war years there was no shortage of engineers. On the contrary, in 1949 there was considerable concern about the employment prospects for new engineering graduates. Early in that year, the post-war boom reached its peak, and employment began to decline. By the middle of the year, unemployment reached 3.8 million, or about 6 percent of the total civilian labor force. The Engineers Joint Council predicted a 21 percent decline from 1948 in the total number of new engineers likely to be hired by all employers. For 1950, a further decline of 30 percent was expected. Meanwhile, the number of engineering graduates was increasing from 31,000 in 1948 to 44,000 in 1949, and 52,000 in 1950.

The salaries received by new engineers reflected these fluctuations in supply and demand. The average monthly salary of graduate engineers with less than one year of experience was $232 in 1946. In both 1949 and 1950 it was about $255, an increase of only 10 percent over 1946. In the same period, the cost of living increased by over 20 percent, so that the real earnings of beginning engineers declined. Since Korea, the average monthly salary has risen to about $330. Salaries for more experienced personnel have fluctuated less sharply, and vary by branch as well as length of experience. The average newly graduated chemical engineer, for example, receives a higher starting salary than his counterpart in mechanical engineering.

Although employment opportunities for newly graduated engineers were declining in 1949 and 1950, employers indicated that they intended to increase their hiring of engineers with advanced degrees. Estimated employment openings for engineers with doctoral degrees were 27 percent higher in 1950 than in 1949. The total number involved, however, was small. The survey estimated only 102 job openings in 1950 for which the doctoral degree in engineering was a requirement. This figure, however, probably understates by a considerable margin industry's willingness to hire additional engineers with a good scientific background.

Its studies led the Engineers Joint Council to advise in 1950 that "intensive cultivation of the smaller organizations for openings not only in engineering, but in production and operations, leading to supervision and sales, offers the best chance for satisfactory placement results." The United States Bureau of Labor Statistics joined in the prediction of a temporary decline in employment opportunities for engineering graduates. It added, however, that demand for some types of engineers would remain high.

The increase in defense expenditures after Korea stimulated the whole economy and created a strong new demand for engineers. A large part of the initial expenditures necessarily went for research, development, investment in new plant and equipment, and other aspects of the "tooling-up" process which require engineering services. Moreover, the demand for engineers was probably enhanced by predictions of shortages. There is evidence that employers sought to "stockpile" engineers while they were still available. This conclusion is supported by a comparison of demand estimates for 1951 and 1952. The estimated civilian demand for new engineers in 1951 was 80,000. No more than 40,000 of these openings, and perhaps as few as 20,000, were filled. Thus, from 40,000 to 60,000 openings remained unfilled at the beginning of 1952. If to this number were added the requirements for engineers to meet further industrial expansion and to replace those leaving the profession in 1952, the 1952 demand should have been at least as high as that for 1951. Yet, the estimated demand for new engineering graduates in 1952 was 40,000. The apparent decline in demand may be accounted for in part by steps taken by industry to improve the utilization of engineers in the face of shortages. Taking this into account, however, it still appears that the drop from 1951 to 1952 can be accounted for largely by more conservative estimates of demand by employers in the second year.

It is far from certain that the demand for engineers will continue at the current very high level. Although defense expenditures are likely to remain high in the next few years, their impact on the demand for engineers will be somewhat reduced. The investment, or "tooling-up," phase of the defense program seems to have reached a plateau, and the production of arms will not require the same degree of engineering effort as the earlier stage. Private investment in new plant and equipment is expected to remain substantial. A recent survey conducted jointly by the U.S. Department of Commerce and the Securities and Exchange Commission indicated that capital investment in 1953 would be almost as high as the record expenditures of 1952.

Moreover, industry has been increasing its research and development capacity. This trend will probably continue with the result that more engineers will find employment in this area. Finally, government expenditures for research and development are not expected to contract significantly. Unless government expenditures for defense purposes increase greatly, changes in the demand for engineers will depend mainly on the level of production for civilian consumption. While the demand for engineers can thus be expected to level off and perhaps even decline slightly, it will probably not fall significantly unless there is a severe recession. The total demand for engineers will probably continue to be strong.

THE SUPPLY OF ENGINEERS

No mechanism exists to reallocate or expand quickly the existing supply of engineers in response to such powerful new demand forces as were created by the defense program. Theoretically, the existing supply of engineers might have been adapted to new demand conditions since 1950 in two ways: through better utilization of engineers in the industries in which they work; and through changes in the salary structure to draw engineers from less to more critical industries.

The most important means of improving utilization is to employ engineers only in positions which make full use of their technical training and experience. At one end of the scale, it has been noted, some engineers are engaged in technical work below the professional level. At the other end, a very large number perform administrative and managerial functions which may make less than full use of their technological skills. The defense program has stimulated better utilization, but efforts to release engineers from relatively low-level technical work are impeded by a shortage of technicians and other auxiliary workers. Moreover, even a temporary reduction in the number of engineers transferred from technological to general management assignments is made difficult by a shortage of men with top-management potential.

The large increase in demand, in short, could not be met solely by improving the utilization of engineers. Nor could the recent shortage be overcome by redistributing the supply to more essential fields of employment through salary changes. Because production for civilian consumption was not curtailed and continued to earn large profits, it was difficult for defense industries to outbid other employers for the services of engineers. Since engineers' salaries were not effectively controlled under the wage and salary stabilization program, the government could not influence the distribution of engineers by instituting differential salary increases for civilian and defense employment. "Pirating" of engineers undoubtedly occurred. But this type of salary competition is expensive, and is likely to result only in a general increase in salaries if the practice spreads. Rapid increases in the salaries of new engineers would have meant costly readjustments for older engineers as well as for all comparable personnel. Large firms, the major employers of engineers, tried to avoid such competition and did not make exceptional salary increases. As has been seen, salaries did increase, particularly for new engineers, but salary adjustments did not generally serve to reallocate the supply of engineers.

Because there have been no fully effective means of adapting the existing supply of engineers to the new demand created by the defense program, concern with the total supply of engineers has developed. Shortages have led to a preoccupation with the supply of new graduates and with the number of engineers in training. It is obvious, however, that present attempts to increase the number of engineers in training cannot relieve current shortages, for they can only expand the size of the future supply.

The supply of engineers at any one time also depends on the rate at which men leave the profession. The Bureau of Labor Statistics estimates that the number of deaths and retirements in the engineering profession for the period 1940 to 1948 was about 43,000 or an average of between five and six thousand per year. The number who shift to other occupations depends upon the incentives in engineering compared to those in alternative occupations. It has been estimated that even in periods of high demand, such as the present, each year about one percent of the total number of engineers shift to other fields. During periods of low demand movement out of the profession is greater.

ADDITIONS TO THE SUPPLY OF ENGINEERS

The long-term trend in the number of engineering graduates has been consistently upward, and has not even been halted by war or depression. There were 5,000 graduates in 1920 and an average of 7,000 per year in the decade ending 1929. During the depression of the 1930's, the proportion of students studying engineering declined. Apparently, young men recognized that industry was not hiring many who completed engineering training, and hesitated to invest in a four-year course of specialized instruction. Nevertheless, for the decade 1930-39 the average number of graduates per year rose to 11,000. In spite of the wartime interruption of training, the annual average for the 1940's was 19,000. After the war, as after World War I, the proportion of college students studying engineering increased substantially. This is not surprising, since both wars intensified the application of scientific knowledge to manufacturing, encouraged the development of new industries, and speeded the growth of older industries which employed engineers in considerable numbers. Because of this development, together with the large number of veterans who enrolled in college after the war, graduating classes rose spectacularly to a high of about 52,000 in 1950.

The number of graduates fell to about 40,000 in 1951 and to 30,000 in 1952, primarily because of the completion of training by most veterans. In addition, the population of college age fell after 1950 as a result of the decline in the number of births twenty years earlier. The shortage of engineers which resulted primarily from increased defense expenditures after the beginning of hostilities in Korea was intensified by the decline in the number of engineering graduates in 1951 and 1952. At the same time, moreover, many of the graduates were drawn into the armed forces.

The decline in the supply of new engineers since 1950, however, seems certain to be only temporary. The proportion of college students studying engineering is increasing, just as it did after both World Wars, and apparently for much the same reasons. In the fall of 1951, total male freshman enrollment declined from 1950 by 12 percent, but engineering freshman enrollment rose about 15 percent over 1950. In the fall of 1952, total male freshman enrollment increased some 15 percent, while freshman engineering enrollment rose about 30 percent. In addition to the abundance of job openings and the rising salaries of new engineers, extensive publicity campaigns to attract students to engineering also contributed to the increasing proportion of freshman students in engineering schools in 1951 and 1952. Because of these recent increases in the numbers beginning engineering training, the upward trend in the supply of new engineers will probably be resumed after graduating classes reach a low of about 20,000 in 1954. If the present student deferment program remains in effect, the average annual number of graduates in this decade will probably be over 30,000. The armed forces, of course, will continue to claim a substantial, and probably a rising, proportion of graduates. On the other hand, some young engineers are now completing their terms of service and returning to civilian life.

Over the years, the additions to the supply of engineers have changed substantially, not only in numbers, but in the character and quality of training received. Even today, almost one-fifth of all engineers do not have a degree in engineering. The proportion with little or no formal training, however, is higher among older engineers. Undoubtedly the opportunities for professional work in the field for men without a degree will continue to decline.

The nature of college training in engineering has also changed. Toward the end of the nineteenth century, engineering schools began to place greater emphasis on the theoretical bases of engineering rather than concentrating exclusively on practical, empirical knowledge. Today, the major employers of engineers recognize that the newly graduated engineer requires extensive practical training before he is able to make full use of his theoretical knowledge. One survey found that a third of the industrial employers of engineers have formal training programs for new engineers. Most firms shift new engineers from one job to another to provide broad practical experience. The new engineer who is hired by a company which does not provide special training must frequently work as a draftsman or in some other sub-professional capacity until he gains the necessary experience. In recent years arrangements between employers and colleges to provide for a mixed program of work and education have become increasingly common. This often adds to the years that a young man must spend before he receives his degree, but it has certain marked advantages for the student, including the opportunity to gain practical experience along with formal training, and to earn part of the costs of attending college.

A recent trend in engineering school curricula is the expansion of courses outside the engineering field, including courses in the humanities and social sciences as well as in business administration and industrial relations. One result has been the overcrowding of the curriculum, which has led several major engineering schools to adopt a five-year course.

Still another important trend in the training of engineers is the increasing number who are securing post-graduate degrees. Between 1934 and 1946, the number of engineers with doctoral degrees increased from 0.6 percent to almost 4 percent. The number with master's degrees increased from 5 percent to over 15 percent. Many firms encourage post-graduate academic study, and some of the larger companies and some government agencies operate formal post-graduate training programs in conjunction with local universities or engineering schools.

In short, the great increase in the number of engineers trained has been accompanied by an increase in the duration and diversity of formal training. Many in the field of engineering education are concerned with extending still further the engineer's training in the sciences, the humanities, and in business affairs. The graduate engineer today bears little resemblance to the engineer of fifty or sixty years ago. Yet, much of the work he performs is still the routine application of practical knowledge, which makes small demand upon his professional equipment. Thus, there has arisen a need for sub-professional technicians, to release the engineer for the more difficult work his training fits him to do. Although some employers estimate that they need several technicians for each engineer, the number of engineers who graduate from college each year is much greater than the number of technicians in engineering and science who graduate from recognized technical schools and institutes.

One of the important factors which affects both the number and the quality of engineering graduates is the ability and motivation of entrants to engineering schools. While the average scholastic ability of engineering students is higher than that of students in most fields, there is some evidence that too many begin training without the requisite aptitude or interest in the field. One reason is that a high proportion of engineering students are enrolled in land-grant state universities which are usually required by law to admit any high school graduate who is a resident of the state. As a result, it has been estimated that attrition in engineering courses may run as high as 60 percent in some schools.

An increase in the supply of new engineering students, as has been indicated, is not the sole means of preventing future shortages. Industry is interested in securing large numbers of executives with some degree of technological background, but not necessarily full engineering training, for work in general management and in sales. If the curricula of liberal arts colleges and schools of business administration, which educate so many young men for business careers, insured some measure of technological training, industry could have an additional source of supply to draw upon for work in general management and sales. Current trends in engineering education which seek to deepen the knowledge of fundamentals, particularly in mathematics and physics, should result in developing more convertible engineers. If a larger proportion of new graduates are better equipped to meet the challenges of a rapidly changing technology, it will be easier to meet sudden, high demands in the future.

The fact that the nation does not have an inexhaustible supply of brain power gives these considerations special pertinence. The number of able young persons interested in pursuing a scientific or professional career is limited. While the number can be increased, major obstacles stand in the way of a very rapid and large expansion. The claims of any one field, therefore, even one so important as engineering, must be balanced against all of the other fields requiring highly trained persons capable of rigorous thought and high performance. This means that estimates of requirements for engineering manpower must be set within a framework which includes both the claims of other professional fields and the advantages of increasing the supply of technicians so that professional engineers can work at a higher level of skill.

CHAPTER IX

Physicists

Wʀɪᴛɪɴɢ in 1940 on "The Fundaments of Theoretical Physics," Albert Einstein defined science as the attempt "to make the chaotic diversity of our sense-experience correspond to a logically uniform system of thought." He went on to say that physics comprises "that group of natural sciences which base their concepts on measurements; and whose concepts and propositions lend themselves to mathematical formulations." Einstein claimed that with the progress of science, the realm of physics— "the sum total of our knowledge which is capable of being expressed in mathematical terms"—has so expanded that its only limitation seems to be the method itself.

In a recent communication, Lee A. DuBridge, President of the California Institute of Technology, expanded Einstein's definition in these terms: "More specifically, the aim of physics is to achieve a greater understanding of the nature, structure and behavior of matter and energy. The 'experimental physicist' contributes to this understanding by making careful, systematic observations using an experimental arrangement which allows certain quantities to be measured while others are subjected to a controlled variation. The 'theoretical physicist' seeks to correlate such observations and to construct a theory or a system of equations which states the relations between various observed quantities and enables one to predict the results of new experiments or observations. . . .

"The field of physics is a broad one and as Einstein points out is continually changing as new areas of knowledge open up. In general, however, the science of physics is thought of as including knowledge in the fields of mechanics, heat, light (optics), sound, electricity and magnetism, and the whole field including molecular, atomic, electronic and nuclear phenomena.

"A physicist then is a person who has been trained in the field of physics, usually to at least the Bachelor's Degree level and frequently through the level of the Ph.D. Degree. A physicist may be engaged in a wide variety of professional activities. He may be teaching in a high school, junior college, college, or university. He may be carrying on 'research,' that is, seeking additional knowledge in some chosen area using for this purpose the laboratory facilities provided in a university, in an industrial corporation, in a private institute or in a government agency. If carrying on research, he may have as his primary goal seeking new knowledge in the field or he may be concerned with applying recently acquired knowledge to some practical end—a new industrial product or a new weapon of war. Sometimes the same physicist will be doing both 'pure' and 'applied' research or he may turn from one to the other as times change or his interests alter. If in a university, he is more likely to be engaged primarily in 'pure' research and is also likely to be carrying on teaching of undergraduate or graduate students at the same time."

Although physicists are engaged in a wide range of activities, this chapter is concerned mainly with those whose primary activity is research, frequently in association with teaching responsibilities. Some attention will be paid, however, to the increasing employment opportunities for physicists in industry. Physicists have been selected for study in order to assess the ways in which a representative group of scientists resembles and differs from such larger professional groups as teachers, engineers, and physicians.

THE SCIENTIST AND THE PROFESSIONAL MAN

One kind of difference is suggested by the size of other professional groups in contrast to the number of physicists. While there are more than one million teachers, over a half million engineers, and over 200,000 physicians, estimates of the present number of physicists in the country range from 15,000 to 20,000. The Director of the American Institute of Physics considers 18,000 a reasonable figure. The 1950 Census, however, listed only 11,000 physicists, of whom under 4,000 were college professors and instructors and over 7,000 were employed outside of universities. The wide range of these estimates is largely the result of variations in the criteria used to define a physicist. These may include training in the field, employment in the field, membership in professional societies, or the individual's own evaluation. The borderline between physics and such fields as chemistry and engineering is not always clear. Moreover, teachers of physics may sometimes be classified as teachers, sometimes as physicists.

The person who has a doctoral degree in physics, however, is very likely to be considered a physicist, regardless of any other criterion. In 1950, there were approximately 3,500 men who had such degrees. At least four-fifths of these were then working in the field of physics and almost all of the remainder were in closely related fields. In analyzing the supply of physicists, therefore, this chapter will be concerned primarily with those who have acquired a doctorate. An additional reason for limiting the analysis of supply to those with a doctoral degree is that most of the basic research in physics is conducted or supervised, and most of the important new knowledge is contributed, by men who have achieved at least this level of education.

The difference between the very small number of physicists and the numbers of teachers, engineers, and physicians can best be explained in terms of differences in the order of work which they perform. Most professional persons are practitioners. Trained in the theory and practice of a particular discipline, they spend their lives in applying what they have learned to meeting important social and economic needs. In America, it is considered essential to have teachers for the young and physicians for the ill. It would be impossible to exploit the practical potentials of modern science without large numbers of engineers. A limited number of persons trained in these professions may spend their lives as research scientists, and many trained as scientists may work as practitioners. Nevertheless, the work of most professionals is directed toward providing services, while the work of most scientists is the discovery of ideas. The great majority of physicists are engaged primarily either in teaching or in some form of basic or applied research, and even those who are primarily teachers generally devote considerable time to research.

Another distinction follows from this. Although aptitude and character play a significant part in the development of every professional person, the key to successful performance is often the excellence of training. Hence, to the extent that uniform minimum standards of training have been established, there is some justification for a statistical analysis which adds together all members of a given profession. Formal training, of course, is also essential for the scientist, but effective performance, measured, for example, by the discovery of new truth, depends to a still greater extent on the qualities of the individual. There can be little question that the training of more scientists would increase the number who make significant discoveries. The relationship between the total number trained and the number of outstanding scientists, however, is very indirect. The inherent limitations of the quantitative approach to manpower problems in the professions are discussed in the chapters dealing with teachers, engineers, and physicians. The difference between the roles of the professional practitioner and the scientist indicates that still greater caution must be exercised in evaluating statistics on the supply of physicists.

Since most physicists are members of the American Physical Society, the membership of that organization provides a rough index of growth in the field. Between 1900 and World War I, membership increased from less than 100 to almost 1,000. By the beginning of World War II, membership had reached about 4,000. In 1947, it was 6,700, and in the next four years increased to over 10,000.

The number of physicists with doctoral degrees also increased rapidly. Between 1900 and 1950, slightly more than 3,500 doctoral degrees in physics were awarded. During the first two decades of the century, the annual number of degrees awarded averaged about twenty. Around 1930, the annual number had risen to nearly 100. The upward trend continued until World War II. Between 1937 and 1942, the figures fluctuated between about 140 and nearly 200. The rise since the end of World War II has been spectacular, representing the completion of education by individuals whose studies had been interrupted during the war, as well as growing interest in the field of physics. From a low of about 40 in 1945, the figure rose to almost 500 for the academic year 1951-52.

It is difficult to interpret trends since the early 1940's because the impact of World War II cannot easily be distinguished from other developments more permanent in nature. Confused as they are, however, recent trends in the numbers specializing in physics in colleges and graduate schools must be examined because they will determine the number of doctorates to be awarded in physics during the next few years.

Bachelor's degrees granted to physics majors rose steadily from the World War II low to a high of 3,400 in 1949-50, and then declined to 2,200 in 1951-52. Master's degrees granted in physics also rose rapidly to a high of about 1,000 in 1950-51, declining slightly in the next year to about 900. In the opinion of one of the best informed students of the problem, Marsh W. White, the recent downward trend of degrees awarded at the bachelor's and master's levels may be expected to continue at least for the next few years. The number of doctoral degrees awarded, however, is likely to continue upward for several years. Dean Harrison of the Massachusetts Institute of Technology has pointed out that the long-term upward trend in the number of physicists trained will undoubtedly continue. For several decades, the number of physicists has been doubling every eight years, and there is no reason to expect that this expansion will be halted in the near future.

The general factors which determine the supply of persons completing graduate studies have been summarized in previous chapters. In the case of graduate study in physics, four factors are particularly important. Together they indicate that any large and rapid increase in the number receiving doctoral degrees in physics would be extremely difficult to achieve. They are: the number of people with high intelligence; the constellation of personality factors which leads to interest in theorizing about the properties of the physical world and a desire to pursue a research career; the special attraction of physics for some individuals; and the opportunities available for training from high school through the post-graduate level.

The most obvious limitation is the very high level of intelligence required for a doctoral degree in physics. The majority of persons receiving doctoral degrees in all fields are drawn from the most intelligent 6 percent of the population, as measured by standard tests of mental ability. This relatively small group must provide the supply of advanced students, not only in physics and the other natural sciences, but in all other fields of study as well. In addition, many positions of great responsibility which do not require advanced degrees also require very high intelligence. Moreover, sample studies using standard tests suggest that graduate students in the physical sciences are even more intelligent than graduate students as a whole. These studies show that two out of every three are in the top 40 percent of the entire graduate student body, and only one out of six is in the lowest 40 percent. Either the requirements for work in the physical sciences include very high intellectual ability, or else individuals with a high order of ability are especially attracted to the physical sciences. Both are probably true.

Personality factors, particularly an interest in the type of work represented by physics and the type of life represented by research, are also an important influence on the number of persons who study for doctoral degrees. In the absence of such personality requirements, it might be expected that the high demand for physicists and the growing prestige of physics would induce many highly intelligent students to enter this field rather than others. That this has occurred to some extent is suggested by the fact that the number of doctorates in physics has increased more rapidly than the total number of doctoral degrees during the past decade.

On the other hand, many young people of high intelligence are not attracted to mathematics, the basic tool of physics, or to theorizing about the physical universe in concrete and measurable terms, which is the basic method. Moreover, many who might make their peace with the method have no special desire to spend their lives in research or teaching, the primary career opportunities for physicists with doctoral degrees.

In positive terms, many individuals who pursue advanced study in physics give evidence of a special kind of enthusiasm for the field which DuBridge has expressed as follows: "Being attracted to physics is very much like falling in love. It is almost unexplainable and an almost emotional experience."

The character of the educational facilities available to persons of high intelligence also influences the number who receive doctoral degrees in physics. Many intelligent individuals attend secondary schools which do not impart a basic knowledge of algebra, geometry, and trigonometry, and which fail to provide any introduction to the essential qualities of natural science, either as a field of knowledge or as a possible career. The fact that it is difficult to progress in mathematics unless one has acquired reasonable control over the fundamentals, together with the conspicuous weakness in the teaching of mathematics at the high school and even college level undoubtedly reduces the number who are later able to qualify for work in the sciences. Many who might be attracted to studying science in college will decide not to if they must strive belatedly to learn the principles of mathematics. The fact that mathematics has been dropped as a required subject in many high schools compounds these difficulties.

The absence of a stimulating science teacher at the high school level is less serious, but may also be important. The interests and values of many individuals are not firmly set by their fifteenth or sixteenth year. Some find stimulation outside the school which puts them on the road to a scientific career. But for many others the presence or absence of an inspiring teacher can have a determining influence.

A relatively small number of colleges and universities produce a high proportion of the undergraduates who eventually acquire the doctorate in physics. Only thirty-seven institutions awarded bachelor's degrees to ten or more individuals who acquired a doctorate in physics between 1936 and 1948. At the top of the list was Massachusetts Institute of Technology with sixty-one, followed by California, Chicago, Columbia, California Institute of Technology, and Harvard, all with more than thirty-five each. Although the list consists mainly of large universities and specialized scientific institutions, several liberal arts colleges which are not part of a large university are also on it, including City College of New York, Oberlin, Reed College, Miami University (Ohio), and Brooklyn College. These thirty-seven institutions provided the undergraduate education of almost half of the 1,700 persons who acquired a doctorate in physics during the period. The other half received their bachelor's degrees from 302 institutions, of which 135 provided but a single graduate who eventually earned the doctorate.

A recent study of *Origins of American Scientists*, by Robert Knapp and H. B. Goodrich, attempted to discover the qualities of a college or university which are responsible for the fact that a high proportion of its graduates go on to secure a doctoral degree in the sciences. One of the most important factors, they found, was an academic atmosphere which emphasizes intellectual achievement and minimizes social and athletic activities. The authors also found that the intelligence and background of the students which a college or university attracts and the teaching ability of its faculty were more important than such factors as its wealth, its physical facilities, or the scientific distinction of its faculty members.

Obviously the characteristics of undergraduate education which are likely to lead students to advanced scientific study are highly intangible. This observation adds point to the fact that a few graduates from each of a large number of institutions account for over half of those who eventually acquire a doctorate. Although the graduates of some institutions are more likely than others to pursue advanced studies, much depends on the student himself. Apparently a young man who enters college with a strong interest in the natural sciences or physics and who possesses good intelligence is quite likely to complete advanced training no matter where he goes to college. The college, of course, must provide him with the opportunity of acquiring a knowledge of calculus and must guide him through the standard theories and laboratory experiments of college physics. This does not imply, of course, that every embryonic physicist will develop. Some will shift to other fields of science and many will lose interest in pursuing a scientific career. Undoubtedly, the character of the college exercises a strong influence on the decisions of those students who are only slightly motivated to study physics when they begin college.

Even more than undergraduate enrollment of physics majors, graduate instruction leading to the award of the doctorate is heavily concentrated in a relatively few large universities. Of the approximately 3,000 physicists with doctoral degrees who were listed in *American Men of Science* in 1949, 60 percent had received their degrees from one of the thirteen institutions listed in Table 10, each of which conferred a total of at least 100 degrees. Another twenty institutions, each of which conferred between 20 and 100 degrees, accounted for another 25 percent. These thirty-three institutions, together, then, awarded 85 percent of the doctoral degrees in physics. Between 1936 and 1948, the total number of institutions which awarded one or more doctoral degrees was only sixty-four. Several of the institutions which are listed in Table 10 did not award a significant number of doctorates in physics until the 1920's. These are California, Michigan, the California Institute of Technology, and the Massachusetts Institute of Technology. More recently, graduate enrollment in physics has expanded at certain other institutions, particularly Ohio State, New York University, Maryland, the University of California at Los Angeles, Cincinnati, Brooklyn Polytechnic Institute, and Catholic University.

Table 10. Institutions Granting the Most Doctoral Degrees in Physics[a]

DOCTORAL DEGREES AWARDED

RANK	INSTITUTION	Pre 1921	1921- 25	1926- 30	1931- 35	1936- 40	1941- 45	1946- 49	TOTAL
1	Chicago	40	31	35	33	41	28	22	230
2	Cornell	41	19	26	24	25	29	15	179
3	California (Berkeley)	9	8	25	33	42	34	20	171
4	Michigan	8	7	26	30	42	21	16	150
5	California Institute of Technology	..	10	35	37	25	22	19	148
6	Johns Hopkins	45	19	19	17	20	12	12	144
7	Harvard	24	8	14	31	22	15	27	141
8	Massachusetts Institute of Technology	1	15	4	14	39	35	41	139
9	Columbia	19	11	16	23	26	15	14	124
10	Yale	17	13	12	23	22	14	20	121
11	Wisconsin	12	11	18	26	22	14	13	116
12	Princeton	17	11	17	15	24	12	13	109
13	Illinois	12	4	14	18	22	26	6	102

Total   1,874

[a] Source: John N. Cooper, "American Physicists and Their Graduate Degrees," *American Journal of Physics*, November 1952. The table shows the number of doctoral degrees awarded to physicists listed in the 1949 edition of *American Men of Science*.

No thorough analysis has yet been made of the costs involved in the advanced education of physicists and such related specialists as astronomers and oceanographers. Since scientists can be trained only if research facilities are available to them, a true estimate of training costs would have to include at least part of the cost of such research facilities as the 200-inch telescope at Palomar; Columbia's synchrocyclotron at the Nevis Estate, Irvington, N. Y.; and the Brookhaven National Laboratory, where many graduate students in nuclear physics do their research. It may well be that training in physics is the most costly type of training, even more costly than training in medicine. Although the availability of training facilities does not now limit the number who can study for the doctoral degree, any large increase over the present number would require further expansion of very expensive facilities. It should also be noted that a considerable part of the recent expansion of facilities has been financed by the government. Any cut-back of government funds for research would make the problem of expanding facilities for advanced training even more difficult.

Another aspect of the facilities problem is their geographical concentration. There are twenty-one states in which no institution granted a doctoral degree in physics between 1936 and 1948. The cost of advanced training for students from those states is increased since they cannot live at home while studying.

PATTERNS OF WORK AND EMPLOYMENT

In light of the substantial increases in the number of persons who have acquired a doctorate in physics and of the striking progress in the field in recent years, it is inevitable that the patterns of work and employment of the younger physicists are strikingly different from those of the older men in the field. The younger men, quite naturally, are found in the newer fields. A physicist's competence, moreover, is greatly influenced by his age. Physics is definitely a young man's field and probably has become even more so in recent years because of major changes in its theoretical structure and rapid advances in its specialized branches. It has often been remarked that a physicist tends to do his best work in basic research in his thirties, which is perhaps a little older than the most creative age for mathematicians, but very much younger than for the humanities and the social sciences. Einstein has repeatedly called attention to the tragedy of the older physicist because of "the increasing difficulty of adaptation to new thoughts which always confronts the man past fifty."

Just under 3,000 physicists holding a doctoral degree replied to the questionnaire of the National Scientific Register early in 1951. Over 10 percent of the entire group were under thirty; over 30 percent were under thirty-five; and half were under forty. Each respondent was asked to indicate the field of his highest competence. Twenty-two percent stated nuclear physics. Electronics was named by 15 percent, and optics by 12 percent. The remainder were about evenly divided among classical theory, quantum theory, mechanics and heat, acoustics, atomic and molecular physics, solid state physics, and general physics. The age factor was most conspicuous in the case of nuclear physics. Slightly more than one-third of the men under thirty-five specialized in this field. Of those under thirty, about 25 percent were in the field of quantum theory. The importance of the age factor in these two fields is indicated by the fact that in both men under the age of thirty-five accounted for roughly half of all those who considered these fields as their area of highest competence. Conversely, the older men were concentrated in the traditional fields. Two-thirds of those who were sixty-five or older were in general physics, classical theory, mechanics and heat, or optics. The rapidly changing relations of mathematics, physics, and engineering, however, point to the need for caution in interpreting statistics by field of specialization. A doctoral degree in electronic engineering, for instance, frequently involves training very similar to that required for a doctoral degree in classical physics.

A survey undertaken in 1948 found that four out of five persons who had a doctoral degree in physics were working in the field at the time. Most of those who had left were in closely allied types of work, particularly in engineering, chemistry, and mathematics. The survey reported in *Manpower Resources in Physics, 1951* indicated that over 90 percent of those with doctoral degrees were then employed in physics.

According to the same survey, just under three out of every five physicists with a doctoral degree work for colleges and universities. The actual figure is probably somewhat lower. Almost 30 percent are employed by private industry, and 11 percent by government. Almost 90 percent of the physicists with doctoral degrees are employed in research and teaching jobs; most of the rest are engaged in management. The type of employment, however, varies markedly with age. Of those below thirty-five, almost three out of five are engaged primarily in research. Of those fifty or older, this is true of only one out of five. Teaching is the primary function of less than 40 percent of the men under thirty-five years of age, but of more than 60 percent of those fifty or above.

This difference reflects two facts. First, a smaller proportion of the younger men are employed by educational institutions. Over half of those who are forty-five or over, but less than 40 percent of those under forty-five, work for colleges and universities. Secondly, even when they work for a college or university, the younger men are more likely to be engaged primarily in research. In the past colleges and universities loaded teaching responsibilities on the younger men. One had to "earn" the right to carry fewer classes and do more research. Now the situation is reversed and many younger men are given staff appointments solely for research without any teaching responsibilities. This is true even in the case of men who have been offered tenure. Vastly expanded research activities in physics are still in the process of being fitted into the structure of the universities. In some institutions efforts have been made to place the expanded research work within the departmental framework, but the more typical approach has been to establish an independent research institute within the university. Many problems remain to be solved, especially those which bear on increasing the work satisfaction of the research personnel who do not have professorial rank and teaching responsibilities.

Twenty-five percent of the physicists with doctoral degrees—most of those working in private industry—are employed in manufacturing. Approximately a third of this group are in the electrical machinery industry. About a fourth are in the professional and scientific equipment industry, chemicals, or transportation equipment. The remainder, about 40 percent of the group, are distributed in small numbers among a variety of industries. The great majority are engaged primarily in research.

The earnings of physicists with doctoral degrees depend to a considerable extent upon the type of employer. As Table 11 shows, median income is considerably higher in government and industrial work than in university employment. Industry, moreover, offers the physicist a much greater chance of increasing his earnings substantially as he grows older and gains experience.

Table 11. Median Annual Income of Physicists with Doctoral Degrees by Type of Employer and Age Group, 1951[a]

Age	University	Government	Industry[b]
All Ages	$6,400	$8,000	$8,000
25-29	4,700	. .	5,900
30-34	5,800	6,700	6,900
35-39	6,600	8,300	8,600
40-44	7,700	8,100	9,300
45-49	7,300	9,300	11,100
50-54	7,500	8,600	12,200
55-64	6,500	. .	. .
65 and over	6,000	. .	. .

[a] Source: *Manpower Resources in Physics, 1951.*
[b] Includes business firms, consultants, and self-employment.

Like other scientific and technological fields, physics is dominated almost completely by men. Of the nearly 3,000 physicists with doctoral degrees reported in the 1951 survey, only 66 were women.

TRENDS IN THE DEMAND

Up to this point, the analysis has been concerned exclusively with physicists who have acquired the doctoral degree. An adequate analysis of the supply of and demand for physicists, however, requires consideration of physicists of all levels of training from the bachelor's degree through the doctorate. This is especially true since the demand for physicists with less than doctoral training has expanded greatly in the last few years. Before World War II, a career in physics generally meant research and teaching at a college or university. A career of this kind almost always required a doctoral degree. A few physicists had made their way into industry, disguised as chemists, for most industrial research laboratories had positions for chemists but not for physicists. A few others had also found positions in the research laboratories of the government.

Developments during World War II created a very heavy demand for physicists with a high level of theoretical and experimental competence, particularly in the fields of nuclear physics, atomic physics, and electronics. These same developments also increased the demand by university, governmental, and industrial laboratories for men who could apply theoretical advances to practical ends. Younger men who had not yet acquired their doctorates were needed in substantial numbers to assist senior personnel who were working against time to apply knowledge in the new fields to military purposes. After the war, the field of applied physics continued to expand in both the military and civilian sectors of the economy. As has been seen, the numbers completing training also increased rapidly in the immediate postwar years, but the number of job openings for persons at each level of training increased even more rapidly. The major shortages, however, were those of senior men. The Armed Services were unable, even before Korea, to meet all of their research and development requirements for men of high competence.

Requirements were increased after the outbreak of hostilities in Korea, which brought with it a rapid acceleration in the research and especially in the developmental work of the Department of Defense and the Atomic Energy Commission. The situation is summarized in the opening paragraph of *Manpower Resources in Physics, 1951,* in the following terms:

> The shortage of physicists now confronting the country is one of the most serious problems in the field of scientific manpower. The development of atomic weapons, experimental research in the application of atomic energy, and expanded research activity in electronics and other fields have created an unprecedented demand for physicists. Even before the outbreak of hostilities in Korea, additional personnel were needed in this branch of science. The demand has been greatly intensified by the mobilization program.

Table 12 shows the trends in the number of job openings for physicists and the number of physicists who registered for employment with the American Institute of Physics in the past three years. Since the Institute is just one center for recruitment, these data cannot be used to measure the absolute level of demand, but only the direction of changes.

Table 12. Openings and Registrants for Employment as Physicists, 1950-52[a]

OPENINGS AND REGISTRANTS	FEB., 1950	FEB., 1951	FEB., 1952
Openings			
Academic	78	85	74
Government	107	1,012	228
Industry	93	238	928
Institutional research	7	87	74
Total openings	285	1,422	1,304
Registrants			
With doctorates	193	169	151
With other degrees	241	192	120
Total registrants	434	361	271

[a] Source: Based on data provided by the American Institute of Physics.

In the first stage after the outbreak of hostilities in Korea the government increased its demand for physicists tenfold compared to the preceding year. As the government was able to place research and development contracts with industry, the increased demand for physicists was shifted to that area. The number of industrial openings in February 1952 was ten times as high as two years previously. At the same time, the number of applicants for jobs declined steadily.

SHORTAGES OF PHYSICISTS

The limitations of a purely quantitative approach to problems of professional and scientific manpower have been stressed throughout these chapters. These limitations are especially important in considering a group like the physicists who number no more than 20,000, including only about 4,000 who have a doctoral degree. Among these 4,000, moreover, only a small number can be expected to make major contributions to theoretical physics.

There is always a shortage of first-rate minds capable of making major advances in the sciences. The present shortage of creative minds is not unusual. There have never been and there are not now as many creative minds as the country could use. To the extent that there is a new factor in this situation, it must be found in the tense international situation. The future security of this country depends to a very great degree on the ideas which physicists have already contributed and are likely to contribute in the future to methods and systems of defense. The most intractable facet of the shortage of physicists consists, therefore, in the production of an additional number of first-rate creative minds.

A second kind of shortage is the insufficient number of mature men who can supervise projects in government and industrial laboratories seeking to apply new knowledge to civilian and military uses in such important fields as nuclear energy, communications, and electronics. Both the shortage of creative minds and the shortage of project leaders are shortages primarily but not wholly of men with doctoral degrees, for this degree alone is no guarantee of competence for high level work.

There remains another aspect of the shortage problem. Since the fields of electronics, nuclear energy, solid state physics, and such new industrial fields as television and industrial electronic control are all built on recent discoveries in physics, physicists are needed to translate these new ideas and techniques from the field of physics into the field of engineering. Whenever a new technology emerges from basic discoveries in science, it is the scientist who must do the critical technological development. How long they continue to work on development problems depends on how long it is before a new field of technology (engineering) arises. This kind of work requires physicists with all levels of training from the recent graduate with a bachelor's degree to the experienced man with a doctoral degree. At present, many physicists are doing the work of engineers because most of the latter have not been solidly grounded in physics. During the past few years, there has been a particularly severe shortage of engineers with adequate background to cope effectively with the application of knowledge in the field of nuclear energy.

This brief analysis of three different kinds of shortages of physicists indicates that merely increasing the numbers of men who complete each level of training will not automatically solve the problem of shortages. In addition, there is need for men with very particular kinds of abilities which are not necessarily provided by formal training. There is no obvious and ready method for increasing the number of first-rate creative minds, and even if there were, this shortage would persist since the latent demand is almost insatiable. There is no substitute for the experience which comes with time for relieving the second type of shortage, that of mature project leaders for applied research and development. If the level of governmental and industrial spending for research and development is not radically increased in the near future, this particular shortage should be somewhat relieved as the large number of younger men who have completed training in recent years acquire more competence and mature judgment.

The third type of shortage is that of men who are capable of performing the applied research and development necessary to carry new ideas into practical application. One remedial step is suggested by the efforts of the Atomic Energy Commission to provide additional training in physics for engineers and in engineering for physicists. As a result of these steps, the shortage of personnel for applied research and development in the field of nuclear energy is now on the way toward solution. If the new developments in physics are to become effective throughout the civilian economy, however, it is likely that steps will have to be taken to increase the amount of mathematics and physics that are currently included in engineering curricula. The better engineering schools are increasingly aware of the need for this type of broadened training and are taking steps to provide it. For some considerable time, however, there will surely be a heavy demand for physicists to assist in the technological development of the new discoveries in physics.

Although increasing the number of young men being trained in physics would not automatically solve any of the shortage problems, it would undoubtedly facilitate their relief through the measures described above. The difficulties of attaining a substantial and rapid increase in the numbers trained have already been indicated. In addition to the problems which apply specifically to this field, training in physics shares with all fields the problems created by the recent decline in the population of college age. One of the most serious barriers to an increase in the number of college students interested in physics is the weakness of many high schools, particularly in their teaching of mathematics. It will clearly be no easy matter to improve this situation rapidly.

Another problem which has received too little consideration derives from the fact that a young man attracted to physics and research is unlikely to prepare himself for this work unless he can see a reasonable opportunity for a meaningful career. The true scientist is unlikely to want to spend his life as a civil servant or as an employee of industry engaged in the solution of practical problems. During the last few years, a considerable number of physicists, including many with doctoral degrees, have looked for new employment opportunities. Almost all of those who registered with the American Institute of Physics, however, indicated that they had a strong preference for college teaching and research, in spite of the higher salaries available in government and industrial employment. The rate at which the number of academic posts, or their approximate equivalent in first-rate research laboratories in government and industry, expands and the conditions of employment that are established will exercise a strong influence on the numbers of superior individuals who will choose physics as a career. Any increase in the numbers trained which does not include a high proportion of superior persons will contribute little to relieving the shortage of creative persons.

It would be unfortunate if the attention devoted to the recently expanding demands of government and industry for relatively large numbers of physicists for development work should obscure the core of the manpower problem in physics. This remains the need for more first-rate research minds. Several years ago the American public was almost complacent because it had a monopoly of the atomic bomb. Only the experts understood clearly that this complacency was uncalled for on two grounds: there was every likelihood that the Russians would learn to build atomic bombs; and, secondly, the American accomplishment was built upon the theoretical work of outstanding European scientists, including Einstein, Fermi, Meissner, Szilard, Bohr, and many others. The American scene is not conducive to what Einstein calls the monotony of a quiet life that stimulates the mind. Yet the security and progress of the country depend as never before upon the nurturing of creative minds that can push back the frontiers of the unknown.

CHAPTER X

Teachers

THE TEACHING PROFESSION has a double importance for a study of scientific and professional manpower. The services of teachers are vital for the welfare of the country and of every individual. Beyond this, the nation's teachers directly influence the quantity and the quality of the services provided by all the other professions. In recent years there have been repeated warnings of an alarming shortage of teachers. It is estimated that there will be shortages of elementary school teachers in forty-five states during the next three years.

Public school enrollment increased over 80 percent between 1900 and 1953, as Table 13 shows. The number of teachers, supervisors, and principals more than doubled between 1900 and 1950, the last date for which full information is available. In that year, there were 914,000 teachers and 48,000 principals and supervisors. In addition, there were 23,000 professional administrators, 22,000 clerical employees, and 133,000 health, transportation, and custodial employees working in the nation's schools. The National Education Association estimates that since 1950 the number of teachers, principals, and supervisors has increased to over one million.

Both enrollment and academic staffs have increased at a slightly more rapid rate in private schools than in public schools.

Table 13. Academic Personnel and Enrollments in American Public Elementary and Secondary Schools, 1900-53[a]

Year	Teachers, Principals, and Supervisors	Enrollments
1900	443,000	15,503,000
1910	548,000	17,814,000
1920	711,000	21,579,000
1930	896,000	25,678,000
1940	917,000	25,434,000
1942	903,000	24,562,000
1944	870,000	23,267,000
1946	872,000	23,300,000
1948	907,000	23,945,000
1950	962,000	25,111,000
1952	. .[b]	26,774,000
1953	. .[b]	28,196,000

[a] Source: U.S. Office of Education and George J. Stigler, "Employment and Compensation in Education," *Occasional Paper 33*, National Bureau of Economic Research, 1950.
[b] Not available.

Almost 12 percent of the total elementary and secondary school enrollment and faculties in the country are now in private schools. Because of the paucity of data relating to private schools, however, this chapter will consider only public school teachers.

Like civilian employment in other professional fields, the number of teachers in the public schools declined during World War II. The teaching profession lost personnel, not only to the Armed Forces, but also to higher-paid clerical and semi-skilled defense jobs. The decline in the number of teachers, however, was proportionately less than the decline in school enrollments. The steady decline in the birth rate, which reached an all-time low during the 1930's, together with enhanced job opportunities for older students were primarily responsible for the decline in enrollments. Nevertheless, there were teacher shortages which reached their peak in 1945. They were evidenced by the increased employment of emergency teachers, that is, persons with inadequate academic preparation according to existing standards.

There was also a substantial shift from men to women teachers.

The clearest sign of a shortage of teachers is an increase in the number of emergency teachers. Their employment means that teachers who are qualified according to existing standards are not available and that employment standards have, therefore, been lowered. There are currently about 65,000 emergency teachers employed in the United States.

Other shortage warnings are given when large numbers of teachers change jobs or leave the profession entirely as a result of discontent over salaries, working conditions, and status in the community. These grievances were sharply evidenced late in 1946 and early in 1947 when teachers in a dozen major cities throughout the nation walked out of their classrooms and went on strike.

THE DEMAND

The demand for teachers depends, not only on the number of children of school age, but on several other factors. Among the most important of these are the proportion of children of school age who attend school and the quality of education which the community wishes to provide. In addition, the number of new teachers needed in any period depends on the number of teachers who leave their positions during that period.

The total school-age population provides the basic data for forecasting enrollments. Since over 98 percent of the children of elementary school age are enrolled in schools, elementary enrollments can be predicted on the basis of the number of births six to thirteen years earlier. This figure may then be adjusted to account for expected migration and deaths, for the number who graduate before the normal graduation age, for the number who remain after they reach graduation age, and for the small number who do not attend school even though they are of school age and have not graduated.

One of the most difficult problems in accurately forecasting elementary school enrollment is to account for the influence of retardation, that is, the failure of some children to be promoted in the normal period. The major effect of retardation is to concentrate the demand for teachers in the lower grades and in elementary school rather than in high school. Thus, although not all children in the age group of six to thirteen were enrolled in elementary schools in 1950, the number of elementary pupils was greater than the number of children between six and thirteen. In other words, many children of fourteen and over were still in elementary school.

The determinants of high school enrollment are still more complex. Even though graduation from high school is gradually coming to be considered normal in America, 23 percent of the children of high school age were not enrolled in 1950. Moreover, the number of high school graduates was only about three-fifths of the high school graduation age group. Clearly, high school enrollment depends on factors which are not important in elementary enrollments. These factors collectively are commonly referred to as "school holding power."

The long-run influence of changing social attitudes on the spread of high school education has been discussed in earlier chapters. At any one time, however, school holding power varies from community to community, largely in response to local economic conditions. Where per capita income is high, families can afford to allow children to remain in school and local governments can support good schools which retain the interest of students. In prosperous communities, there are likely to be greater economic incentives for education, in the form of job openings which require high school graduation. On the average, whites earn more than Negroes, Northerners more than Southerners, and city-dwellers more than those who live in rural areas. Consequently fewer Negro than white children, fewer Southern than Northern children, and fewer rural than urban children are enrolled in high school. The percentage is lowest among Southern Negroes in rural areas. Even compulsory school attendance laws, which followed rather than led increased enrollments, could not have succeeded if communities had not been prosperous enough to support continued school attendance.

The direct relationship between income and high school enrollment, which may be observed by comparing different communities at the same time, is one of the main reasons for the long-term increase in high school graduation. There is, however, some evidence that the number of graduates increases in depression periods. The most rapid increase in the last sixty years in the percentage of seventeen-year-olds graduating from high school occurred in the decade of the 1930's, probably because, for much of the period, employment was not a possible alternative to high school attendance.

Enrollment is the most rigid of the factors which determine the demand for teachers. Elementary enrollment in any one year is determined largely by the number of births in prior years. Better enforcement of school attendance laws could raise the number of six- to thirteen-year-olds enrolled in school but by no more than about 2 percent. Better schools could lower enrollments by reducing the number of children who do not graduate from grammar school by the time they reach thirteen. If the legal school-leaving age were raised in those states where it is relatively low, elementary school enrollment might be increased substantially. Otherwise, elementary enrollment is only slightly influenced by actions of the community. High school enrollments, which are influenced by school holding power, are more responsive to changing conditions. The number of children for whom teachers must be provided really depends on average daily attendance rather than on formal enrollment. Data on attendance, however, are not reliable enough to permit conclusions about the effect of absence from school on the demand for teachers.

The demand for teachers also depends on the number of pupils assigned to each teacher. As the United States has become wealthier, the average number of pupils per teacher has declined. Nevertheless, the decline in the ratio of students to teacher has always lagged behind the reduction in the standard or desirable ratio established by educators. Teacher organizations have held that elementary classrooms should contain no more than thirty pupils, but the average class in 1950 contained thirty-three. Urban classes generally have more pupils per teacher, and rural classes fewer, because of differences in population density. In 1950, there were still about 60,000 one-room schools with an average of only seventeen pupils each. The ratio is being increased in many rural areas, however, by the consolidation of schools and provision of bus transportation. This, of course, results in a reduction of the demand for rural teachers.

Attitudes toward education and the community's ability to support its schools are also important determinants of teacher demand. Community support is reflected by the level of appropriations for salaries, transportation, buildings, and facilities, and other educational costs. If a community does not provide enough teachers or classrooms, the number of pupils per teacher rises and teachers may even work double sessions. Thus, what would otherwise have been a demand for two teachers may become a demand for one teacher with twice as many pupils. Even though state and Federal educational contributions have more than doubled since the depression, over half of all school revenues were still derived from relatively inflexible local property taxes in 1950. For this reason, school budgets frequently fall behind increasing enrollments even in prosperous communities. In the high schools, prolonged poor support may reduce the quality of the schools so severely that many students leave prematurely, thus reducing the demand for teachers.

The demand for teachers is always stated in terms of a specific kind of person. The ideal teacher has pedagogical skill, subject-matter competence, an attractive personality, and a fine character. Since such paragons are always in short supply, the ideal is compromised, and people who lack one or more of these characteristics to some extent are hired. The degree to which the ideal is compromised in any community depends largely on the support the community gives to its schools.

The potential supply of teachers is limited by the number of educated people in the community, by the number who want to teach, and by the number who are acceptable to the school systems. From the applicants for teaching jobs, communities select those who best meet their standards of teaching ability, knowledge, personality, and character. Frequently, knowledge and teaching ability are measured only by the amount of formal academic and pedagogical preparation. Only those persons who have had the required amount of training are certified, or licensed, by the states to teach in the public schools. Certification requirements may change, but generally they move upward rather than decline. In practice, however, this limitation on supply is overcome by employing emergency teachers when certified teachers are not available.

Almost all states now require at least a bachelor's degree for high school teachers. The minimum requirements for elementary school teachers are now approaching this level. The academic preparation of teachers has risen along with the increase in requirements. In 1920, four-fifths of all teachers had less than two years of training beyond high school, and one-fourth had less than two years of high school. In 1952, about 55 percent of all elementary teachers had a bachelor's degree. Another 33 percent had completed at least two years of college and most of the others had attended college for at least one year. The proportion of elementary teachers with a bachelor's degree varied from less than 9 percent in South Dakota to 97 percent in Arizona.

The amount of preparation, however, is at best only a rough measure of the quality of a teacher. Many teachers are trained in small, impoverished colleges, where admission requirements, faculties, curricula, and libraries are below the standards prevailing in other colleges. Teachers' colleges in general have been criticized for giving courses which lack depth and intellectual content, and for emphasizing teaching methods at the expense of subject matter. Although students majoring in education vary widely in ability, they generally rank below other college students on the basis of most objective measures of mental ability. Thus, only 44 percent of the male students in their junior year who were majoring in education were eligible for deferment on the basis of their scores on the Selective Service System's College Qualification Test given during the spring and summer of 1951. In comparison, 88 percent of engineering majors and 71 percent of all college juniors were eligible. However, many students preparing to teach, including a high proportion of those preparing for high school teaching, do not major in education. If these were included with the education majors in the data the future teachers would compare more favorably with other students. Nevertheless, the figures do show that students preparing for elementary teaching and for physical education, who constitute most of the education majors, have less ability on the average than do other college students.

The number of college graduates who decide to teach is affected by several factors. For some, teaching is a career in the same sense as medicine or physics. For others, it is a form of "job insurance." Only about two-fifths of all bachelor's degrees in education are awarded by teachers' colleges, and many students qualify for teaching positions with a degree in another field. Many students in liberal arts schools take enough pedagogy courses to qualify as teachers, in case they cannot find preferred employment. In addition, even though most states now permit married women to teach, a high proportion of teachers are women who fill the interval between graduation and marriage with a job which provides professional status. Over four-fifths of all teachers are women, many of whom do not regard teaching as a lifelong career. For these reasons, teachers tend to leave the field when better positions become available. Moreover, teachers' salaries become a crucial factor when recent college graduates decide whether to enter teaching or some other field.

Because school budgets are relatively inflexible, salary reductions and increases for teachers tend to lag behind changes in the general price and wage levels. As a result, throughout most of the last depression teachers' salaries were relatively high. As late as 1940, the average salary of teachers, supervisors, and principals in the public schools was $1,441. Although the average salary of classroom teachers was slightly less, it still compared favorably with the average of only $1,306 earned by all employed workers. By 1944, when salaries in the rest of the economy had increased sharply, the average salary of teachers, supervisors, and principals was approximately $500 less than that of all employed workers. Some of this loss has since been made up. In 1950 salaries averaged $3,010, almost the same as the average for all employed persons, but well below the average for other professionals and for non-professional college graduates. The generally low level and narrow range of teachers' salaries discourage bright college students, especially those from well-to-do backgrounds, from becoming teachers. On the other hand, teaching may attract those who desire long vacations and the security provided by tenure and pensions. While the desire for security increases during depressions, it declines when attractive alternative employment becomes available in prosperous times.

The factors which determine the supply of teachers operate within very restricted and local employment markets. Because of varying certification requirements, some persons who are qualified to teach in one state are not in another; elementary teachers may not be eligible to teach in the high schools, nor high school teachers in the elementary schools of the same state; high school teachers of one subject may not be permitted to teach some other subjects in the same school. Although most states require at least a bachelor's degree for high school teachers, only eighteen states require a bachelor's degree for elementary school teachers and three states, Mississippi, Nebraska, and North Dakota, require less than one year of post-high school preparation for some teaching certificates. Although the barriers are sometimes informal, there are also different employment markets for urban and rural teachers and for Negroes and whites.

Because of these conditions, there may be a shortage of some kinds of teachers while there is a surplus of others. Thus, the segregated school system of the South, together with the paucity of attractive alternative employment for educated Southern Negroes has resulted in a surplus of all types of Negro teachers, while at the same time there is a shortage of white elementary school teachers in the South. Some shortages would even be intensified by reducing the barriers to the movement of teachers. A reduction of the barriers between urban and rural schools would stimulate the movement of rural teachers to better-paying positions in the cities and increase the shortage in rural schools.

Surprisingly, the shortage of qualified teachers is smallest where certification requirements are high. The eighteen states which require a bachelor's degree for elementary teachers have less difficulty in finding teachers than the other states. This situation is probably explained in part by the fact that high requirements, good community support, and adequate salaries generally go together.

SUPPLY AND DEMAND IN THE FUTURE

An attempt to forecast the future demand for teachers must begin with an estimate of future enrollment. Although the precise number of children enrolled in elementary school depends on many factors in addition to the number of children of elementary school age, these factors affect very few children. Consequently, future enrollment changes will probably correspond closely to past birth-rate changes.

Because of the rapid increase in the birth rate which began in 1940, elementary school enrollment began to rise rapidly in 1947. Eighteen million elementary pupils were enrolled in 1940; by 1950, there were almost 23 million. If all factors except the number of births in previous years are disregarded, it may be estimated roughly that total elementary enrollment will increase to about 28 million by 1957 and will continue to grow at least until 1960. Thus, there will be a steadily increasing demand for elementary school teachers for the rest of this decade. The increase in elementary school enrollment will be much larger in some states than in others. Since 1940, the annual number of births has increased only 8 percent in Kentucky compared to over 163 percent in the District of Columbia.

High school enrollment also depends in part on the size of the school-age population. The decline in the population of high school age which began after 1940 was reversed in 1950. If the percentage of children between fourteen and seventeen who are enrolled in high school remains the same as it was in 1950, high school enrollment will increase gradually each year through 1955, and more rapidly between 1955 and 1965. By the latter date, it will reach 10.8 million, compared to slightly more than 6 million today. If the proportion enrolled increases from approximately three-fourths today to as much as 85 percent, present enrollment will be almost doubled by 1965. If the school-leaving age is raised in some states, school holding power could be improved artificially. On the other hand, preliminary estimates by the Office of Education suggest the possibility that since 1950, high school enrollment, as a percent of the age group, has declined, just as it did during World War II when older boys left school for war industry jobs and for military service.

Still other factors might influence the demand for teachers. For example, a substantial change in national immigration policy could alter the whole picture. In any particular community, of course, migration also affects enrollments. Thus, in addition to a record increase of 133 percent in the number of live births from 1940 to 1951, California has experienced a huge in-migration of families with school-age children. The extent to which communities provide additional financial support to meet predicted increases in enrollments and the teacher-utilization practices of local school systems will also help to determine the number of additional teachers needed. In some places, a few additional children will result in the demand for an extra classroom and an extra teacher. In schools where present facilities and teachers are underutilized, additional personnel may not be needed. Rural areas will probably need fewer additional schools and teachers to serve increased enrollment than will urban areas. Although the birth rate is still higher in rural areas than in cities, the recent increase in births has been relatively small in rural areas. Moreover, there are now fewer students per teacher in rural than in urban schools.

The community's willingness and ability to support education will affect the supply of as well as the demand for teachers. The salaries offered to teachers influence both the quantity and quality of the supply. The level at which certification requirements are fixed depends on the extent to which salaries offered by a community attract qualified teachers. These requirements express the qualitative aspect of the demand for teachers. At the same time, however, they help to determine the quantitative supply. Thus the demand for teachers' services is complicated by the fact that some of the factors which determine demand are closely interwoven with the factors that determine supply.

Predictions about the supply of teachers are as hazardous as those about future demand. The number of persons who prepare for teaching, the number of qualified persons who elect to teach, and the length of their teaching careers will depend upon a multitude of individual decisions. These will be influenced, in turn, by community decisions about teachers' salaries and other career incentives. The number who elect to teach also depends on the opportunity for more attractive employment, and the cost of living trend, over which the schools have no control. Even a minor depression, for instance, could produce an oversupply of teachers. Persons qualified to teach would lose other jobs, while married women who left teaching would return to supplement the family income. A deflationary period of several years would raise the relative earnings of teachers. The number of qualified teachers, moreover, can be changed quite arbitrarily by changing certification requirements. Requirements for specific kinds of preparation for different kinds of teaching positions may also be changed, either to increase or decrease the difficulty of matching qualified teachers with job openings. Finally, the actual number of teachers at any time depends on the extent to which the schools are willing to waive their requirements and accept emergency teachers.

SHORTAGES

Judgment on the extent of the present shortage of teachers is a function of the criteria used. The U.S. Office of Education has estimated that in the fall of 1952 the nation needed about 53,000 more qualified new teachers than were available to take care of increased enrollment and to replace teachers leaving the schools. Almost all of this requirement was for elementary school teachers. The National Education Association estimated that there was a shortage of 57,000 elementary school teachers. This estimate, however, is based on the number needed to reduce "teacher load" and to replace half of the emergency teachers, as well as to meet increased enrollment and to replace retiring teachers.

It has been estimated that all but two states were short of qualified elementary teachers for rural schools in the fall of 1952, and that all but five states were short of elementary teachers for urban schools. More states reported shortages for both rural and urban schools in 1952 than in the preceding year.

Other means of judging the adequacy of the supply yield different results. As has been seen, the number of emergency teachers is one index to the shortage of qualified teachers. Before World War II, less than three-tenths of one percent of all teachers held emergency certificates, but the estimated 64,000 emergency teachers in the fall of 1952 comprised about 6 percent of the total. Part of this increase, however, reflects the raising of certification requirements during the last decade. Moreover, the number of emergency teachers has declined steadily since 1948, at first rapidly and then more slowly. In 1951 and again in 1952, the number decreased by about 6,000, in spite of the shortage of new qualified teachers in those years. This improvement apparently occurred because many teachers hired with emergency certificates later completed the requirements for regular licenses.

Still another shortage index is the number of children deprived of a full school-day because teachers must be used to teach double sessions. It is estimated that the number of children attending short sessions increased by about 100,000 between 1951 and 1952. Even so, only about 2½ percent of all school children were attending short sessions, most of them because of classroom rather than teacher shortages.

From all of the efforts to estimate the size of the teacher shortage, three facts stand out quite clearly: there are not as many qualified teachers as school officials would like to hire; the shortage is more serious in rural than in urban areas; and it is confined, for the most part, to the elementary schools.

Part of the shortage of elementary teachers is accounted for by rapid and substantial changes in elementary and high school enrollment which are the result of the fluctuation of the birth rate during the last two decades. Preliminary estimates indicate that public elementary school enrollment was about a million higher in the fall of 1952 than in the preceding year. The U.S. Office of Education predicts that by the fall of 1955, elementary enrollment will be 5 million above the level of the fall of 1951. On the other hand, the increase in high school enrollment from the fall of 1951 to the fall of 1952—the first in over ten years—was less than 100,000.

The demand for elementary school teachers, consequently, is far greater than the demand for high school teachers. Incomplete data indicate that twice as many new elementary teachers as high school teachers were hired in 1952. The difference would have been even greater had more qualified elementary teachers been available. Training, however, has not paralleled these developments. The same study (*Teacher Supply and Demand in the United States*, National Education Association, 1952) showed that three high school teachers were being trained for every two grammar school teachers, and that the number of newly qualified high school teachers was a third greater than the number of job openings. The surplus of high school teachers does not offset the shortage of elementary teachers because there are two separate markets resulting from the different certification requirements for each group.

To the extent that it is the result of sudden and substantial changes in the birth-rate trend, this type of imbalance will correct itself within a few years. By 1954, the children born in the early 1940's will begin to enter high school. After 1955, barring another major change in the birth-rate trend, the high-school-age population will begin to expand at a rate more nearly equal to that of the elementary school population.

The recent changes in the birth rate, however, may have a more lasting effect on teacher shortages than the creation of a temporary imbalance between the demand for elementary and for high school teachers. From the beginning of the nineteenth century, the birth rate declined steadily. As a result, the school-age population did not increase as rapidly as the population as a whole. Between 1870 and 1950, the population in the age group of five through seventeen fell from over 30 percent to barely 20 percent of the total. The long-term decline of the birth rate, however, was halted in 1933. Since 1940 there has been a substantial increase, and it now appears that the school-age population will grow at least as fast as the rest of the population in the immediate future. Unless communities adjust their support correspondingly, the shortages resulting from the rapid growth in the school-age population may become chronic.

While the demand for elementary teachers has been increasing, the supply has been curtailed by prosperity, high employment, and inflation. Teachers' salaries have increased less rapidly than the earnings of the rest of the labor force. High employment has made attractive jobs with industry and government available to both women and men. As the desire for security and "job insurance" becomes less urgent, relatively fewer students undertake teacher training. Twenty-one states reported that enrollment in teachers' colleges in the fall of 1952 was less than or about the same as in 1940-41, when the demand for teachers was much smaller. Moreover, many persons who qualify for teaching certificates never teach. The outflow from the profession becomes even larger when attractive non-teaching jobs are abundant. The National Education Association forecasts that almost 700,-000 teachers, roughly 70 percent of the number of teachers in 1950, will leave the profession between 1950 and 1960, and there are indications that this is a low estimate. Rural schools are hit particularly hard by these developments because their teachers, whose salaries are generally below the national average for teachers, leave for higher-paid city school jobs as well as non-teaching occupations.

It should be noted that a good portion of the high school teacher surplus mentioned above is more apparent than real. Certification requirements in most states require considerably less pedagogical training for high school teachers than for elementary teachers. Consequently, those college students who look upon a teaching certificate as a form of "job insurance" are more likely to prepare for high school than for elementary school teaching. Because they have taken a few education courses, they are counted as qualified teachers. Yet, at present high employment levels, the schools have little chance of attracting them into teaching jobs. Even though high school enrollment is still below the 1940 level, eighteen states reported a general shortage of high school teachers for rural schools in the fall of 1952. Only six states, however, had a shortage for urban high schools. Teachers of some subjects, including mathematics, natural sciences, and home economics, were short in most states. In other subjects, such as English and the social sciences, there were substantial surpluses.

In light of the impact of increased enrollment on demand, and of economic conditions on supply, it is perhaps surprising that the shortage of teachers is no greater than it is. This, however, is no reason for complacency. Every community can get enough teachers by compromising its standards of quality. The crucial question, therefore, always concerns quality rather than quantity. From this viewpoint, there are indications of basic deficiencies. Inadequate salaries in periods of high employment and very slight chances of earning a large income at any time deter bright students from entering the profession. Most Americans appear unwilling to sacrifice good salaries in prosperous periods for a job which offers security in bad times. Men, especially, are discouraged from entering a career which requires college training but offers little chance for earnings possible in other professions and in business. In 1870, two-fifths of the teachers were men, but since 1910, men have been about one-fifth of the teachers. The predominance of women, who frequently do not regard teaching as a career, aggravates the problem of high turnover in the profession. The predominance of less able students in teachers' colleges and among education majors in other colleges makes it difficult to maintain high standards in elementary school training. In turn, low standards attract poor students and add to the unwillingness of bright students to prepare for elementary school teaching. In the light of these circumstances some of the improvement in the quality of elementary school teachers which is implied by increases in their formal preparation and in certification requirements must be discounted.

REMEDIES FOR SHORTAGES

The value of various plans to alleviate teacher shortages must be judged by the extent to which they eliminate the basic causes of shortages. The attempt to alleviate the present shortage of elementary school teachers has resulted in strong reliance on stopgap measures which have little effect on basic causes. In addition to issuing emergency teaching certificates, communities have attempted to increase the number of students in teacher training through Future Teacher of America Clubs and other devices. Although over 75 percent of all students majoring in education, including almost 100 percent of all students in teachers' colleges, are enrolled in colleges which are already subsidized by state funds, many states are increasing their subsidies in order to attract more high school students. Tuition and room and board fees have been reduced at state teachers' colleges, and at least seventeen states have recently begun to award special scholarships to students of teaching. Some communities have used newspaper and radio advertisements to urge former teachers to return to teaching.

To make elementary school teaching more attractive, over 90 percent of all city school systems now provide equal pay for teachers with the same amount of collegiate preparation regardless of the level of school taught. At least sixteen states have approved programs to retrain high school teaching candidates for elementary school positions. In a few states, liberal arts graduates may also qualify under these programs. The retraining varies in length from a few months to about a year, and in many cases temporary teaching certificates are granted after very short periods of study.

These measures do no more than touch the surface of the problem. While a few more teachers may be secured through a large increase in the number of college students majoring in education, there is no assurance that many of the new teaching graduates will elect to teach if better jobs are available. Few former teachers currently employed in higher paying jobs will leave them in response to advertising appeals. Many retired teachers are too old or are out of touch with new teaching developments. Single salary schedules raise elementary salaries to the high school level, but they do not significantly lift the generally low salary level of the profession. Conversion programs temporarily sidestep, rather than reduce or eliminate, the barriers between elementary and secondary teacher markets. These measures do not correct any of the major causes of shortages such as the weak career incentives offered by the teaching profession or the weak curricula for teaching preparation.

Some efforts have been made, however, to eliminate the basic causes of qualified teacher shortages. At least thirty-nine states now have reciprocity agreements, usually on a regional basis, which are intended to reduce the barriers to the movement of teachers across state lines. Thus, they would facilitate the movement of some of Michigan's surplus teachers into Indiana or Illinois which do not have enough qualified teachers. On the theory that highly specialized training programs for elementary and high school teachers do not provide better teachers, dual certification programs and single preparatory curricula have been adopted in at least two states. These programs will provide greater flexibility in meeting changes in the relative demands for elementary and high school teachers.

There is also a trend toward greater state and Federal aid for local school systems, which reduces the inflexibility of school budgets based on local taxes. One of the major causes of teacher shortages may be reduced if this aid can be used to raise teachers' salaries. It is equally important to make salaries more responsive to changing economic conditions and to provide a higher ceiling on earnings as well as higher average earnings. If a better salary structure induces more men to become teachers, personnel turnover will be reduced. Turnover is also dependent, however, on other aspects of the teacher's job. So far, educational administrators have shown little interest in discovering and attacking the circumstances which are responsible for the loss of at least 10 percent of the nation's experienced teachers each year.

In the attempt to enhance the quality of their teachers, many states are increasing their requirements for elementary teaching certificates to include a bachelor's degree or even five years of college preparation. Higher standards in teachers' colleges and in the education departments of other colleges will also help to improve the quality of teachers. More careful screening of entrants, and better vocational guidance, could help to raise the proportion of education majors who have a firm interest in teaching as a career. This would reduce the large investment now made by many states in the training of students who are not really interested in teaching.

Most of these measures will be unable to raise both the quantity and quality of the nation's teachers unless they are undertaken simultaneously. Thus, increased certification requirements will result in the substitution of emergency teachers for certified teachers in communities which persist in offering low salaries. Moreover, salary increases must more than offset increases in academic requirements to enable the schools to attract more well-trained persons. Similarly, reciprocity agreements will only increase shortages in low salary states, such as Georgia, if teachers are attracted by higher salaries in neighboring states, such as Florida. Before teachers' colleges can hope to raise their standards, the profession must be made attractive to better students. Although few of the other measures to reduce teacher shortages will be effective without an improvement in the salary structure, salary increases alone cannot be relied upon to raise both the quantity and quality of teachers.

The simultaneous introduction of a number of adjustments will be necessary to relieve the major causes of teacher shortages. The complexity of the remedies reflects the complexity of the problem of shortages and emphasizes the fact that the necessary adjustments are long-term in nature.

CHAPTER XI

Physicians

I_T IS WIDELY BELIEVED_ that for some time there has been a shortage of physicians in the United States. Almost everyone concerned with the problem recognizes that there are inadequate numbers of physicians in certain areas and perhaps in certain fields of specialization. Some believe that these specific shortages can best be relieved by increasing the total number of physicians. Others are not especially concerned about the total number of physicians, but emphasize their redistribution. These diverse conclusions are based on the same body of evidence, but different experts are impressed by different sets of facts or interpret the same facts differently. This chapter examines the evidence, the assumptions underlying the various interpretations of the evidence, and the major policy implications growing out of these interpretations.

THE SUPPLY OF PHYSICIANS

Physicians are more readily identifiable than many other professionals and can therefore be counted more accurately. The length and basic content of the medical school curriculum have become standardized as a result of the reform of medical education which began early in the century. Since no one can practice medicine without a license, since no one who has not graduated from an approved medical school can obtain a license, and since

220   SCIENTIFIC AND PROFESSIONAL MANPOWER

almost all medical graduates obtain licenses and remain active in the profession during their working lifetimes, estimates of the current number of physicians are highly reliable.

At the end of 1952, there were approximately 214,000 physicians in the United States. This figure is based on the 201,300 physicians in the continental United States in 1949 who are listed in the 1950 Directory of the American Medical Association, and the estimated gains between 1949 and 1952. The following table indicates recent changes in the employment of physicians.

Table 14. Employment of Physicians, 1938 and 1949[a]

Status	1938	1949	Increase
Private practice	137,700	150,400	12,700
Hospital service and others not in private practice	19,200	28,700	9,500
Federal service	4,400	12,500	8,100
Total active	161,300	191,600	30,300
Retired and not practicing	8,300	9,700	1,400
Total	169,600	201,300	31,700

a Source: Frank G. Dickinson and Charles E. Bradley, "Comparisons of State Physician-Population Ratios for 1938 to 1949," Bulletin 78, Bureau of Medical Economic Research, American Medical Association, 1950.

In 1949, three-fourths of all physicians were in private practice. During the preceding eleven years, however, the number in private practice increased far less rapidly than the number in Federal service, or in hospital service and other non-private practice. The latter category includes interns and residents; full-time teachers in medical schools; physicians engaged in research; employees of insurance companies and other business and professional organizations; and full-time health officers for local and state governments. It is estimated that the number of residents undertaking advanced training increased from approximately 3,000 in 1938 to about 14,000 in 1949.

One of the most noteworthy developments has been the trend toward specialization. In 1923, 15,400 physicians, or 11 percent of the total, limited their practice to a specialty; by 1938, the number had increased to 33,600, or 20 percent of the total; by 1949, it was 62,700, or 31 percent of the total. The trend toward specialization has been even more marked among physicians in private practice. The number of general practitioners and physicians not limiting themselves to a specialty in private practice actually declined from 109,700 to 95,500 between 1938 and 1949.

The supply of doctors is usually stated in terms of the ratio of physicians to population. The use of this ratio as an indication of the relative adequacy of the supply of doctors in particular localities has limited validity. The size of the population is not an accurate measure of the need for doctors in any particular locality. Patients frequently seek medical care in nearby communities. As the size of the area in question increases, this criticism loses force, since few individuals travel great distances for physicians' services. Nevertheless, the metropolitan areas, as well as certain other localities where comprehensive hospital facilities and large numbers of specialists are found, attract many patients from other areas. The amount and kinds of medical care which a community needs and seeks also vary, depending on such factors as the income, education, age, birth rate, cultural background, housing, environmental sanitation, and occupation of the residents, and even the climate.

The number of doctors in a locality does not measure the amount of medical care provided any better than the size of the population measures the care needed. Differences which may exist among states or regions in the quality of physicians cannot be measured. Fortunately, the marked improvement in medical education means that doctors in all localities have at least adequate scientific training. The amount of care provided by each doctor also depends on prevailing patterns of doctor utilization, which is influenced in turn by the age of doctors, the amount of time they spend in traveling between patients, the length of their usual work week, the character of nearby hospital facilities, and the supply of auxiliary medical workers such as nurses and technicians. The physician to population ratio is used here only because there is no superior measure of the supply of doctors.

Over the last thirty years the number of doctors and the population of the United States have expanded at almost the same rate. The ratio of doctors to population is now about what it was in 1920, though somewhat higher than in either 1930 or 1940. In 1949, the ratio for the United States as a whole was 121 active doctors per 100,000 population. This ratio excludes doctors who were employed by the Federal government. Figure 5 shows the ratio by states. In Mississippi, there were only 64 doctors per 100,000 population, while in New York there were 196. Differences of approximately the same magnitude have persisted for some time. They reflect the fact that there are generally fewer doctors in rural areas, in low-income regions, and in areas which have few or no medical schools and medical centers, as well as a host of other factors. The scattered pattern of the map indicates both the variety of factors influencing the ratios in different states, and the limits of ratios as measures of the adequacy of medical care. Some tendency for the highly industrialized states to have higher ratios is apparent, but there is no clear pattern based on region, income levels, or other economic differences.

Unlike the future supply of most other professional groups, the number of doctors in the United States some years from now may be predicted with reasonable accuracy. Because of licensing requirements, additions to the supply will consist almost entirely of the graduates of American medical schools, plus a small number trained abroad. Since the number of applicants for admission to medical school will undoubtedly exceed the capacity of the schools in the near future as it has in the past, the number of new doctors will depend almost entirely on the capacity of the medical schools. As a result of the high cost of expanding medical training facilities, and the necessity for maintaining the quality of medical training, the rate of expansion of the schools is not likely to increase suddenly in the next few years.

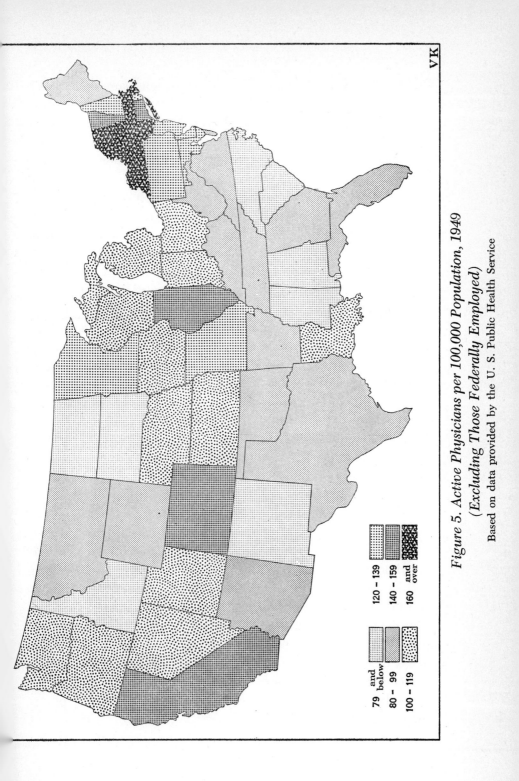

Figure 5. Active Physicians per 100,000 Population, 1949
(Excluding Those Federally Employed)
Based on data provided by the U. S. Public Health Service

79 and below

80 – 99

100 – 119

120 – 139

140 – 159

160 and over

Finally, because medical training takes so long, any unexpected change in the capacity of the schools will not be reflected in the number of new doctors until after 1960. In short, the number of new doctors during the rest of this decade can be estimated with fair accuracy. Moreover, since doctors seldom leave the profession except when they retire or die, the percentage of the present supply that will still be active in 1960 can also be predicted. It was estimated in 1949 that there would be about 215,000 active physicians in 1960, a net gain of almost 25,000.

REQUIREMENTS FOR PHYSICIANS

During the last decade several agencies of the Federal government have estimated the nation's requirements for doctors. Each estimate relates to some date five or ten years in the future, usually 1960. No statistical attempt has been made to evaluate the extent to which the available supply of physicians is adequate to meet the current needs of the public. The various estimates of requirements for and availability of physicians in 1960 indicate shortages ranging from 17,000 to 45,000 physicians. Recently, the President's Commission on the Health Needs of the Nation estimated that the supply of physicians would be from 22,000 to 45,000 short of requirements in 1960. The size of the estimated shortage depends largely on two factors: the estimated size of the population in 1960, and the criterion selected to measure physician requirements.

The difficulties of predicting the size of the population are well known. Estimates prepared in 1948 assumed a probable population of 158 million in 1960 and a maximum of 162 million. In 1951, however, one population authority predicted that the 1960 population would number no less than 161 million and no more than 180 million. The President's Commission on the Health Needs of the Nation estimated that the 1960 population would be 171 million. Far more formidable difficulties are involved in establishing the requirements of any given population for physicians.

Discussion of requirements for physicians is complicated by the fact that the ability of the patient to pay for medical care is not usually accepted as the criterion of the amount of care he should receive. There is a tradition that an individual should receive the medical services that he needs. The concept of need is different from demand in two respects. It ignores the individual's ability to pay for doctors' services, and it assumes that he appreciates and actively seeks the benefits of medical care. Most recent estimates of need for physicians have drawn on the pioneer work of Roger I. Lee and Lewis W. Jones in 1931 for the Commission on the Cost of Medical Care. They defined the need for medical care "in terms of the physical conditions of the people and the capacities of the science and art of medicine to deal with them. Thus, it is not always a conscious need, still less an active desire backed by willingness to pay." Drawing on good prevailing medical practice, their aim was to develop a conservative and reasonable standard of required services which members of the medical profession would accept.

Their estimates drew on the best available information on the incidence of diseases and injuries. They then estimated the number of physician-hours required for the prevention, diagnosis, and treatment of each major disease and injury category. Requirements in physician-hours were converted into requirements for physicians by assuming that doctors spend on the average 2,000 hours a year caring for patients. It was concluded that 135 physicians per 100,000 population were required for the individual care of patients.

The validity of the Lee-Jones method is subject to question at every step. Adequate basic data on the incidence of disease and injury are not available. Even if they were, there is no known technique for translating disease incidence into physician-hour requirements. The problem is complicated by constant changes in the incidence of disease and injury and in methods of patient care. The translation of requirements for physician-hours into requirements for physicians entails further difficulties. The number of hours a year a physician can be expected to devote to patient care has been estimated at 2,000 by those who use the Lee and Jones formula, at 1,440 by the report of the New York State Legislative Commission on Medical Care in 1946, and at 1,200 by others.

Even if these essentially technical problems were solved, it is doubtful whether a community's need for physicians' services can be ascertained independently of its level of economic development and of its needs for other types of goods and services. No community can afford all the goods and services it desires. Ours is a world in which most goods and services can be produced only by utilizing scarce resources. It is always necessary, therefore, to consider the conflicting claims of such diverse objects of expenditure as housing, nutrition, clothing, and education, as well as of medical care.

Even if costs were no obstacle, further problems would remain. The amount of medical care which individuals and groups purchase depends, not only on their ability to pay for various goods and services, but also on their knowledge and evaluation of the benefits of doctors' services. Certain groups rely more on physicians and derive considerable emotional support from them, while others with the same income are much less likely to call upon a doctor unless they are seriously ill. Some groups prefer the services of osteopaths. In many parts of the country, chiropractors, nature healers, religious practitioners, and others are frequently called upon in place of licensed physicians to treat illness. This raises the question of whether need for medical care can be appraised realistically except within rather localized social and cultural contexts.

As Lee and Jones understood, calculating requirements for physicians according to the standard of need involves an implicit commitment that a given volume of physicians' services will be financed in some way. In short, even if the predicted shortage is accepted as valid, the remedy must consist of far more than the indicated increase in the supply of doctors. It is also necessary to insure that the "needed" volume of medical care will be demanded and paid for.

Other methods for calculating requirements are based, not on need, but on physician to population ratios reflecting existing conditions. One approach is to assume that the whole country should have as high a ratio as now exists in some selected group of states or localities, such as the twelve states with the largest number of doctors in relation to population. This method of estimating requirements, as well as any of the many variant methods, inevitably yields a shortage of physicians. If one calculated shortage is made good, another will take its place as long as states or localities have different physician to population ratios. Indeed, as the national ratio rises, absolute differences among state ratios may well increase, resulting in an increase in the calculated shortage.

This method may also be questioned on the ground that there is no good reason to assume that the areas selected to provide the standard have just the "right" ratio of doctors to population. Nor is there any reason to assume that the right ratio for one state is right for another. Like the method based on need, this procedure ignores differences in the economic resources of communities, in their needs and desires for other goods and services, and in their knowledge of and attitudes toward the benefits of medical care.

Another use of the physician to population ratio to determine future requirements assumes that the number of doctors should be large enough to maintain the national ratio in a selected base year, and to make up well-defined deficiencies in the existing supply as well as to cover any important new requirements likely to develop in the future. This method assumes that people will continue to require about the same amount of physicians' time as they do in the base year. In this connection, it is worth stressing that individuals require a definite amount of medical care only in certain instances, such as serious injury or major illness. At other times the amount of medical care that is sought depends on the anxiety of the patient, the attitude of the physician, and the play of economic conditions. In wartime the patient recognizes that he is entitled to less service and is more cooperative. At such times, many retired physicians return to practice and most physicians work longer hours, spend less time per patient and insist upon office visits whenever possible. The experience during World War II, when the Armed Forces had as many as 60,000 physicians on active duty at one time, or approximately one-third of all active physicians, suggests that these factors are significant for planning for a period of mobilization.

ECONOMIC ANALYSES OF PHYSICIAN SUPPLY

Some economists who have applied their techniques to the study of medical care have concluded that there is a substantial shortage of physicians. One expert has found signs of an impending surplus.

Much of the discussion has centered around the perennial surplus of applicants for medical schools. The annual number of applicants ranged between 16,800 and 24,500 between 1948 and 1952, while the number accepted did not exceed 7,700. Many of those who are rejected by the schools possess the qualifications required for a successful medical career. To some economists, these facts are prima facie evidence of a shortage of physicians in the sense that there are barriers to the training of qualified applicants.

This conviction is reinforced by evidence of the high earnings of physicians. In 1951, according to a survey by *Medical Economics,* the median net income before taxes of doctors in private practice was over $13,000. This compares, for instance, with a median net income of about $8,000 for physicists with doctoral degrees employed by private industry. The average net income of physicians increased by two-thirds between 1943 and 1951. General practitioners gained much more than specialists. Their average net income more than doubled between 1943 and 1951 and increased by almost half between 1947 and 1951. The relatively high earnings of doctors, even when the length of their training and the great demands made on them are taken into account, indicates, according to this type of analysis, that the supply of physicians' services is not in balance with the community's demand for their services.

This analysis, however, has been challenged on a number of grounds. In the first place, the demand for medical training cannot be measured entirely in terms of the number of applicants for admission to medical schools. Only a part of the very high cost of training a doctor is borne by the student. The rest is paid for through some form of subsidy. Consequently, the demand for training is reflected partly by the willingness of individuals, and partly by the willingness of society to bear the costs. It may be argued that communities should be educated to understand the need for more doctors and to increase their contribution to the cost of expanding medical training, but it has also been argued that many communities would not be willing to undertake such expansion if they were aware of the true costs.

Moreover, the problem of expanding the medical schools is complicated by the scarcity of competent teachers and of clinical material, as well as of funds. These considerations are crucial because of the necessity for maintaining the quality of medical training. Some have cautioned that the quality of medical training may be impaired at a relatively early point in the expansion of medical schools. The problem is probably not insurmountable, simply because no single problem is insurmountable in a wealthy country in which conflicting policy views are reconciled by discussion and compromise. It is, nevertheless, extremely difficult to provide for any sudden large-scale increase in the number of physicians without jeopardizing the quality of their training.

The conclusion that the high average earnings of doctors indicate a shortage has also been questioned. Their incomes reflect in part the high demands made on them, including a longer average period of training than is required for any other profession, especially if the doctor is a specialist; long and uncertain hours; great responsibility and nervous strain; and the element of individuality which is inherent in this type of personal service.

Some medical authorities have also warned against the dangers that may result from jeopardizing the accustomed earnings of doctors through a large increase in their number and consequently increased competition for patients. Physicians are in a position to modify the amounts and types of medical services they prescribe for patients in terms of their own requirements for income to maintain a customary level of living.

Other economists conclude that there is a shortage of physicians because of the fact that certain indices of economic growth, such as national income, total consumer expenditures for medical care, the number of college graduates, or the number of professional persons, have increased much more rapidly than the number of physicians. One economist has suggested that the country could easily afford and make good use of 400,000 doctors by 1960. It has been pointed out in rebuttal that in recent years the ratio of physicians to population has been rising, although slowly. Between 1940 and 1950, the number of physicians increased 17 percent, while the population increased 14.5 percent. The annual production of new physicians is increasing as new schools are opened, two-year schools are converted to four-year schools, and existing schools expand enrollments. Enrollment of undergraduates in medical schools rose from 21,400 in 1940-41 to 27,100 in 1951-52, or 27 percent. Moreover, the ratio of physicians to population in the United States is already higher than in any other major industrial country.

The argument that the number of doctors has increased less rapidly than certain other indices of growth is essentially an argument that the number of doctors should bear some fixed relation to these factors. As we have seen, however, the health of the nation depends on many considerations besides the amount and quality of medical care. Nor does the amount and quality of medical care depend exclusively on the number of doctors. The effectiveness of the care provided by each doctor has increased greatly since the time of the medical diploma mill, forty or fifty years ago. Except for professional nurses, trainèd personnel acting as assistants to physicians are increasing rapidly. According to a recent report by the Brookings Institution, they increased by more than 70 percent between 1940 and 1950.

One expert in medical economics has even suggested that the slowly increasing ratio of doctors to population, and the increasing effectiveness of the care which each doctor can provide per hour of work may well presage a surplus of physicians by 1960. Increases in physicians' productivity can be ascribed to other developments in addition to improvements in medical education and the great increase in the number of auxiliary medical personnel. The development of the antibiotics and other highly effective drugs has materially reduced the time needed to cure a number of serious illnesses, and greatly reduced the incidence of others. Improved transportation has reduced the travel time of physicians, but the largest part of this gain probably occurred before 1940. The large increase that has taken place in the treatment of patients in hospitals in recent years results to some extent in the more efficient use of physicians' time.

On the other hand, some of the increase in the amount of effective care per hour that can be provided by each physician is balanced by new demands. Thus, some of the work performed by assistants, particularly in hospitals, is new work required and made possible by improved diagnostic techniques. Part of the increased use of hospitals represents a new demand for medical care. As medical knowledge advances and medical care can accomplish more, people like to obtain more of it, and do, if they can pay for it. Although there is no concrete quantitative evidence, it is probable that the demand for medical care by individuals has been rising. Certainly all the factors favorable to an increased demand have been present, such as the growth of medical insurance, national prosperity, medical advances, and a rising health consciousness on the part of the people. In short, while there is no doubt that each doctor can provide more effective care per hour than he once could, there is no way to determine whether the demand has increased equally with, or more or less than this gain in physicians' productivity.

OTHER CRITERIA OF A PHYSICIAN SHORTAGE

The course of the discussion up to this point suggests that there is no simple and direct way of determining whether the country faces a shortage of physicians; or what the magnitude of such a shortage, if any, is or will be. The statistical analyses of requirements and supply that have been attempted are subject to serious question, largely because there is no clear-cut standard of how much medical care the country requires, and because ways of using doctors vary greatly from place to place and are constantly changing. The economic analyses of physicians' earnings and productivity are likewise inconclusive.

This does not mean that these estimates and analyses are irrelevant, but rather that these approaches must be supplemented by other kinds of evidence which have not yet been considered except in passing. It means also that no precise, indisputable conclusion about a physician shortage is possible, and that conclusions must be based on the burden of a great many different kinds of evidence.

The existence, on a large scale, of preventable health deficiencies among the population is frequently cited as evidence of a shortage of physicians. Draft rejections during World War II called attention to the large number of young men with some form of health defect. Roughly one-fourth of all men examined were rejected because of some medical deficiency. The relevance of this fact, however, is open to question. The diagnosis of mental diseases was notoriously inaccurate. Many physical shortcomings which disqualified men for military service were relatively minor and were not hindrances to a satisfactory adjustment in civilian life. Finally, there is no way of knowing how many of the rejections were the result of inadequate medical care, and how many were the result of other factors, such as poor diet, ignorance of elementary hygiene measures, accidental injury, or inherited defects. While the draft rejection figures undoubtedly indicate considerable room for improvement in the medical care of the nation, they provide no basis for a quantitative estimate of the adequacy of medical care.

It has also been pointed out that there are over 300,000 preventable deaths a year in the United States. This figure, however, includes all accidental deaths as well as those caused by disease. An increasing proportion of the preventable deaths, moreover, are preventable only for short periods and at very high costs to the patient, his family, and society. Thus, the life of the patient with advanced cancer may be prolonged for a few months by modern surgical techniques, or that of the patient suffering from the degenerative diseases of old age by constant medical attention and the use of expensive drugs. Because of the increasing proportion of deaths which are a result of such diseases, or of accidents, the opportunities for a further reduction of the death rate through more and better medical care are constantly decreasing. New medical knowledge, of course, could improve the opportunities for important gains in postponing death.

Another kind of evidence to support the claim of a shortage of physicians is the fact that doctors in general are badly overworked. One recent survey showed that the work week of general practitioners averages sixty-two hours. Doctors are harassed by day and frequently unavailable for emergency or night calls. The difficulty in many areas in obtaining a doctor at night or on week ends reflects primarily the increasing desire of doctors for a regular schedule, rather than a shortage of doctors. Yet, it may not be irrelevant to note that because of the abundance of patients, doctors can now afford the financial cost of refusing to be on twenty-four-hour call.

There is widespread agreement that there are too few doctors in many rural areas. The effects of the lower ratio of doctors to population in these areas are aggravated by the longer distances which the rural doctors must travel, and the generally higher age of rural doctors which means that they are, on the average, less active than urban doctors. The actual number of doctors in some rural areas has declined in recent years, as doctors who have died or left the area have not been replaced. Some communities are without a physician and without ready access to one. These conditions are offset to some extent by improved transportation and the declining size of the rural population. There is no question, however, that medical care is inadequate in many rural localities.

Other kinds of specific shortages are also widely recognized. Generally, there is great difficulty in filling salaried medical posts, such as those in public health departments and state hospitals. One expert has declared that there are shortages of doctors for teaching, medical administration, public health, industrial medicine, pathology, radiology, psychiatry, and pediatrics. Each of these shortages, while limited to a specific field of medical practice, may have widespread consequences. Thus, the shortage of teachers is one of the major limitations on any expansion of the capacity of the medical schools. The shortage of administrators may well impede efforts to utilize doctors' services more efficiently. The shortage of doctors for public health and industrial medicine limits advances in the application of preventive medicine which might ultimately reduce the amount of care required for treating illness. It is well known that adequate psychiatric care is generally available only to the upper income groups. The major limitation on medical research today is a shortage, not of research funds, but of trained and experienced medical scientists.

Recent increases in the average earnings of doctors, while not conclusive proof of a shortage, are a clear indication that the demand for the services of doctors has increased substantially. The average income of physicians increased at the same rate as that of all employed persons between 1929 and 1949, and at a considerably faster rate since 1949. These gains have been made at the same time that the number of physicians has been slowly increasing. They reflect the fact that physicians work

longer hours, make better use of their time, charge higher fees
and collect a higher percentage of their bills.

FUTURE DEMAND FOR PHYSICIANS

Because it takes so many years to train a physician, any
analysis of the desirability of increasing the supply of doctors
must consider the future, as well as the present, demand for their
services.

One of the main reasons for the present high level of demand
is that prosperity has produced a rapid increase in expenditures
for medical care. A depression would undoubtedly reduce expenditures to some extent. However, once people become accustomed to and are educated to appreciate the benefits of medical
care, they tend to sacrifice other expenditures, if necessary, to
maintain their purchases of medical services. A depression, therefore, would probably cause a smaller decline in medical than in
many other consumers' expenditures. The decline in medical
services received would be even smaller, since free services and
services provided by government would be increased.

The long-term increase in the amount of medical care received
by the population is also the result of advances in medicine. As
doctors learn to do more, people increase their demands for
services. Many new services, moreover, are of increasing complexity and take more physicians' time. On the other hand,
because medical progress reduces the incidence of some illnesses
and reduces the time needed to cure others, the net effect on requirements for doctors is difficult to forecast. There is no ground
for believing, however, that new medical knowledge will significantly reduce the need for doctors in the near future.

A number of other developments may also influence future
demand. Periodic physical examinations for all persons of thirty-
five years of age or over would require, at least for the immediate
future, approximately 40,000 additional physicians. However,
there is no agreement among physicians regarding the relative
value of such examinations and their priority in a medical care

program. The gradual growth of medical pre-payment plans will probably increase somewhat the demand for physicians' services. The population of the United States is growing at a rate considerably faster than anticipated even five years ago. This development has a double impact upon physician requirements. In addition to the larger number of people requiring care, it leads to high demands for obstetrical and pediatric services.

The increasing number of older people in the population may also affect the demand for doctors. It is generally believed that older people use more than an average amount of physicians' services, although data published by the Health Insurance Plan of New York indicate that this has not been their experience. It should be noted, however, that the number of older doctors is also increasing. Consequently, some of the recent and expected gains in the number of doctors are counterbalanced by the inability of older physicians to work as long and as hard as younger men.

The military demand for doctors must also be taken into account. In 1949, there were 7,000 physicians in the armed forces; today, there are 13,000. The number varies with the number of men in service, and with the authorized physician to troop ratio. Since World War II, the number of doctors in service per 100,000 men has been reduced from about 600 to about 350, a ratio still nearly three times as high as the average for the civilian population. The number of doctors required to care for a given number of men in service depends, of course, upon both the efficiency with which the services use doctors and the extent to which the armed forces are engaged in active combat. Full mobilization would greatly increase requirements of the armed forces for doctors. All of these considerations seem to point to a continuing high level of demand for the services of physicians.

PROBLEMS OF POLICY

Medical care is only one of many factors upon which the health of the nation depends. The adequacy of medical care, moreover, is determined by far more than the number of doctors. The number and complexity of relevant factors are so great that there is little possibility of proving that the health needs of the country require or do not require an increase in the number of physicians, and even less possibility of determining the precise size of any required change.

Nevertheless, the burden of the evidence seems to point clearly to certain conclusions. There is no question that important health deficiencies could be reduced if some large groups in the population received more adequate medical care. It also seems clear that the present level of medical care is achieved at the cost of exceedingly long hours and hard work by many doctors. The total number of physician-hours of care is probably approaching the maximum possible, which means that the volume of services which physicians provide can be increased—short of changes in utilization patterns—only by increasing their number.

It is very likely that the present high demand for doctors' services will continue for some time. In spite of the recent expansion in the capacity of the medical schools, moreover, it is probable that, at least until 1960, the expansion of the population will keep pace with the increase in the number of doctors. Since the capacity of the medical schools is by far the major determinant of the number of new doctors, one method of increasing the adequacy of medical care and of relieving the current pressure on doctors is to increase the number and capacity of the schools.

Against this conclusion must be set the difficulty and the high cost of expanding medical training. Even if cost were no barrier, there are other important limits on the rate at which the schools can be expanded. To increase the number of doctors trained at the expense of the quality of training would be worse than useless. Good medical schools require competent teachers, who are already in very short supply in part because of the current high earnings of physicians in private practice.

Cost, however, is also an important obstacle. The universities which operate medical schools, like colleges and universities generally, are now under severe financial pressure because of rising costs and relatively stable incomes. The financial difficulties of some universities are in large part the direct result of the high costs of operating their medical schools. A substantial expansion of capacity requires a solution for this problem. Many states are increasing their appropriations for medical education. Proposals for substantial Federal subsidies have met with strong objection from parts of the medical profession, and from others, largely on the ground that Federal funds might lead to Federal control.

An increase in the total number of doctors would not automatically solve all of the serious shortage problems. Widely recognized shortages of physicians for specific functions are the result of a number of different circumstances. Shortages in rural areas are apparently the result of several characteristics of rural medical life which doctors find less attractive than practice in cities. Since the average income of rural doctors is almost as high as the average for all doctors, the problem is not essentially economic. Increasing the number of doctors with rural backgrounds and orientation might help. Positive incentives to attract new doctors to rural areas, such as are being tried in some states, may also be necessary.

Shortages of doctors for salaried positions, and particularly for government positions, are largely, though by no means entirely, an economic problem. Low salaries compared with earnings in private practice, combined with lack of professional prestige and unfavorable working conditions in many governmental medical programs, have long made it difficult to fill authorized positions in many state hospitals and public health departments. Temporary shortages of specialists in particular fields are inevitable as new fields are developed. Most of these shortages will probably disappear in time without special efforts. The shortage of pediatricians reflects the rapid increase in the number of births since 1940 as well as changing medical practices. Certain specific shortages would probably be easier to remedy if the total number of doctors were expanding more rapidly. Nevertheless, enlarging the number of doctors without also paying attention to the special circumstances underlying each kind of shortage would not eliminate shortages.

As has been noted, moreover, an increase in the number of physicians is only one of the many possible methods of improving medical care. It is equally important, for instance, to maintain and improve the quality of America's doctors. In this connection the residence limitations imposed by the large majority of medical schools operated by state governments are properly an object of concern. In spite of the overall surplus of qualified applicants, some medical schools in sparsely settled states, which restrict admissions to residents of the state, have difficulty in filling their classes with well-qualified candidates.

One of the essentials for the maintenance of high quality in medical practice is the development of means whereby the practicing physician may keep abreast of rapid changes in medical knowledge and methods. Hospital staff appointments and postgraduate teaching conferences are highly effective for this purpose.

In addition to the number and quality of doctors, the adequacy of medical care depends also on the ways in which the time of doctors is used. Since the number of graduates in any one year represents only 3 percent of the total number of physicians, utilization patterns are far more important than the size of graduating classes in determining the adequacy of medical care at any one time. Patterns of medical care are far too complex to permit systematic discussion in this chapter. The amount and effectiveness of care provided by any given number of physicians depend upon a host of influences, including the number, fields, and use made of specialists; the number and utilization of nurses, technicians, and other auxiliary personnel; the extent to which specific medical needs are met by home or hospital care; the attitudes of patients and doctors concerning the need for a doctor's care in particular circumstances; and the number of physicians withdrawn from civilian life for military duties.

At present about 13,000 doctors, or nearly 7 percent of the nation's total number, are on active military duty. Consequently, although the armed forces have recently made great progress in providing better medical care with relatively fewer doctors, continuing efforts to improve the utilization of doctors by the services are indicated.

One of the most promising opportunities for improving the utilization of physicians lies in the expanded use of various groups of auxiliary health personnel so that the physician can serve a larger number of people, while keeping the costs of his services within bounds.

Another way to improve the utilization of physicians has been suggested by the President's Commission on the Health Needs of the Nation. The Commission recommends that the limitations imposed upon the practice of certified specialists by the medical specialty boards should be reviewed. Pointing to the possibilities of a more flexible pattern of specialization, the Commission concludes that the scope and limitation of a specialist's professional services should be determined by the needs of the community in which he serves as well as by his professional capabilities.

The increasing tendency of doctors to work in conjunction with other doctors, through hospitals, health centers, and group practice clinics also promises more effective utilization. It usually permits a more efficient division of practice between specialists and general practitioners, helps the physician to keep up with new developments through constant contact with other doctors, and in many cases provides him with more and better equipment and auxiliary assistance than he could afford working alone.

A judgment about the level of medical care is not the same as a judgment about the number of doctors, for the number of physicians is only one factor determining the level of medical care. New patterns of medical practice that will result in the improved utilization of the available supply of physicians provide a major opportunity for raising the level of medical care. Nevertheless, although the number of doctors being trained is

already increasing slowly, the evidence points to the desirability
of a greater rate of increase. Great care must be taken, however,
to maintain and even further improve the quality of medical
training. Moreover, no foreseeable increase in the number of
graduates is likely by itself to solve some of the most serious types
of shortages such as currently exist in rural areas and in many
state hospitals. The successful solution of these problems requires
the combined efforts of the nation, the affected communities, and
the medical profession.

CHAPTER XII

Manpower Policies in a Democratic Society

Except in periods of crisis, manpower policies in a democratic society are everybody's business and nobody's business. Responsibility for the development and utilization of the society's human resources is widely distributed. No single agency, private or public, defines the society's manpower needs or decides on the best ways to meet them.

Every employer and trade union influences the use of manpower. Every community helps to educate and develop its citizens through the schools it maintains. Professional societies establish minimum standards of formal education and competence for their members. Each individual decides what kind of education and career he will pursue. The identification of individuals of unusual ability and talent, to the extent that this is done at all, occurs both within and outside the schools. Many governmental policies have far-reaching implications for the development and use of manpower resources.

MANPOWER POLICIES IN PEACE AND WAR

In times of peace the manpower objectives of a democratic society are not clearly defined and the ways in which they are attained are many and uncoordinated. The society hopes that it will develop and have available all the human skills and capacities it requires. While it does seek to provide the opportunity for each individual to develop his potentialities, it neither blueprints its manpower objectives nor does it formulate a grand design by which they can be realized. The result is that a democratic society normally does not establish specific manpower policies and that the development and utilization of its manpower result from the interplay of many forces, institutions, and social and individual decisions.

Under the pressure of war, however, manpower policies cannot be left so completely to the uncoordinated actions of individuals and groups. Responsibility for the training and use of military manpower is assumed by the national government with the result that the freedom of the individual to choose his education, career, and employment is temporarily restricted. Authority may even be vested in the government to control and direct non-military manpower. Manpower objectives, moreover, tend to be expressed in precise numerical terms and the measures for realizing them are carefully planned.

Today, the United States, as well as other democratic nations, faces an emergency situation which contains the elements of both war and peace. There is little in the nation's past experience which provides guidance for dealing with a crisis situation of undetermined length and intensity. Tested policies of past periods of war or peace are not directly applicable to present manpower problems, particularly those concerning the country's resources of scientific and professional personnel.

The present situation compels consideration not only of current manpower needs but also of long-range policies to provide the country with the highly trained manpower it will require in the future. In this consideration, the following questions are pertinent: What can be said about the nature of future demands? What lessons can be derived from past efforts to develop the supply of highly trained manpower? What sort of knowledge is essential to the making of sound policy? What American values and attitudes significantly affect those policies?

THE PROBLEM OF FUTURE DEMAND

At best, assertions about the future demand for manpower are informed guesses. The growth of scientific and professional groups has been irregular, and the projection of past trends of demand into the future provides a very uncertain guide. There is no way in a formal calculation of taking into account all the possible changes in the factors which could affect the future demand for any one group of scientists or professionals. The general, total demand for scientific and professional manpower, however, can be forecast with some confidence. It is safe to assume that, barring a catastrophe which would destroy the bases of Western civilization, the major factors which have been responsible for the very rapid growth of the professions and the sciences in recent years will continue to operate in the future. The rate of progress in science and technology will certainly not be slowed and will probably be accelerated. The gain in productivity, estimated at about 3 percent per year in recent decades, is not likely to be less in the near future. An expanding national income will result in a greater capacity to consume the services of professional personnel. A dynamic economy, high levels of employment, rising living standards, and the aspiration for improved health, education, and social security all point to the need for larger numbers of scientifically and professionally trained workers. In spite of the uncertainties which must qualify any judgment on the future, a long-run view clearly points to a continuing high level of demand for scientific and professional manpower.

In any shorter-run view of the years ahead, the questions of the level of employment and of a third world war are crucial. Although large scale unemployment would reduce the demand for the services of many scientists and professional persons, this development would probably be only temporary. The strategic position of scientists and technologists in modern production and their relatively small numbers suggest that the demand for their services might remain quite high. Short-run changes in employment levels, moreover, have to be seen in relation to the general development of the economy. The report of the President's Materials Policy Commission, *Resources for Freedom*, issued in 1952, observes that "economic history certainly records more underestimates of the future than overestimates. Depressions and recessions, historically viewed, become smaller episodes in a longer and more heroic tale. There is no reason to assume that the world which has been growing economically by leaps and bounds for many generations will suddenly become static in this generation."

Behind the measures of partial mobilization which have been adopted since Korea is the assumption that a continuation of the existing crisis in the relations between the free world and Soviet Russia and its satellites is more likely than the outbreak of a major war in the near future. At the same time, however, no one dares operate on the assumption that a major war is improbable. Should war break out, the demand for most scientists and technologists would expand still further.

The build-up of the military and economic strength of the United States and its allies and a posture of readiness against total war are seen as the foundation stones of long-term national security and peace. As long as the cold war exists, it will stimulate the demand for scientific and professional personnel. The technology of modern warfare requires large expenditures on research and development activities in virtually every conceivable field—in communications, health, nutrition, human behavior, meteorology, and history, as well as in weapons and military equipment. For such work, scientists and professionals from almost every field, in or out of uniform, are indispensable. No reasonable view of the proximate future permits the conclusion that a drastic cut in the demand for scientists and professional persons for defense work is likely.

These considerations reinforce the basic judgment that the overall demand for scientific and professional personnel will continue to be high. They do not, however, permit precise arithmetic estimates of the size of the demand for each group within that larger manpower category ten, fifteen, or twenty years from now. They do not even permit more than very rough guesses about which kinds of manpower are likely to be more important in the future. In the absence of much more precise knowledge or of willingness by a society to forego the fulfillment of certain goals in favor of others, attempts to rank manpower groups according to some hierarchy of importance are hardly feasible. A system of manpower allocation becomes practical when a country engaged in war is prepared to sacrifice certain objectives in order to survive.

THE ROLE OF GOVERNMENT

Although the adequacy and competence of the country's resources of scientific and professional manpower have become important questions of national policy only in recent years, the policies of Federal, state, and local governments have long influenced the supply and quality of highly trained personnel.

Immigration policy has a direct influence on the nation's resources of scientific and professional manpower. The laws of 1921 and 1924 which ended the era of unrestricted immigration treated persons trained as professionals differently from other immigrants. The racial and quota barriers of these laws did not apply to certain professional persons. If they had two years of professional experience and wished to continue their vocation in the United States they were freely admitted. While the McCarran-Walter Act of 1952 also contains special provisions governing professional persons, it is far more restrictive than the earlier legislation, and almost all professionals are subject to quota regulations.

The licensing of professional persons is a state function. State laws which make a license mandatory for professional practice have been enacted largely in response to the demands of organized professional groups. These laws restrict the supply of certain professional groups, but they also protect the public from improperly trained practitioners and contribute to raising professional standards and improving the educational institutions in which professional persons are trained. Most states have tended to adopt the standards for licensing proposed by professional societies.

Some licensing laws go beyond the protection of the public, however, in limiting the supply of certain professional groups. This can perhaps be most clearly seen in the provisions which affect aliens. Although immigration policy has facilitated the entrance of professionally trained persons to the United States, the states have made it difficult for immigrants to engage in some professional occupations. At the close of World War II, there were over 500 state laws which limited certain occupations to American citizens or to aliens who had filed their first papers. Today, almost thirty states bar aliens from the practice of medicine, while almost as many require full citizenship for the practice of law. Similar restrictions affect pharmacists, teachers, dentists, nurses, engineers, and still other professional persons. Thus, the influence of professional societies and nationalist sentiment has deprived the country of the skills and capacities of many highly trained aliens.

The major governmental influence upon the supply of scientific and professional manpower is the result of educational measures of various kinds. The creation of a national university was unsuccessfully championed by the country's first six presidents. The Federal government took its first step toward providing facilities for the education and training of certain kinds of personnel in founding the Military Academy at West Point in 1802. Annapolis was founded in 1845, and training facilities were later established for the Marine Corps, Coast Guard, U.S. Merchant Marine, and the Air Force. Other facilities are maintained by the Federal government for the advanced training of its employees. The U.S. Department of Agriculture Graduate School, which is open to all government employees, offers courses in economics, statistics, and other fields. Different kinds of more specialized training are provided by the State Department's Far Eastern school, the Bureau of Standards, the U.S. Public Health Service, the Atomic Energy Commission, and other government agencies.

In recent years, the Federal government has made contracts with universities for the training of State Department officials, officers in the armed forces, civilian employees of the Department of Defense, and other government employees. Such governmental institutions as the Library of Congress and the Smithsonian Institute, whose branches include the National Museum, the National Gallery of Art, the Bureau of American Ethnology, and the Astrophysical Observatory Stations, have also enriched the country's supply of highly trained and specialized personnel.

The most important, single governmental step in connection with the training of scientific and professional personnel was the Morrill Act of 1862, which laid the basis for the country's extensive state college and university system. This measure provided for grants of public land or land-scrip to the states for the support of "at least one college where the leading object shall be, without excluding other scientific and cultural studies, and including military tactics, to teach such branches of learning as are related to agriculture and the mechanic arts . . . to promote the liberal and practical education of the industrial classes." The state universities and land grant colleges have provided low-cost education, have contributed to the supply of specialized manpower, and have stimulated by their example the development of other scientific, technological, and graduate schools.

In addition to universities and colleges, the states support normal schools, which are the traditional training institutions for elementary and high school teachers. In New York, for example, there are more than twenty such teachers colleges. For about a century, the training of teachers has been viewed in greater or lesser degree as a state responsibility. Coincident with the decline in denominational education and the enormous expansion of popular education, the number of normal schools or teachers colleges has grown greatly since 1920.

A number of municipal governments have also established and maintained institutions of higher learning, the largest being the four institutions which make up the College of the City of New York. Municipalities have also established junior colleges. These institutions, both public and private, have multiplied in recent years, particularly in Indiana, Michigan, and California. The junior colleges serve several needs. They "feed" students to the four-year colleges; they provide a two-year terminal education in liberal arts; and they train young men and women as technicians. The importance of publicly supported institutions of higher education in the development of scientific and professional manpower is suggested by the fact that they award about half of all degrees and almost three-fifths of the professional degrees granted in the United States.

The Federal, state, and local governments have also influenced the development of educational institutions through their tax policies. All property used for non-commercial purposes by privately supported educational institutions is normally, but not universally, exempt from taxation. Publicly supported institutions are not subject to state or Federal taxation. In the past, states exempted faculty members and students from certain forms of taxation and thus provided a modest incentive for study and the pursuit of a teaching career. Federal income tax provisions, particularly since 1934, have encouraged gifts to universities, research foundations, and other non-profit organizations. Because they are deductible for tax purposes, such gifts result in a loss of revenue to the Federal government and so are a form of governmental subsidy to the institutions which receive them.

Direct governmental aid to students, through scholarships, fellowships, and veterans' benefits, also influences the supply of scientific and professional manpower. Almost four-fifths of the states sponsor scholarship programs of varying kinds. New York provides some 3,000 scholarships worth from $250 to $750 annually. Some seventeen states have established scholarships specifically to encourage the training of teachers. For 1952-53, the National Science Foundation awarded 624 graduate fellowships in the physical and biological sciences, mathematics, engineering, and other fields.

The enactment after World War II of Public Laws 16 and 346 was a significant new venture by the Federal government in the field of education and training. The educational benefits which they provide for veterans were one of the primary causes of the great expansion in the number of college students during the post-war years. In 1947, the peak year, about 2.8 million veterans were enrolled in institutions of higher education. By 1950, almost 8 million veterans had used their educational benefits for college and post-graduate education and for apprenticeship, on-the-job, on-the-farm, or some other form of training.

SIGNIFICANCE OF PUBLIC POLICIES

Although the number and quality of the nation's resources of scientific and professional personnel have been profoundly influenced by the actions of government, the development and utilization of this critical segment of the labor force have been shaped primarily not by public but by private policies and actions. Historically, the growth in the numbers of scientific and professional personnel has been accompanied by a minimum of governmental policy and direction, except in the field of education. In spite of the rapid expansion of publicly supported higher education, however, about half of the country's college and university graduates still receive their degrees from private institutions.

Government—whether local, state, or Federal—is only one of many centers of policy-making with respect to manpower. Public policies in this field have been limited in scope and fragmented in the sense that they have not been the product of a coordinated approach. To say this is only to emphasize once more the extent to which manpower policies in a democratic society emerge from the countless decisions and acts of individuals and voluntary groups. A stimulating high school teacher of science may be far more influential in shaping the decisions of students to study engineering or science in college than the school's counselling and guidance program. Word that the employment market for engineers looks poor results in a decline in registration at engineering schools. The inability to secure first-rate teachers for a well-equipped Negro medical school in the South limits the

supply of Negro physicians. High wages for semi-skilled or unskilled work induce young men and women to take jobs after
high school rather than continue their education.

Recent developments have given a new importance to public
policies relating to scientific and professional manpower, particularly to those made by the Federal government. Compulsory
military service, the operation of the Selective Service System,
the Reserve Officer Training Corps program, the policies governing men in the reserves, other aspects of military manpower
policy, and educational benefits for veterans—all have far-reaching
consequences for the development and utilization of highly trained
personnel. So do the Federal government's expenditures for education, for research and development, and for defense production.
The Federal government, moreover, is a major employer of civilian
scientists and professional persons, and, through the Bureau of
the Census and the Bureau of Labor Statistics, it has major responsibility for the collection of basic manpower data.

The present emergency has led to a search for greater integration and consistency among the different government policies
with implications for manpower. For example, Dale Yoder and
Herbert G. Heneman of the University of Minnesota, in a report
prepared for the Subcommittee on Labor and Labor-Management
Relations of the Senate Committee on Labor and Public Welfare
and released early in 1953, argue that "manpower considerations
should be made a major responsibility of some Federal Agency.
. . . our present practice divides responsibility. We have no
realistic manpower departments in Federal or State or local governments. We have no Secretary of Manpower. Our labor departments have no such broad and inclusive responsibilities as have
been suggested. They have neither the authority nor the expert-
ness necessary to supply leadership in this field."

Whether or not the establishment of a Department of Manpower is desirable or practicable need not be debated here. The
important point is that this proposal reveals a recognition of the
difficulties involved in the manpower problems which the nation

now faces and of the new position which the Federal government occupies with respect to them.

The United States has only about 6 percent of the world's population. America's position as a world power, its ability to produce almost half of the world's output of goods, and its standard of living depend far more upon an advanced technology and the quality of its manpower than on the size of its working force. Underlying the high quality of the American labor force, which is a major reason for the country's remarkable productivity, is a large and complex educational structure which makes possible the training of the nation's scientific and professional personnel. The scale of the present system of higher education is indicated by the fact that the young men and women who now enter college each year will account for about 1.5 million student-years by the time they terminate their higher education. This figure includes the time spent in study by those who do not receive a degree, as well as by those who do and those who go on to post-graduate work. Normally, it may be added, only about 1 percent of those entering college eventually receive doctoral degrees.

Because very highly trained manpower occupies a peculiarly strategic position for America's security and well-being, the nation would be making a mistake if it failed to consider the many long-range problems involved in the maximum development and utilization of its human resources. In the solution of these problems, the Federal government has a major responsibility to develop, within its authority, such new approaches to manpower problems as are required. The government took one step in a new direction in September, 1952, when the Office of Defense Mobilization issued Defense Manpower Policy No. 8, "Training and Utilization of Scientific and Engineering Manpower." Its purpose was to insure an adequate supply of such personnel by coordinating appropriate governmental and private policies aimed at (a) securing "more efficient use of existing resources of scientific and technical skills in private industry, in the civil government, in the Armed Forces, and in educational institutions";

(*b*) developng "increasingly reliable information regarding requirements and resources of scientists and engineers to meet both immediate and long-term national needs"; and (*c*) attracting and training "the additional number of men and women required for professional, scientific, and technical fields." The issuance of a policy statement, of course, does not itself solve problems. The objectives of Defense Manpower Policy No. 8 cannot be attained without the concerted, cooperative efforts of government, business, higher education, and the professional societies.

KNOWLEDGE AND POLICY

The point has been made repeatedly in preceding chapters that the basic information available for the solution of scientific and professional manpower problems leaves much to be desired. Because the supply of highly trained personnel cannot respond rapidly to frequent and severe fluctuations in demand, the need for better methods of predicting both short- and long-run requirements has been emphasized recently. It has already been observed, however, that not too much can be expected from efforts to improve estimating techniques. Even if it were possible to forecast future requirements accurately, there would still be a great many deficiencies in the information available about human resources, particularly with respect to problems of supply.

An important contribution in this area will come from the work on which the Commission on Human Resources and Advanced Training has been engaged since 1950. Established by the Conference Board of Associated Research Councils and financed by the Rockefeller Foundation, this Commission has been studying the supply of persons distinguished by high intellectual ability and intensive formal training and the supply of persons who are capable of but are not currently undertaking advanced training, as well as the nation's needs for scientific and professional personnel. This and related investigations will lay the basis for critical thought about a whole range of problems in the human resources field.

The conditions which contribute to the development of potential ability and talent and the causes of poor motivation and attrition among students mentally equipped to do good college work warrant far more intensive study than they have yet received. So do the factors which are responsible for the failure of able individuals to continue study after graduating from college, and the conditions which encourage and discourage high performance in employment.

The complicated processes involved in the choice of education and career have only recently begun to be investigated effectively. Greater knowledge of the factors which determine training and career decisions will discourage the tendency to induce young men and women to enter fields in which there are shortages through techniques which may have undesirable long-term consequences. Spot radio announcements have been used, for example, to attract young men and women into such fields as engineering, teaching, and nursing. The wisdom of employing the same kind of advertising approach in the selling of a career as in the selling of a hair tonic may be questioned.

In view of the extended period of education required for work in scientific and professional fields, there is also reason to investigate the ways and results of reducing the time which able students spend in high school. The program developed by the Ford Foundation's Fund for the Advancement of Education to facilitate entrance to college by exceptionally able sixteen-year-olds who have not graduated from high school provides a new basis for research on these problems.

In addition to studies of the factors which influence the development of potential ability, investigations of utilization practices are needed to point the way to reducing waste in the employment of persons already highly trained. The problem of finding the most effective balance among professional personnel and technical and skilled manpower in various work situations calls for purposeful investigation. It may also be noted that little is known about the effects which changes in technology and changes in the demand for and supply of scientific and professional manpower have upon each other.

It is not necessary to detail a comprehensive research program to stress the importance of building a more adequate body of basic information and theory in the human resources field which will contribute to the development of sound public policies and to wise and informed individual decisions and actions. Much has been accomplished in recent years in this respect, but what still remains to be done should be of major concern to a nation so dependent upon its resources of scientific and professional manpower.

AMERICAN VALUES AND ATTITUDES

Soviet Russia's current Five Year Plan calls for specified percentage increases in the numbers of natural scientists and engineers. In a totalitarian society such targets can be set, and all the power of a monolithic state can be employed to fulfill them. A democratic society can seek to expand its engineering and scientific personnel to meet an anticipated demand, but it must rely on voluntary and primarily indirect methods of attaining its goal.

Since a democracy is barred from using means that conflict with its fundamental values involving individual freedom, it must reject the use of compulsion to direct people into fields of study and work. It cannot institute a coercive system for controlling the development and utilization of its human resources according to a master plan and still retain the essential qualities of a free society. It must, therefore, run the risk of having either a shortage or a surplus of specific kinds of personnel at any given time.

A democratic society promises each individual the opportunity to develop his potentialities as fully as he can in accordance with his own desires. It is committed, furthermore, to enlarging the individual's freedom in the choice of field of study, career, and employment. Consequently, when an increase in the supply of certain groups of scientific or professional personnel becames desirable or necessary, a free society can bring it about only by creating favorable conditions. It can, for example, make the teaching profession more attractive both in terms of earnings and prestige; it can reduce the costs of training to the individual through free tuition or scholarships; it can expand training facilities. But it may not order young men and women to prepare for teaching careers nor to remain in the profession after they have become qualified to teach.

These considerations indicate that the development of an adequate supply of scientifically and professionally trained personnel can be attained only by a large-scale concerted effort in which different kinds of action are taken by various groups. Contributions to the success of such an effort may take the form of changing existing immigration laws to facilitate the admission of foreign-born scientists; of modifying state law governing the gifts of corporations for educational and philanthropic purposes; or of providing greater opportunities for satisfying academic careers for able young scientists. The creation of conditions which make for a reasonable balance between the supply of and the demand for scientific and professional manpower can only be the product of a vast, cooperative undertaking which becomes possible when the society as a whole has an understanding of its problems and shares a common purpose.

Consequently, the attitudes of the society toward the work of its scientists and professional persons are extremely important. Many of the professions, most notably medicine and law, have long been highly regarded in the United States. Belief in the social and economic worth of a college education is widely held by Americans. Yet, intellectual endeavor and intellectuals themselves are not very highly esteemed and occasionally are even somewhat suspect. Enjoyment of the goods and services which science and technology make possible has not been accompanied by a high regard for the men and women who are responsible for scientific discoveries and their application. No other nation maintains as large a college and university structure, but the term "professor" has invidious overtones in the United States, and the most eminent scholar enjoys neither the salary nor the prestige of the leading football coach. It is not without significance that "brain trust" is a term of opprobrium rather than praise. The salaries of industrial research directors, it may be added, compare poorly with those of vice presidents in charge of sales.

As long as there is lively competition for able persons among the many fields of study and of work, the training and career decisions of young men and women will be enormously influenced by the attitudes of the society which condition the prestige, the status, and the earnings of those who pursue careers in such fields as the physical and social sciences, the humanities, and university teaching. To insure an adequate supply of scientific and professional personnel of high quality it is necessary to develop a more positive and sympathetic climate for intellectual endeavors which will make them attractive to able young men and women.

Bibliography[a]

Anthony, Robert N. Management Controls in Industrial Research Organizations. Boston, 1952.

Bachman, George W., and associates. Health Resources in the United States. Brookings Institution. Washington, 1952.

Baehr, George, and Neva R. Deardorff. "Experience of the Health Insurance Plan of Greater New York with Its Older Enrollees," in Illness and Health Services in an Aging Population, *Public Health Service Publication No. 170*, Washington, 1952.

Blauch, Lloyd E. The Professions in Transition. Address to the Inter-Professional Conference, Southern Regional Education Board. Atlanta, August 19-20, 1952.

Bureau of Labor Statistics, "Employment Outlook for Engineers," *Bulletin No. 968*. Washington, 1949.

—— "Employment Outlook for Elementary and Secondary School Teachers," *Bulletin No. 972*. Washington, 1949.

—— "Employment, Education, and Earnings of American Men of Science," *Bulletin No. 1027*. Washington, 1951.

Bureau of Labor Statistics and Research and Development Board. Industrial Research and Development. A Preliminary Report. Washington, January, 1953.

Bureau of Labor Statistics and U. S. Office of Education. Manpower Resources in Physics, 1951. Washington, 1952.

Bush, Vannevar. Modern Arms and Free Men, New York, 1949.

Cooper, John N. "American Physicists and Their Graduate Degrees," *American Journal of Physics*, XX, No. 8 (November 1952), 484-87.

Cattell, Jacques (ed.). American Men of Science. 8th ed. Lancaster, Pa., 1949.

Commission on Financing Higher Education. Nature and Needs of Higher Education. New York, 1952.

[a] Based primarily on items referred to in the text.

Department of Defense. Annual and Semiannual Reports of the Secretary of Defense and the Secretaries of the Army, the Navy, and the Air Force. Washington, 1950-52.

Department of the Air Force. United States Air Force Training Prospectus. Washington. Various revisions.

—— Officer Personnel: Assignment of Research and Development Officers. Air Force Regulation No. 36-65. Washington, October 8, 1952.

Department of the Army. Organized Reserve Corps: Utilization and Training of Officers in Research and Development. Special Regulations No. 140-190-2. Washington, May 2, 1950.

—— Enlisted Personnel: Selection of Specialists and Scientific and Professional Personnel. Special Regulations No. 615-25-38. Washington, January 11, 1952.

—— Enlisted Personnel: Identification, Classification, Assignment, and Utilization of Scientific and Professional Personnel. Special Regulations No. 615-25-11. Washington, August 7, 1952.

Dewhurst, J. Frederic, and associates. America's Needs and Resources. New York, 1947.

Dickinson, Frank G. "Supply of Physicians' Services," Bulletin 81. Bureau of Medical Economic Research, American Medical Association. Chicago, 1951.

Dickinson, Frank G., and Charles E. Bradley. "Comparisons of State Physician-Population Ratios for 1938 to 1949," Bulletin 78. Bureau of Medical Economic Research, American Medical Association. Chicago, 1950.

Educational Testing Service. A Summary of Statistics on Selective Service College Qualification Test of May 26, 1951, June 16, 1951, June 30, 1951, July 12, 1951. Princeton, January 22, 1952.

Einstein, Albert. Out of My Later Years. New York, 1950.

Engineering Manpower Commission of Engineers Joint Council. Newsletter. Various dates.

—— Proceedings of Conference on Manpower Utilization and National Security. New York, 1952.

Engineers Joint Council. The Engineering Profession in Transition. New York, 1946.

Engineers Joint Council, General Survey Committee. 1949 Employment Programs for Engineering Graduates. New York, 1949.

—— 1950 Employment Programs for Graduates in Engineering and Physical Science. New York, 1950.

Ewing, Oscar A. The Nation's Health. Washington, 1948.

Frederiksen, Norman, and W. B. Schrader. Adjustment to College. Princeton, 1951.

Friedman, Milton, and Simon Kuznets. Income from Independent Professional Practice. New York, 1945.

Ginzberg, Eli, and associates. Occupational Choice, New York, 1951.

Ginzberg, Eli, and Douglas W. Bray. The Uneducated. New York, 1953.

Harris, Seymour. Hearings on National Health Program, 1949, Part 1. Before a Subcommittee of the Senate Committee on Labor and Public Welfare, 81st Congress, First Session. Washington, June, 1949.

—— The Market for College Graduates. Cambridge, Mass., 1949.

Harrison, George R. "The Role of the Secondary School in the Teaching of Science," Physics Today, V, No. 6 (June, 1952), 10-15.

Havemann, Ernest, and Patricia S. West. They Went to College. New York, 1952.

Hertz, David B., and others. A Study of Team or Group Research. Columbia Studies of Research Administration, School of Engineering, Columbia University. New York, 1952.

Hollingsworth, Helen, Margaret C. Klem, and Anna Mae Baney. "Medical Care and Costs in Relation to Family Income," Social Security Administration, Bureau Memorandum No. 51, 2nd ed. Washington, 1947.

Hospital Council of Greater New York. Hospital Staff Appointments of Physicians in New York City. New York, 1951.

Kistiakowsky, George B. The Public and the Training of Scientists Today. Remarks as a Participant in a Panel on Science, Industry, and Education. Mt. Holyoke College, South Hadley, Mass., October 3, 1952.

Kline, J. R. "Soviet Mathematics," in Soviet Science, ed. by Ruth C. Christman. Pages 80-84. American Association for the Advancement of Science. Washington, 1952.

Knapp, Robert H., and H. B. Goodrich. Origins of American Scientists. Chicago, 1952.

Lee, Roger I., and Lewis Webster Jones. The Fundamentals of Good Medical Care. Chicago, 1933.

Long, Clarence. "Nothing to Lose But Its Brains," The John Hopkins Magazine, III, No. 9 (June, 1952), 8-10, 26-27.

Maul, Ray C. Teacher Supply and Demand in the United States. National Education Association. Washington, 1952.

Mountin, Joseph W., Elliott H. Pennell, and Anne G. Berger. "Health Service Areas: Estimates of Future Physician Requirements," Public Health Bulletin No. 305. Washington, 1949.

National Education Association. Advance Estimates of Public Elementary and Secondary Schools for the School Year 1952-53. Washington, November, 1952.

National Manpower Council. Student Deferment and National Manpower Policy. New York, 1952.

National Science Foundation. The Second Annual Report of the National Science Foundation. Washington, 1952.

National Society of Professional Engineers. How to Improve the Utilization of Engineering Manpower. Washington, 1952.

Notestein, Frank W. "Population," Scientific American, CLXXXV, No. 3 (September, 1951), 28-35.

Office of Defense Mobilization. Manpower for Defense, Policies and Statements of the Office of Defense Mobilization. Washington, 1953.

—— "New Resources Bring New Opportunities," Seventh Quarterly Report to the President by the Director of Defense Mobilization. Washington, October 1, 1952.

—— "The Job Ahead for Defense Mobilization," Eighth Quarterly Report to the President by the Director of Defense Mobilization. Washington, January 1, 1953.

Oxtoby, Toby, Robert Mugge, and Dael Wolfle. "Enrollment and Graduation Trends: From Grade School to Ph.D.," School and Society, LXXVI, No. 1973 (October 11, 1952), 225-31.

Pennell, Maryland Y., and Marion E. Altenderfer. Health Manpower Source Book. Section I: Physicians. Public Health Service. Washington, 1952.

President's Commission on Higher Education. Higher Education for American Democracy. 6 vols. Vol. I: Establishing the Goals. Washington, 1948.

President's Commission on the Health Needs of the Nation. 5 vols. Vol. I. Building America's Health. Washington, 1952-53.

President's Materials Policy Commission. Resources for Freedom. 5 vols. Vol. I: Foundations for Growth and Security. Washington, 1952.

Rappleye, Willard C. "Medical Education Data," The Educational Record, XXXII, No. 1 (January, 1951), 81-88.

—— Personnel: The Key to Effective Health Programs. Josiah Macy, Jr. Foundation. New York, 1950.

Report of the New York State Legislative Commission on Medical Care for the People of New York. Albany, 1946.

Research and Development Board. Staff Studies. Washington, 1951-52.

Rusk, Howard A. "Medicine, Mobilization, and Manpower." Proceedings of the American Congress of Medical Education and Licensure, Reprinted in the Journal of the American Medical Association, CXLVII, No. 2 (September 8, 1951), 5-9.

Scates, Douglas E., Bernard C. Murdock, and Alice V. Yoemans. The Production of Doctorates in the Sciences, 1936-1948. Washington, 1951.

Securities and Exchange Commission and U. S. Department of Commerce. Plant and Equipment Expenditures of U. S. Business. Washington, 1953.

Stigler, George J. "Employment and Compensation in Education," *Occasional Paper 33*. National Bureau of Economic Research. New York, 1950.

Turkevich, John, "Soviet Physics and Chemistry," in Soviet Science, ed. by Ruth C. Christman. Pages 70-79. American Association for the Advancement of Science. Washington, 1952.

U. S. Congress. HR Report No. 1517, to Accompany HR 7072. Independent Offices Appropriation Bill, 1953. 82nd Congress, Second Session. Washington, March 14, 1952.

U. S. Office of Education. Earned Degrees Conferred by Higher Educational Institutions. Washington, various years.

—— National Survey of the Higher Education of Negroes. 3 vols. Vol. II: General Studies of Colleges for Negroes. Miscellaneous No. 6. Washington, 1942.

—— "Statistics of State School Systems, 1949-50," Chapter 2 in Biennial Survey of Education in the United States, 1948-50. Washington, 1952.

Wolfle, Dael, and Toby Oxtoby, "Distributions of Ability of Students Specializing in Different Fields," *Science*, CXVI, No. 3013 (September 26, 1952), 311-14.

Volen, Lazar. "Science and Intellectual Freedom in Russia," in Soviet Science, ed. by Ruth C. Christman. Pages 85-99. American Association for the Advancement of Science. Washington, 1952.

White, Marsh W. "Production of Professional Physicists Decreasing," *American Journal of Physics*, XX, No. 8 (November, 1952), 469-70.

Wrenn, C. Gilbert. "Potential Research Talent in the Sciences," *The Educational Record*, XXX, No. 1 (January, 1949), 5-22.

Wright, David McCord (ed.). The Impact of the Union. New York, 1951.

Yoder, Dale, and Herbert G. Heneman, Jr. Staff Report to the Subcommittee on Labor and Labor-Management Relations of the Committee on Labor and Public Welfare, United States Senate, Eighty-Second Congress, Second Session, on Manpower Blueprint for a Free Economy. Washington, 1953.

"Your Economic Weather Vane: Results from the Seventh *Medical Economics* Survey," *Medical Economics*, XXX, No. 2 (November, 1952), 85-102, and No. 3 (December, 1952), 71-87.

Date Due

DEC 8 69			
NOV24'74			
DEC 8 74			